MISUNDERSTANDING FINANCIAL CRISES

MISUNDERSTANDING

FINANCIAL CRISES

Why We Don't See Them Coming

GARY B. GORTON

OXFORD
UNIVERSITY PRESS

OXFORD
UNIVERSITY PRESS

Oxford University Press is a department of the University of Oxford.
It furthers the University's objective of excellence in research,
scholarship, and education by publishing worldwide.

Oxford   New York
Auckland   Cape Town   Dar es Salaam   Hong Kong   Karachi
Kuala Lumpur   Madrid   Melbourne   Mexico City   Nairobi
New Delhi   Shanghai   Taipei   Toronto

With offices in
Argentina   Austria   Brazil   Chile   Czech Republic   France   Greece
Guatemala   Hungary   Italy   Japan   Poland   Portugal   Singapore
South Korea   Switzerland   Thailand   Turkey   Ukraine   Vietnam

Oxford is a registered trade mark of Oxford University Press
in the UK and certain other countries.

Published in the United States of America by
Oxford University Press
198 Madison Avenue, New York, New York 10016

© Oxford University Press 2012

Library of Congress Cataloging-in-Publication Data
Gorton, Gary.
Misunderstanding financial crises : why we don't see them coming / Gary B. Gorton.
   p.   cm.
Includes bibliographical references and index.
ISBN 978-0-19-992290-1 (cloth : alk. paper)
1. Financial crises—United States.   2. United States—Economic policy.   3. Monetary policy—United States.   I. Title.
HB3722.G674 2012
338.5′42—dc23   2012008750

3 5 7 9 8 6 4 2

Printed in the United States of America
on acid-free paper

CONTENTS

PREFACE

> The effects of the financial catastrophe through which the country had passed in the previous period were seen in legislation for perhaps a decade, but then they were gradually forgotten. The literature of this subject for fifty years had repeated the same inferences, lessons, and warning; but all the doctrines of currency have to be learned over again apparently every ten or fifteen years, if indeed they were ever learned at all.
>
> —William Graham Sumner, *A History of Banking in the United States*, 1896

William Graham Sumner (1840–1910), a Yale professor and expert on banking, was describing the half century prior to the U.S. Civil War. The next seventy or so years after the Civil War were marked by repeated financial crises until federal deposit insurance legislation was passed during the Great Depression, and could be described similarly. The global financial crisis of 2007–8 suggests that the lessons were probably never learned. What are the lessons?

One is that financial crises are inherent in the production of bank debt, which is used to conduct transactions, and, unless the government designs intelligent regulation, crises will continue. This is not understood. Prior to the financial crisis of 2007–8, economists thought that no such financial crisis would ever happen again in the United States. Economists thought that a crisis *could not* happen. Then the unthinkable happened; the inconceivable happened. How could economists, myself included, have been so wrong?

Economists misunderstand financial crises, what they are, why they occur, why we didn't have one in the United States between 1934 and

2007, and a host of related questions. But the real question is: What are the origins of this misunderstanding? This is a question about the epistemology of economics, about how economics produces knowledge. That is our subject.

This small book began as an essay that was originally prepared for the Academic Advisory Panel of the Board of Governors of the Federal Reserve System, for a meeting in May 2011. The question posed to me as a topic was: "What will the future financial landscape look like after Dodd-Frank?" Because Dodd-Frank is very complicated—the legislation requires 243 rule-makings and sixty-seven studies in order to implement its various parts—and hinges on the discretion of regulators, it is extremely hard to answer this question. My response: "Who knows?"

I also said that I thought that a more important way to think about the question was to focus on the word "look." What the future "looks" like depends on the observer and what the observer is capable of "seeing." What is the actual process of seeing in economics? Think of economists and bank regulators looking out at the financial landscape prior to the financial crisis. What did they see? They did not see the possibility of a systemic crisis. Nor did they see how capital markets and the banking system had evolved in the last thirty years. They did not know of the existence of new financial instruments or the size of certain money markets, like the sale and repurchase market. They did not know what "money" had become. They looked from a certain point of view, from a certain paradigm, and missed everything that was important. As Sherlock Holmes put it to Dr. Watson: "You see, but you do not observe."

The blindness is astounding. That economists did not think such a crisis could happen in the United States was an intellectual failure. Why did this happen? How could this have happened? Non-economists agree this is an important question and have leveled all sorts of criticisms at economics and economists to explain it. Economics, they argue, is too mathematical, too rational, and so on. Former chairman of the Federal Reserve System Paul Volcker essentially blames economists for the crisis, in so many words. Here's his opening sentence in an article in the *New York Review of Books*: "It should be clear that among the causes of the recent financial crisis was an unjustified faith in rational expectations, market efficiencies, and the techniques of modern finance" ("Financial Reform: Unfinished Business," November 24, 2011).

Never mind that Nobel Prizes in economics were won for rational expectations and the techniques of modern finance. Yet most well-known of the economists' critiques is that of 2008 Nobel Prize–winner Paul Krugman:

As I see it, the economics profession went astray because economists, as a group, mistook beauty, clad in impressive-looking mathematics, for truth. Until the Great Depression, most economists clung to a vision of capitalism as a perfect or nearly perfect system. That vision wasn't sustainable in the face of mass unemployment, but as memories of the Depression faded, economists fell back in love with the old, idealized vision of an economy in which rational individuals interact in perfect markets, this time gussied up with fancy equations. The renewed romance with the idealized market was, to be sure, partly a response to shifting political winds, partly a response to financial incentives. But while sabbaticals at the Hoover Institution and job opportunities on Wall Street are nothing to sneeze at, the central cause of the profession's failure was the desire for an all-encompassing, intellectually elegant approach that also gave economists a chance to show off their mathematical prowess. (Krugman 2009)

It may be easy for economists to dismiss both Paul Volcker and Paul Krugman. Their critiques—economics is excessively mathematical; economists are mesmerized by the idea of efficient markets and rational expectations; and there are conflicts of interest—are standard fare and come up repeatedly. Friedrich von Hayek (1974 Nobel Prize winner) in his Nobel Lecture, "The Pretense of Knowledge," said:

It seems to me that this failure of the economists to guide policy more successfully is closely connected with their propensity to imitate as closely as possible the procedures of the brilliantly successful physical sciences—an attempt which in our field may lead to outright error. It is an approach which has come to be described as the "scientistic" attitude—an attitude which, as I defined it some thirty years ago, "is decidedly unscientific in the true sense of the word, since it involves a mechanical and uncritical application of habits of thought to fields different from those in which they have been formed."

So it is not the critique of economics that is really different. It is the reality of the financial crisis, an event which emphatically emphasizes the critique. That is the difference now. And it is well to keep in mind that Paul Volcker is the former chairman of the Federal Reserve System, in addition to other posts he has held in a long and distinguished career. And Paul Krugman, a professor at Princeton, is a Nobel Prize winner, like Hayek. It should not be easy to cavalierly dismiss them. That would be the height of arrogance. As Hayek put it in his Nobel Lecture, in a different context: "We have indeed at the moment little cause for pride: as a profession we have made a mess of things."

The issue Krugman and Hayek raised concerns the question of how economic knowledge is produced. What is "economic knowledge"? Where do correct economic ideas come from? In the face of the financial crisis, these are important questions. There is a long intellectual history on the epistemology of economics, but it is basically formal, more about how economics should be done than about how it is actually done. In practice, economics proceeds differently than the formalisms. Economists "see" reality by looking through the lenses of models, which are representations of reality, simplified to highlight certain aspects.

Models consist of concepts, like asymmetric information, and rational expectations, arranged together with a particular structure. Models frame reality, give meaning to reality. Although there is formal testing of some economic theories using statistical methods, this requires a well-articulated hypothesis and the relevant data. In many cases, the "test" of a theory has more to do with its ability to provide a useful way of organizing reality for the viewer.

The problem is not mathematical models. The organization of reality using models is a very powerful method for creating clarity. But, of course, there are good models and bad models. One issue involves how it is determined that a model is good or bad. Some models fail statistical tests. As Krugman suggested, sometimes models, and paradigms generally, are rejected only when reality overwhelms them, as in a financial crisis. This was the way in which Keynesianism originally came to dominate macroeconomics. It was the Great Depression that made earlier models unreal. When experience departs from the ordinary, orthodoxy becomes suspect. This is because the "ordinary" is embedded in a model, or paradigm, and becomes the orthodoxy. The financial crisis was an extreme departure from the ordinary. When orthodoxy becomes suspect, one departure is backward-looking, and previous ideas, since superseded, become popular again. So some have revived Keynesianism.

People also now recall the ideas and writings of Charles Kindleberger and Hyman Minsky.

Kindleberger spent most of his academic career at MIT and was president of the American Economic Association in 1985. Minsky, a Harvard PhD, taught at Brown, Berkeley, and Washington University in St. Louis. Their ideas about financial crises have been durable and influential, although they do not lead to any policy recommendations, because they are somewhat imprecise; that is, they do not provide models. But they provide a starting point.

It has been easy for economists to dismiss the criticisms of Volcker, Krugman, and others. And in the process of dismissing the criticisms, we economists have avoided the uncomfortable question: How could economists have failed to foresee the possibility of a financial crisis in the United States? Many economists want to avoid the question. Cognitive dissonance has set in: the crisis happened and yet economics cannot account for it.

One need not endorse all the criticisms to admit the question is important. The gains in economic knowledge in the last thirty years or so, during the rational expectations revolution, have been enormous, to say the least. And there is no turning back. But that is not the point here. Conflating the gains in economics with the criticisms and then dismissing the criticisms may be clever debating, but we all know that it is no more than that.

I think the question is important. The subject of this book, why economists failed to see that there was the possibility of a financial crisis, is a topic in the history of economic thought: What intellectual milieu could account for this belief? How can we explain why economists were in this situation? Addressing these questions, I hope to elucidate crises. Indeed, the many misunderstandings about crises are related to the inability to foresee the possibility of one happening.

Economists did not think there was the possibility of a crisis because either (1) they believed that the problem of crises had been solved, or (2) they believed that crises were simply not inherent to market economies but rather were idiosyncratic, unpredictable, unfortunate events that stemmed from a coincidence of unconnected factors—so rare that they need not be part of mainstream models.

Neither of these alternatives is very attractive. In the case of the former view, that the problem had been solved, economists would have to assume that the world doesn't change, that there is no financial innovation; that somehow solving the problem once meant it was solved forever. Yet proponents of this view could not explain how the problem was solved. The latter view, that crises were not inherent, but random events, flies in the face of the evidence that crises strike more often than apparently thought and empirically have common features. There is a fundamental misunderstanding of crises.

How can this be? There are hundreds of academic papers about crises. Almost all of these papers are theory papers—this fact alone is telling. (This sounds like one of Krugman's points.) How can it be that there are hundreds of papers on a subject that no one thought was of practical relevance? Isn't this fact alone evidence that the critics are on to something? In any case, the number of papers on the subject is, unfortunately, not evidence that the subject is understood. If that were the case, economists (including me) would have warned of a crisis. There were a small number of economists that gave vague warnings. But the fact is no one said clearly that there could be a systemic global financial meltdown. It seems to me that there is a certain amount of denial among economists. I have noticed, in talking about the ideas in this book with my economist colleagues, that there is a fairly clear generational divide on this. To younger economists and graduate students it is obvious that there was an intellectual failure. Some older economists are inclined to hem and haw, resorting to farfetched rebuttals. It is clear that this is a sensitive issue, as like banks no one wants to have to write down the value of their capital.

But if economists want to deny that there is a problem in the field of economics, who cares anyway? Why does economics need to be introspective? Because it will lead to better economics, a better understanding of crises, and better policies. Bad economics leads to bad policies. One need only look at Argentina as an example.

In 1913 real GDP per capita in Argentina was 72% of the U.S. level, and higher than other developed countries such as France, Germany, and Sweden. Between 1900 and 1930 Argentina had an average annual per capita growth rate of 1.8%, compared to that of the United States of 1.2%, Australia with 0.8%, Brazil with 1.2%, and Canada with 1.2%. But since then Argentina has lagged behind. In 1950, real GDP per capita in Argentina was 52% of that of the United States, but still higher than Germany, because of the aftereffects of World War II. In 1990 Argentina's real GDP per capita was 28% of the U.S. level. The growth of real GDP per capita over the period 1913–1990 averaged

0.7% a year in Argentina; it was 1.6% a year in the rest of Latin America and 1.9% a year for the United States. The difference is essentially the result of bad policy rather than bad luck.

In thirty-five years, 1970–2005, Argentina had thirty-two central bank governors, an average term in office of just over one year. The persistent poor performance of Argentina over the last seventy or so years has simply lasted too long to be explained as a response to some exogenous shocks or bad luck. The only reason for this performance must be in the realm of policy. It is the job of economists to produce good policy advice.

The human toll from the financial crisis of 2007–8 will eventually be measured, and future economists and historians will assess the economic policies and legislation adopted. The inability of the economics profession to articulate any lucid narrative of what happened in the crisis meant that reform legislation would be the product of this incoherency. The Dodd-Frank legislation reflects this. The effects of those decisions will be felt by Americans for decades to come.

Finally, let me quote the words of John Maynard Keynes:

> In writing a book of this kind the author must, if he is to put his point of view clearly, pretend sometimes to a little more conviction than he feels. He must give his own argument a chance, so to speak, not be too ready to depress its vitality with a wet cloud of doubt. It is a heavy task to write on these problems; and the reader will perhaps excuse me if I have sometimes pressed on a little faster than the difficulties were overcome, and with decidedly more confidence than I have always felt. (*A Treatise on Probability*, 427)

Some of the ideas in this book are from work with my academic coauthors. I am very indebted to them, in particular Tri Vi Dang, Bengt Holmström, Andrew Metrick, Guillermo Ordoñez, and George Pennacchi. The academic work is briefly discussed in the bibliographic notes at the end of the book.

For their detailed comments on the manuscript of this book I especially thank Andrew Metrick, Guillermo Ordoñez, Roberta Romano, and David Warsh.

For comments and suggestions on the original essay for the Federal Open Market Committee (FOMC), I thank Doug Diamond, Henry Hansmann, Arvind Krishnamurthy, Robert Lucas, Lee Ohanian, Robert Shiller, John

Taylor, Warren Weber, and participants at a seminar at the Hoover Institution and at the FOMC meeting for comments.

Thanks to Michael Bordo, Richard Grossman, Stefan Hunt, Teresa Miguel, Romain Ranciere, Alan Taylor, Aaron Tornell, and John Williams for at least one of the following: making suggestions, answering questions, help with data, locating court cases, sharing data, and assistance in procuring illustrations. I thank Paulo Costa, Thomas Bonczek, and Lei Xie for research assistance. Thanks to Harry Bliss for the cartoon (Figure 12.1).

Throughout the book I try to provide very brief biographies of the economists and historians that I cite. These are eminent people, but I think many of them are largely forgotten forerunners who worked on topics about which I write. I build on their work—stand on their shoulders—academics like A. Piatt Andrew, Allan Bogue, Wesley Mitchell, William N. Parker, and Fritz Redlich; but also regulators and bankers, like George S. Coe, Hugh McCulloch, and Carroll Wright, who are important but forgotten figures in U.S. banking and economic history.

Finally, I should note that I worked as a consultant to AIG Financial Products for twelve years, 1996–2008. This was a transformative experience for me in many ways. I am indebted to my colleagues there for their patience and their camaraderie in the face of difficult circumstances.

MISUNDERSTANDING FINANCIAL CRISES

I. INTRODUCTION

History carries good lessons to all who heed them. All of these extraordinary crises have their most important features in common, though the attending circumstances, preceding and consequent, vary widely in one, from those of every other.

—*Commercial and Financial Chronicle*, August 7, 1875

Why do market economies experience financial crises? That a crisis is the result of a coincidence of a large number of special causes is never a plausible explanation. This is especially so once we recognize how often crises occur. They are fairly frequent internationally and throughout history—indeed, they are pervasive in market economies. Understanding crises is important for avoiding them. But to understand them, it is vital to first understand why we didn't think one could happen again in the United States.

The crisis led many to question why the credit rating agencies and bank regulators never saw the possibility of a crisis coming. Banks held too many assets of the type that later became problems—didn't somebody understand the risks? The idea that no one saw the possibility of a crisis is a widespread idea, so much so that best-selling books have popularized the idea that a small band of misfit hedge-fund operators were actually geniuses who saw the crisis coming when all the others did not. Many saw a crisis looming, but what no one saw was the size of it, that it would be a global systemic crisis.

It is understandable why politicians did not understand the crisis and did not expect one—they are not experts in economics. Nor could they ever be expert on every issue that confronts them, from health care to foreign policy to the federal budget. The same goes for journalists. What about regulators? How could they not have seen the buildup of risk? Their job was to regulate banks, not to be intellectually curious about the financial system. The regulators did not see the shadow banking system; it was not their job to look there.

Politicians, journalists, regulators, and others rely on experts, in this case economists: macroeconomists and financial economists. After all, economists are expected to be experts on crises and should have seen that one was possible, even if the timing was not predictable. In fact, they had the view that a crisis could not occur in the United States, that the problem has been solved.

Would it have been possible to avoid the financial crisis, based on insights from economics? We can't know the answer to this. But that avoiding crises is possible is demonstrated by the "Quiet Period" in U.S. history: the years 1934–2007 saw no systemic financial crises.[1] The Quiet Period shows that properly designed bank regulations can prevent financial crises for a significant period of time, until innovation and change necessitate their redesign. The period is a counterexample to the widespread view that we are stuck in a world where the government cannot help but cause problems. It deserves intense scrutiny.

Yet economists have not found the question of why there were no crises from 1934 until 2007 interesting. Economists implicitly viewed the Quiet Period as related to what macroeconomists called "the Great Moderation," a view based on the observation that starting in the 1980s the volatility of aggregate economic activity had fallen dramatically in most of the industrialized world. One explanation was that there were no longer financial crises or banking panics. The Great Moderation, however, includes a very short period of history. From a longer historical perspective, banking panics are the norm. It seems that there was some implicit view economists had that crises were a thing of the past.

The sharp and tragic termination of the Quiet Period by the recent crisis and the fact of repeated financial crises historically and internationally strongly suggest something deeper than episode-specific, multicausal explanations. Rather, it suggests that market economies have an *inherent* feature that can lead to financial crises if not checked. Although each crisis has specific characteristics, financial crises have a common structural cause, whether they occur in the pre–Civil War period of American history, after the Civil War, after the Federal Reserve comes into existence, after federal deposit insurance legislation is enacted, or in 2007–8. And crises internationally have the same cause. As Wesley Mitchell put it:[2]

> As business cycles have continued to run their round decade after decade in all nations of highly developed business organization, the idea that each crisis may be accounted for by some special cause has become less tenable. On the contrary, the explanations in favor today ascribe the recurrence of crises after periods of prosperity to some inherent characteristic of economic organization or activity.... The influence of special conditions is admitted, of course, but rather as a factor which complicates the process than as the leading cause of crises. (Mitchell 1913, 6)

The cause of financial crises is the vulnerability of transactions media, the privately created debt of financial institutions: private bank notes (in the United States before the Civil War, and historically in other countries as well), demand deposits (checking accounts), commercial paper, sale and repurchase agreements—forms of money that are usually the short-term liabilities of financial intermediaries.[3] These forms of money exist for a reason, to conduct transactions, but they are vulnerable to sudden revocation, withdrawal, or exit—demands for cash. Misunderstanding the reasons for such exits or withdrawals is part of the problem.

Panics are not irrational events. Panics happen when information arrives about a coming recession. It is the fact that there are potential problems with banks that causes a run. It is not the other way around, that runs cause problems for banks. We will see that this underlying problem of runs is distorted when consumers and firms do not run because they expect the government to act; but runs are still the underlying problem.

A financial crisis in its pure form is an exit from bank debt. Such an exit can cause a massive deleveraging of the financial system. It is not the asset side of banks which is the problem (though assets may be impaired) but the liability side. Financial intermediaries cannot possibly honor these short-term debt obligations if they are withdrawn or not renewed. And when the whole banking system cannot honor its contractual demands, it is a systemic problem.

Of course, this systemic problem would not occur if the economy did not have bank debt, or if it had a lot less bank debt. But bank debt is special. The output of a car company is cars. The output of a consulting company is advice. The output of a shipping company is transportation services. The output of a bank is debt. Banks create debt so that people and firms have a way to transact. To produce debt that people and companies find useful for transactions is not easy. It would be best if this debt were riskless, like modern government-produced money, because then it would be very easy to transact. People and companies would accept the money without questions. But private firms cannot create riskless debt, and that is the basic problem. Unlike other products, bank debt comes with a kind of contractual warranty: if you don't want it anymore, the bank has to return all your cash. But there cannot be enough cash, because the cash is lent out, leading to a multiplying process creating more than a dollar of bank debt for each dollar of cash. The cash cannot be returned fast enough.

Whatever the form of the bank money, financial crises are en masse demands by holders of bank debt for cash—panics. Before the Civil War, people in the United States used private bank notes to conduct transactions. If they did not want these notes, they would go back to their bank and ask for specie—that is, gold or silver coins. When everyone in the economy does this, there is a system-wide bank panic. Here is a description of the Panic of 1857 from a *Times* correspondent in St. Louis, Missouri:

> The first effect of the panic here was the common one; it created a universal demand for specie. Every interest that thought itself strong enough to enforce payment of its dues and charges in coin, did so, with very partial and no permanent success. After years of reliance on paper [private bank notes], an abrupt change to an opposite and more solid system was simply impossible. The proprietors of the Mississippi steamers, a strong interest, combined, and announced that they would not take "currency" or notes for freights. They obtained no cargoes.... The wholesale firms would not take "currency" for goods from country customers... the goods are unsold.... All paper was looked at askance.... The shops would not take the money the visitors brought them. Cab-drivers and omnibus-men would not touch it...hotel-keepers rejected it. (Quoted in the *Westminster Review*, January 1858, 90)

The Panic of 1857 started in New York City and spread outwards. The correspondent describes the run, in which no one wanted bank debt (private bank notes), only cash (specie). He then goes on to describe the real effects of having no means of transacting—business cannot be conducted, nothing is transported or sold.

Here is another description of a panic, from a nineteenth-century short story:

> Little sleep did any of us have that night. Morning broke wan and chill, a true dawn of calamity....I went out into the streets, and was impressed by the unwonted throng on the sidewalks,—like a holiday, only the crowd wore no holiday air....I observed...that the motion on every side was towards one central point: the mass of human beings pressed, struggled, and fought onward to the white marble steps of Thorne and Quincy's bank. Near noon a neighbor ran to my house crying that there was a run on the bank, and that she should lose everything...before she could push forward she heard the roar of rage and misery which told her that the bank doors were shut. Thorne and Quincy had suspended. (Octave Thanet, "The First Mayor," *Atlantic Monthly* 64 [November 1889], 622)

Thorne and Quincy bank "suspended"—that is, refused to honor the demands for cash from the depositors. Suspension, though never sanctioned, was usually organized by the banks and happened jointly.

The financial crisis of 2007–8 was also a bank run, but it was not people who ran to their banks but firms running on investment banks. In the modern era there are just different forms of bank debt, as well as a central bank and government that can intervene.

During most of the Quiet Period banks had insured deposits, where insurance premiums were not risk-based; banks paid no interest on demand deposits, or there were ceilings on how much they could pay, regardless of risk; the banking system in the United States consisted of a small number of large banks and thousands of small banks; and there were no binding capital requirements (but there were reserve requirements). Yet there were no systemic crises. Understanding why there was a Quiet Period must be part of the explanation of the crisis itself.

The Quiet Period was never previously viewed as a delimited era, because it was seen as having no end, so there was no puzzle about it—it was simply the future. There was no "Quiet Period" until the recent financial crisis signified the end. That end point, the reality of the recent financial crisis, not only defines the Quiet Period but poses rather firmly the question I started with, namely, why did we think "it" could never happen again?[4]

One reason is that once the government or central bank is active in the financial sector of the economy, a kind of identification problem occurs. Households and firms behave differently if they expect the government to take action during a crisis, even if the government does not take the action expected. And their anticipation of government action can keep them from running on banks. Bank runs are then not observed when they would otherwise occur if not for the anticipated actions of the government. When the government does act, there are large losses, but the real problem is bank runs, and the problem is misdiagnosed. It appears that bank runs are a thing of the past, historical relics. The government's actions in response to a shock are seen as problematic, with no recognition that the government actions were due to the unobserved, inherent possibility of a bank run. Each crisis then seems like an idiosyncratic event, requiring its own explanation and solution.

The failure to understand that a systemic crisis was a real possibility in the United States was an intellectual failure of economists. How could this failure have happened? It is easy to criticize ex post, but that is not the point here. The explanation I seek is one that explains not only why economists thought that a systemic crisis would not happen again but also why they thought what they thought—that is, why certain models came to the fore and seemed sensible and realistic. In other words, economists' hypothesis that a systemic crisis would not happen again is testable in a certain way. If one believed that the Quiet Period would last forever, then one would have had the view that financial intermediation is largely irrelevant for asset pricing theory and for macroeconomics, and that any frictions in the models would articulate complications other than the vulnerability of bank debt. Moreover, one would explain any problems with banks as being due to the actions of the government. But why would one think the Quiet Period would last forever?

I am interested in explaining financial crises, although the approach is quite different than the one usually pursued (at least in economics). I try to provide evidence for a certain explanation of financial crises by accounting for why economists did not think that a crisis would ever occur again and were surprised and intellectually unprepared when it did occur. This is not the usual method of supplying evidence for an argument in economics. In fact, I mostly focus on crises themselves, rather than on economics. We will come to economics only in the middle and at the end of the book.

In sum, my argument is that the output of a bank is short-term debt. Such debt is backed by collateral of some form, maybe the assets of the bank, maybe specific bonds. But it is not possible for the private sector to produce riskless collateral. Because it is not riskless it is vulnerable to not being renewed when depositors suspect problems with the collateral. A financial crisis in its pure form is an exit from bank debt, a bank run. This is an inherent problem in market economies.

When there is a crisis, banks cannot possibly honor all their debt claims; they do not have enough cash. Starting in the early nineteenth century a policy evolved of not liquidating the banking system during a financial crisis. The best articulation of this is in a legal case, *Livingston v. The Bank of New York*. *Livingston* clarified that in times of crisis, bank debt should not be enforced, and banks should not be forced into insolvency. I call this the Livingston Doctrine. In line with this doctrine, the Federal Reserve System helped save Bear Stearns; counter to the doctrine, it let Lehman fail.

Economics has become history-less. Indeed, because the data requirements for models demanded richer data than was available for earlier periods, economists only looked at short timeframes to study macroeconomics, ignoring history. Yet this myopia was viewed as acceptable, because no crisis had happened in the United States since the Great Depression and it was assumed that none would happen again. The latter assumption was based not on an understanding of the root causes of crises but on the view that bank runs were no longer observed. Bank runs are often not observed, because people and firms expect the government and the central bank to act to prevent crises. The government's policies can prevent runs, but if the policies are imperfect then the problem is viewed as the government.

In 1984, Continental Illinois was bailed out because regulators thought its collapse would trigger a crisis. The threatening crisis was never observed, and the bailout was taken as a new policy, one of bailing out large banks in "normal times." Yet Lehman Brothers was allowed to fail, although there was a crisis. The lack of understanding of the evolution of policies led to mistakes.

The confusion about these events—Continental Illinois, Lehman—and about the origins of crises depends on counterfactuals: "What would have happened if…?" What would have happened if there had been no Federal Reserve Bank? What if Continental Illinois had not been bailed out? What if Lehman Brothers had been bailed out? "What if" questions are not ones that economists can currently answer, because the models are inadequate for understanding the expectations and beliefs of people and firms. Such models are needed to build a social consensus about the solutions to crises. This is the task for economists.

II. CREATING THE
QUIET PERIOD

All writers on the subject of money have agreed that uniformity in the value of the circulating medium is an object to be greatly desired. Every improvement, therefore, which can promote an approximation to that object, by diminishing the causes of variation, should be adopted....A currency may be considered as perfect, of which the standard is invariable, which always conforms to that standard, and in the use of which the utmost economy is practiced.

—David Ricardo

In market economies consumers rely heavily on bank-created money to transact: checks, ATM cards, credit cards. Before the Civil War the government did not issue paper money, and banks issued private banknotes for use as money. Firms use checks, as well as other forms of bank-created money. These transactions between firms and consumers occur very frequently, every day and even many times during a day.

But this creates a problem. The bank-created money must be backed by something. In the case of demand deposits—checks—it is a claim to bank assets. But the backing assets ultimately are real investments in the economy, usually loans by banks, and these take a long time to reach fruition, and the payoffs are uncertain. The problem is that the bank money is backed by assets that have an uncertain value. If consumers and firms start to worry about the value of the bank money, because they are worried about the backing assets, it becomes very difficult to transact, and there can be a panic.

If there is concern about the backing assets, the collateral, then the money might lose value and trade at a discount to par. Par value is the amount printed on the bank money—if a private banknote or check for $10 can always buy $10 worth of goods or services, then it is said to trade "at par." If the money does not trade at par, life becomes complicated. This is Ricardo's point.[1] But the problem is this: How can banks create money backed by loans or collateral with uncertain values that always trades at par?

One way to begin thinking about this question, and a way to start to understand financial crises, is by using examples of financial reform that were successful in addressing this question and that helped to eliminate financial crises. There has, of course, also been legislation that failed to rectify crises, but I will not go into these many cases. Internationally, there has also been a wide range of bank regulatory experiences, some successful and some not successful. I start here with the two successes in the United States. These examples help elucidate crises and remind us that success, even if limited, is possible.

The U.S. National Bank Acts and the adoption of federal deposit insurance requirements in the United States were two momentous acts of the U.S. Congress that changed the way that money produced by banks was backed. The legislation also raised questions about the essence of money, its purpose, and how it should be backed, questions that come up over and over again.

FREE BANKING AND THE NATIONAL BANK ACTS

Passed during the U.S. Civil War, the National Bank Acts ended the U.S. Free Banking Era of 1837–63. The National Bank Acts created national banks and national banknotes, essentially money issued by the federal government. Prior to the National Bank Acts, there had been no paper currency issued by the federal government that traded at par.[2] Instead, there were private banknotes issued by state-chartered banks, or free banks. Approximately 1,500 different banks' notes traded in the economy at varying discounts from par. This is hard to imagine today—a ten-dollar bill issued by a particular bank in New Haven, Connecticut, for example, might have been worth only $9.90 in gold in New York City, $9.40 in Baltimore, and so on. The discounts from par were not certain; they changed and could not be known for sure by users of the banknotes (everyone in the economy). The discounts were determined in the market for banknotes, where brokers traded notes.

The Free Banking Era began when Michigan, Georgia, and New York passed "free banking laws" following the Panic of 1837. Free banking laws were motivated in part to eliminate the corruption associated with obtaining bank charters (required to open banks) from state legislatures, and in part to eliminate the banking panics associated with private banknotes. Not all states passed free banking laws; table 2.1 shows those that did and those that didn't.

Free banking laws generally had the following provisions: (1) The state legislature did not have to grant a special bank charter to operate a bank. Instead, anyone with the minimum amount of capital could open a bank

Table 2.1   U.S. States With and Without Free Banking Laws by 1860

Free Banking States (Year Free Banking Law Passed)	States without Free Banking
Michigan (1837[a])	Arkansas
Georgia (1838[b])	California
New York (1838)	Delaware
Alabama (1849)	Kentucky
New Jersey (1850)	Maine
Illinois (1851)	Maryland
Massachusetts (1851[b])	Mississippi
Ohio (1851[c])	Missouri
Vermont (1851[b])	New Hampshire
Connecticut (1852)	North Carolina
Indiana (1852)	Oregon
Tennessee (1852[b])	Rhode Island
Wisconsin (1852)	South Carolina
Florida (1853[b])	Texas
Louisiana (1853)	Virginia
Iowa (1858[b])	
Minnesota (1858)	
Pennsylvania (1860[b])	

Source: Rockoff (1975, 3, 125–30)

a. Michigan prohibited free banking after 1839 and then passed a new free banking law in 1857.

b. Very little free banking occurred under the laws in these states; see Rockoff (1975).

c. In 1845, Ohio passed a law that provided for the establishment of "independent banks" with bond-secured note issue.

Figure 2.1 Free Bank Note of the Mechanics Bank of Memphis
Source: Federal Reserve Bank of San Francisco's American Currency Exhibit. Courtesy of the Federal Reserve Bank of San Francisco.

without a vote by the legislature. (2) State or federal bonds had to be deposited with the state auditor as collateral for all notes issued (the state auditor would typically oversee the printing of each bank's notes). (3) Free banks were required to pay gold or silver on demand for the notes they issued. If they did not, then the state auditor could close the banks and sell the bonds and other assets to pay off the noteholders. In most states, the noteholders had preference over other creditors if the bank's assets were liquidated. (4) Free banks were limited liability companies.

The key innovation of free banking was that note issuance required explicit backing by specified high-grade collateral: state bonds. By backing the notes with near-riskless bonds, the value of the notes would have been ensured, and should have traded at par. But they did not.

Notes of the Mechanics Bank of Memphis, Tennessee, like the one shown here, did not circulate in the East and are not listed in eastern banknote reporters, small newspapers listing note discounts, except for a few instances.

Figure 2.2 shows the note discounts from par in Philadelphia for the notes of the Planters Bank of Tennessee.

The discounts from par were quite volatile and sometimes very high, reaching 25% on one occasion. Imagine trying to buy lunch in Philadelphia with a $10 note of the Planters Bank of Tennessee. What was it worth? How would you know? As David Ricardo put it:

> In the use of money, every one is a trader; those whose habits and pursuits are little suited to explore the mechanism of trade are obliged to make use of money, and are no way qualified to ascertain the solidity of different

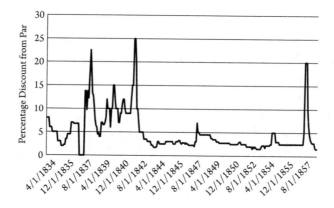

Figure 2.2 Planters Bank of Tennessee Note Discount in Philadelphia
Source: Gary Gorton and Warren Weber, *Quoted Discounts on State Bank Notes in Philadelphia, 1832–1858*, Research Department, Federal Reserve Bank of Minneapolis, http://www.minneapolisfed.org/research/economists/wewproj.cfm.

banks whose paper is in circulation; accordingly we find that men living on limited incomes, women, laborers, and mechanics of all descriptions, are often severe sufferers by the failure of country banks. (Ricardo 1876, 409)

The Free Banking Era was not a totally chaotic monetary system. Since the banks were obligated to honor notes in gold and silver on demand, discounts from par increased directly with the risk of the bank and with the time and distance it took a noteholder to get back to the issuing bank (the time it took to cover this distance is essentially the maturity of the note). In modern parlance, the market for free banknotes was "efficient."

But the "efficiency" of a market is not a normative statement. In fact, it was very difficult to transact with private banknotes. When a note was presented for payment at a shop, the shopkeeper would look up the name of the issuing bank in a small newspaper called a "banknote detector," where the discount on the bank's notes in the market would be listed. Sumner (1896) explains in his *History of Banking*:

The bank-note detector did not become divested of its useful but contemptible function until the national bank system was founded. It is difficult for the modern student to realize that there were hundreds of banks whose notes circulated in any given community. The bank-notes were bits of paper recognizable as a species by shape, color, size, and engraved work. Any piece of paper which had these came with the prestige of money; the only thing in the shape of money to which the people were accustomed. The person to whom one of them was offered, if unskilled in trade and banking, had little choice but to take it. A merchant turned to his "detector." He scrutinized the worn and dirty scrap for two or three minutes, regarding it was more probably "good" if it were worn and dirty than if it was clean, because those features were proof of long and successful circulation. He turned it up to the light and looked through it, because it was the custom of the banks to file the notes on slender pins which made holes through them. If there were many such holes the note had been often in bank and its genuineness was ratified. All the delay and trouble of these operations were so much deduction from the character of the notes as current cash. A community forced to do its business in that way had no money. It was deprived of the advantages of money. We would expect that a free, self-governing, and, at times, obstreperous, people would have refused and rejected these notes with scorn, and would have made their circulation impossible, but the American people did not. They treated the system with toleration and respect. A parallel to the state of things which existed, even in New England, will be sought in vain in the history of currency. (455)

The Free Banking Era is marked by constant complaints about using banknotes as a medium of exchange. The problem was that consumers and firms were at the mercy of note brokers, who could buy the notes at high discounts and profit by taking the notes back to the bank and demanding specie. These broker profits came at the expense of firms and consumers, who did not accurately know the discounts. The note brokers had better information about the value of the notes, about the assets backing the bank debt, and were able to profit from this. The note brokers were competitive, so the discounts were more or less accurate, but still there was a loss to the uninformed consumers and firms. The banknote markets were "efficient," but banknotes were not a good medium of exchange, since they did not trade at par.

A banknote traded at a higher discount when note brokers discovered that the assets backing the note were suspect. They made a business trading on this information, which they would learn privately. This is how markets became efficient, but the problem was that the notes were not liquid. "Liquidity" requires the ability to trade without fear of being taken advantage of by better informed parties like note brokers. The most liquid asset is one that always trades at par. If an asset doesn't trade at par, resources have to be devoted to figuring out its value. Banknotes were not liquid in this sense. Although the free banking legislation tried to make banknotes liquid, they were not.

Because of these problems, contemporary accounts of the use of private banknotes as a medium of exchange are uniformly critical. The editor of the *Historical Magazine* recalls "The History of a Little Frenchman and His Bank Notes. Rags! Rags! Rags!" a story sent in to him by a reader, which he describes as "a correct account of the condition of the currency which followed the War of 1812."

> Travelling lately in the stage [coach] from the South, I fell in company with a little Frenchman. . . . It seems the little man had arrived from Cuba with about eight thousand dollars in gold, which by way of security he lodged in one of the banks in Savannah. When he came to demand his money, he was told they did not pay specie, and he must therefore take bank notes or nothing. Being an entire stranger, and ignorant of the depreciation of paper money arising from the refusal to pay specie. . . he took the worthless rags and began his northward journey. Every step he proceeded his money grew worse and worse, and he was now travelling to Boston with the full conviction that by the time he got there he should be a beggar. ("Origin of the National Banking System," *The Historical Magazine*, August 1864, 253)

It is difficult to measure the waste of resources elicited by the difficulty to transact, even if the discounts were accurate in the efficient-markets sense. Thus "disputes were of frequent occurrence as to the goodness of notes and as to the proper discount" (Bayles 1916, 247). Today, we take it for granted that when we offer a ten-dollar bill in payment, it is accepted as being worth ten dollars. Private banknotes attempted to achieve that and failed. However, the free banking legislation, which would become the basis for the National Bank Acts, was momentous in recognizing that the backing of the notes was a key problem. While states without free banking continued with the system of backing bank liabilities with portfolios of loans, free banking attempted to make the collateral clearly and credibly safe. If the collateral backing was riskless, then the notes would not have discounts when they circulated.

Table 2.2   U.S. State Bond Defaults

State	Date of Default	Action	Date of Resumption or Repudiation
Indiana	January 1841	Resumed	July 1847
Florida Territory	January 1841	Repudiated	February 1842
Mississippi	March 1841	Repudiated	February 1842
Arkansas	July 1841	Resumed	July 1869
		Repudiated	July 1888, Holford Bonds
Michigan	July 1841	Resumed	January 1846
		Repudiated Partially	Partly paid bonds, July 1849
Illinois	January 1842	Resumed	July 1846
Maryland	January 1842	Resumed	July 1848
Pennsylvania	August 1842	Resumed	February 1845
Louisiana	February 1843	Resumed	1844

Source: English (1996) and Kim (2003)

This explicit recognition of the need for riskless collateral for banking money issuance was a very important observation. But its execution, using state bonds as the backing collateral for the notes, had a flaw. The collateral was explicitly required to be U.S. state bonds (varying by state), but state bonds were not riskless. States often defaulted on bond interest payments, and if they did not resume payments, they simply repudiated their debts. And many free banks held the bonds of these states. Even without state bond defaults, a decline in the price of the bonds could cause a free bank to fail.

Table 2.2 lists the states that defaulted on bond interest payments, the date of the default, whether the state resumed payments or repudiated their debts, and, if they resumed, the date of resumption.

Of the thirty-four free banks that failed in New York State during the period 1838–63, most of them failed in 1841 or 1842 and held the bonds of Indiana, Illinois, Michigan, and Arkansas. The attempt of using free banking laws to improve the collateral backing of bank money did not ultimately work—though it led the way for the momentous legislation that did.

With passage of the National Bank Acts of 1863–64, the federal government took over the production of paper money, and national banknotes replaced private banknotes, which were taxed out of existence. The legislation

Figure 2.3A and 2.3B National Bank Note of South Reading and First National Bank of Seattle Federal Reserve Bank of San Francisco's American Currency Exhibit. Courtesy of the Federal Reserve Bank of San Francisco.

was radical.[3] Thousands of state banks were eliminated by essentially forcing them to become "national" banks and eliminating their profitable note-issuing business. A new category of banks was authorized to issue the new legal tender that was required to be backed by U.S. Treasury bonds, creating a demand for U.S. Treasuries.

With a better form of collateral than state bonds, paper money traded at par everywhere for the first time in U.S. history. This was an enormous achievement. The explicit requirement for money backed by U.S. Treasuries was an improvement over the best collateral that could be provided by states or by bank loan portfolios. This was the innovation of the National Bank Acts, an improvement in the collateral backing money, and the troublesome problem of banknote discounts was eliminated.

Two national banknotes are shown in figures 2.3A and 2.3B. The top note is a $2 bill from the National Bank of South Reading, Massachusetts, and the bottom note is a $50 bill from the First National Bank of Seattle, Washington. Each national banknote was issued by a specific national bank, but was backed by U.S. Treasury bonds.

Ironically, the National Bank Acts were not passed to provide an efficient medium of exchange but to finance the U.S. Civil War. "Vast armies must be maintained. Immense armies must be raised and supported; war must be immediately waged. Money must be borrowed. Money, and money alone, will maintain and support armies. The money markets of the old world are closed against the Government" (Lyman Tremain, counsel for the government; see Lord [1863]). Nevertheless, as Judge Alphonso Taft wrote in a letter to Secretary of the Treasury Salmon P. Chase, "If the Civil War resulted in nothing else than providing the country with a uniform currency [that trades at par] it would not have been fought in vain" (Andrew 1913, 609).

This achievement would be remembered later. John W. Faxon, a banker from Chattanooga, Tennessee, recalled this in a speech at the twenty-fourth American Bankers' Association Annual Convention in Denver, Colorado, in August 1898:

> That there has been great progress, in our system of banking, in the past half-century, none will deny; and that we have the satisfaction of seeing every dollar of currency worth a dollar of gold, every day we live, is an evidence of that progress. Many there are in this audience who can easily remember the uncertainties which surrounded commercial enterprises and industrial development not so many years ago, when in every business house there hung a Thompson or Dye's Bank Note Reporter, giving the latest quotations of discounts on the constantly fluctuating currency with which our country was flooded. It was utterly impossible for a business man at that time to tell the profit on a transaction, for by the time such money had circulated, to any great extent, it might have fallen or risen in value from ten to twenty per cent. ("Banking as it Relates to Industrial Development," *Bankers' Magazine* 57 (1898): 498)

The principle that money needs to be backed by collateral that is safe was established. Also, importantly, the conclusion was that only the government is able to provide completely riskless collateral. Other countries have variations on this same principle. Still, through financial innovation the private sector continued to try to produce collateral for the production of private money, thus maintaining the risk of panics and financial crises.

And by the time of the National Bank Acts, financial innovation had already started. Another form of private money had grown to a great amount: demand deposits, or checking accounts. The first financial crisis after the Civil War was the Panic of 1873. This was an en masse run by depositors on banks demanding not gold and silver but currency—national banknotes. The *Financier* called the Panic of 1873 "The Depositors' Panic" (September 27, 1873). According to the *Nation* (October 2, 1873):

> A good many of the admirers of an irredeemable paper currency have begun to admit, sorrowfully but frankly, within the last few days, that whatever other virtues this currency may possess, it does not possess the power of preventing panics, for we are now passing through a well-developed panic.... If they recall their talk of a few years ago, they will find that the reason they gave for believing that inconvertible paper would protect us against crises was that, unlike gold, it would be increased indefinitely in quantity whenever the occasion called for it. Panics, they said, consist in the sudden withdrawal of money from circulation; if money can be supplied in sufficient quantity to fill up the vacuum, the panic passes away.... Nobody has any legal authority to stifle a panic with fresh issues.

Ironically, the Panic of 1873 was evidence that the National Bank Acts were a success; money did trade at par—at least national banknotes did. But the economy had changed; there was financial innovation. In the panics of the National Banking Era, bank liability holders wanted to turn in their checks and withdraw national banknotes.

The Panic of 1873 began on September 13, and by September 20 there was a full-fledged crisis. The New York Stock Exchange closed for ten days, and President Ulysses S. Grant rushed to New York to confer with bankers and business people. Economic activity declined by 10.83% between 1873 and 1875 (Davis 2004). Unemployment was rampant, and, much like today, there were cries for "a complete overthrow of the social and political system" and "to hang the thieves and robbers in Wall and Broad Streets" (see Rezneck 1950, 500).

In fact, demand deposits played a crucial role in the Panic of 1857, the only panic during the Free Banking Era. The superintendent of banking of New York noted:

> A more fearful and mightier power lay dormant, as yet, behind this disturbed currency [private banknotes]—the depositors in our banks, usually quiet, stable, and reliable...a steady and fearful contraction was begun.... Capital, in the shape of deposits, for the first time in the history of this country, and, I think I may say, the world, sided with the business men against the banks.... [To say that deposits are a problem] is heresy, as compared with opinions heretofore entertained upon this question by men of experience.... The idea that deposits were a dangerous element to the banker six months ago would have stamped its promulgator as a tyro in banking.... The element of weakness in banking lies in what has heretofore been considered its strength, its deposits. ("Annual Report of the Superintendent of Banking of the State of New York, December 31, 1857, in "Condition of the Banks of throughout the United States," report of the U.S. Treasury Department, in *Executive Documents*, House of Representatives, during the first session of the thirty-fifth Congress, 1857–58, [Washington, DC: James B. Steedman], 115–16)

The world had changed, and another form of bank money had grown to be very large—demand deposits. A check is a claim first of all on an individual's account at a bank, and then on the bank itself. Checks do not circulate like banknotes, and checks never traded at discounts from par during noncrisis periods. Partly this was due to the fact that they did not circulate, and they were mostly used, at least initially, in cities, where a person's identity could be checked. But also the private bank clearinghouse system, which oversaw check clearing, monitored individual banks. Clearinghouses were private bank regulators starting in New York City in 1853 and spreading to all major cities during the next seventy years.

The problem with checks, as we will see later, was that if leading indicators of a recession got sufficiently high, then the fear of the sudden appearance of a discount on checks led to bank runs. The panics during the National Banking Era were such events, when holders of demand deposits ran on their banks and demanded money. Panics are associated with many of these business cycles, and tended to occur at or near business cycle peaks. Table 2.3 shows the business cycles of the time according to the National Bureau of Economic Research. The two columns in table 2.3 following the panic date show the percentage change in the currency-deposit ratio and the percentage change in pig iron production. These are measured from panic date to the trough of the recession.

Even though banks suspended convertibility of deposits into currency during panics, as checking accounts are withdrawn there are large increases in the currency-deposit ratio, the proportion of all currency in circulation to that which is deposited in banks. Pig iron production, important because of railroad construction during this period, is a measure of economic activity. The dramatic declines in pig iron production are an indication of the severity of the recession. The final two columns show the losses on demand deposits at national banks, measured from panic date to trough, and, finally, the number of national banks that failed during the period of the panic date to the recession trough.[4]

Two important points stand out from table 2.3 (which I will also return to later). First, the timing of the panics near business cycle peaks is important. Panics are not random. This has also been largely confirmed using more modern data. Second, the losses on demand deposits and the number of banks failing are quite small numbers. The largest realized loss on checking accounts at national banks was two cents per dollar of deposits in 1873. Although all banks faced runs—these panics were systemic events—once the dust had settled, the banking system was not insolvent, although the banks could not honor their debts during the panic and had to suspend convertibility.

The panics shown in table 2.3 all involved demand deposits, as currency was now backed by the federal government and was no longer subject to runs. The rise of checking accounts was not well understood for decades. Checks were a kind of "shadow banking system." For example, forty years after the Panic of 1857, a famous economist, David Kinley, president of the American Economic Association in 1913, studied checking and tried to determine the extent of check usage:

> There is no part of industrial life whose record is more strikingly indica-
> tive of the progress of the past fifty years than is the history of the extent
> and course of banking development. In some respects, indeed, banking

Table 2.3 U.S. National Banking Era Panics

NBER Business Cycle Dates Peak–Trough	Panic Date	% Change in C/D	% Change in Pig Iron Production	Loss per Deposit $	% and # of U.S. National Bank Failures
October 1873–March 1879	September 1873	14.53	–51.0	0.021	2.8 (56)
March 1882–May 1885	June 1884	8.8	–14.0	0.008	0.9 (10)
March 1887–April 1888	No Panic	3.0	–9.0	0.005	0.4 (12)
July 1890–May 1891	November 1890	9.0	–34.0	0.001	0.4 (14)
January 1893–June 1894	May 1893	16.0	–29.0	0.017	1.9 (74)
December 1895–June 1897	October 1896	14.3	–4.0	0.012	1.6 (60)
June 1899–December 1900	No Panic	2.78	–6.7	0.001	0.3 (12)
September 1902–August 1904	No Panic	–4.13	–8.7	0.001	0.6 (28)
May 1907–June 1908	October 1907	11.45	–46.5	0.001	0.3 (20)
January 1910–January 1912	No Panic	–2.64	–21.7	0.0002	0.1 (10)
January 1913–December 1914	August 1914	10.39	–47.1	0.001	0.4 (28)

Source: Gorton (1988)

had reached a high plane before the present century, but its sphere was, after all, a very limited one. That the possibilities it offered for facilitating trade were not well understood is shown by the fact that the comparatively unimportant matter of note-issue was the banking function long regarded as worthy of the most serious attention of legislators. The progress of the past century has shown the error of this view. "The check and the clearing system are the main lines upon which banking is destined to run,"—on which it has run for a generation. The issue of notes is no longer regarded as a necessity either for the welfare of the bank or for that of the public. "To us the living fact is the substitution of a new instrument of credit,"—the check. (Kinley 1897, 157)

Kinley prepared a questionnaire, which was sent to U.S. banks by the comptroller of the currency, asking for information about deposits as of July 1896. Replies came back from 5,750 institutions and showed that the percentages of the transactions conducted with checks were 68% in retail, 95% in wholesale, and 92.6% in "all other" transactions, subject to various caveats. Even before Kinley's survey, the comptroller of the currency in 1871 had requested fifty-two selected national banks to analyze and report their receipts for six days. They found that money substitutes (checks, bills, and drafts) accounted for 87.7%, while 12.3% was currency.

The attempts to determine whether demand deposits are "money" would continue, effectively ending only with the passage of deposit insurance. Currently, the same issue is at play with respect to sale and repurchase agreements (repo), which played a leading role in the crisis of 2007–8, but for which there are no accurate measurements. Echoing the earlier surveys, the U.S. Financial Crisis Inquiry Commission sent out a questionnaire about repo usage. During a panic in the National Banking Era the problem of checks trading at a discount from par arose again and again. Currency went to a premium. (A "currency premium" is the counterpart to a discount from par.) In crises, checks could not be used. For example, the contemporary press often reported stories like this one: "It was stated on good authority, yesterday, that Adams & Co's expressmen were specially instructed to receive no checks in payment from anybody, no matter how well they might stand in the mercantile community" ("The Panic," *New York Times*, September 19, 1873). With checks unacceptable and currency hoarded, there was a "currency famine"—a shortage of money and no way to conduct transactions.

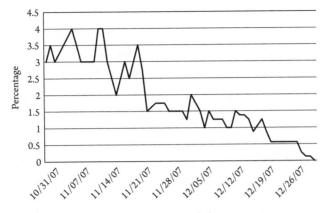

Figure 2.4 Currency Premium during the Panic of 1907 (%)
Source: Andrew (1908a); missing values (for weekends, holidays, and Election Day) interpolated.

But the clearinghouse would stamp some checks "certified," and the currency premium was quoted in terms of these checks. For example, a 3% currency premium meant that a dollar of currency was equal to $1.03 worth of certified checks. The discounts from par, or the currency premium, recalled the private banknotes of the pre–Civil War era. Figure 2.4 shows the currency premium during the Panic of 1907.

The Federal Reserve System was established in 1914, but there were panics during the Great Depression. Later I will discuss the period between 1914 and 1934, between the time that the Federal Reserve System came into existence and when deposit insurance was established.

FEDERAL DEPOSIT INSURANCE

Even after the Federal Reserve System was established in 1914, the United States endured continual panics through the National Banking Era and during the Great Depression until federal deposit insurance legislation was passed in 1934, the second momentous financial legislation in U.S. history.

Despite the experience of the extensive bank runs during the Great Depression, there was a bitter and extended national debate over deposit insurance. It was the only important legislation during Roosevelt's famous first one hundred days that was not initially supported by the administration. Finally, deposit insurance was adopted as part of the Banking Act of 1933 and at first was planned to be temporary, lasting from January 1 to July 1, 1934, but was later extended. The Banking Act of 1935 made deposit insurance permanent. The Banking Act of 1933 also included the separation of commercial and investment banking activities, authorized federal regulators to remove officers and directors of member banks, regulated the payment of interest on deposits, increased minimum capital requirements for national banks, and included other less important provisions. Deposit insurance was part of this full set of reforms.

Deposit insurance had been tried previously in U.S. history, at the state level, with mixed success. It was thus not a new idea, but it had never been tried at the federal level. Some states were not always able to provide sufficient backing for bank deposits, relying on insurance funds that were sometimes too small. And some state designs created misaligned incentives. The U.S. state experiences were later echoed in the international experience, which also had a mixed history. Like the National Bank Acts, deposit insurance was also radical. It forced banks to make a payment into a government fund, a kind of tax. It is interesting to note the justification for this tax, which had come in an earlier court case concerning the Oklahoma state deposit insurance system. In the case, the U.S. Supreme Court faced the question of the constitutionality of forcing banks to pay a deposit insurance fee. The case was *Noble State Bank v. Haskell*, decided January 3, 1911 (219 U.S. 104; 31 S. Ct. 186; 55 L. Ed. 112). In this case, the bank stated that it was solvent and did not want the help of the Oklahoma Guaranty Fund. Further, it claimed that the enforced payment charged by the fund was unconstitutional. The U.S. Supreme Court ruled that it was not unconstitutional. Justice Holmes, writing for the Court, said:

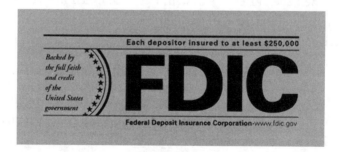

Figure 2.5 The Federal Deposit Insurance Logo
Source: FDIC.

Probably few would doubt that both usage and preponderant opinion give their sanction to enforcing the primary conditions of successful commerce. One of those conditions at the present time is the possibility of payment by checks drawn against bank deposits, to such an extent do checks replace currency in daily business. If, then, the legislature of the State thinks that the public welfare requires the measure under consideration, analogy and principle are in favor of the power to enact it....*It is to make the currency of checks secure*, and by the same stroke make safe the almost compulsory resort of depositors to banks as the only available means for keeping money on hand. The priority of claim given to depositors is incidental to the same object and justified in the same way. (emphasis added)

The court states that the primary purpose of the insurance is to ensure that successful commerce can be maintained because there is a credible money system. That requires that bank checks be made secure. In other words, the decision was not based on the idea that the wealth of small depositors was to be protected. Rather, it was to make checks trade at par.

Deposit insurance was another success, as no further systemic crises were experienced in the United States until 2007. Deposit insurance was radical also because the federal government essentially guaranteed the value of one kind of private liabilities issued by all firms in an industry, banking. There were claims that it would create "moral hazard" by allowing all banks to borrow at the same rate regardless of risk, and despite the fact that the capital requirements were very low.

Yet despite prognostications to the contrary, deposit insurance was a success. Whether a deposit insurance system will succeed or not depends on the details of the design. The details that were critical to the success of federal deposit insurance in the United States were interest rate ceilings on demand deposits, limited entry, and bank examination. The legislation included limitations on the payment of interest on demand deposits, so that banks could not attract money by raising rates. Banks were examined regularly, a key feature for making deposit insurance work.

The advent of federal deposit insurance in the United States was the start of a long period in which effective regulation eliminated the threat of systemic financial crises—the Quiet Period.

Another bank regulatory system that sometimes works is one in which there is a small number of large banks that are in an implicit club with the central bank. The banks do not want to lose their club membership because it provides special benefits, the value of which is called "charter values." Charter value is created by the maintenance of the club oligopoly. The banking systems of many of the world's developed economies follow this model. A leading example is Canada, where there has been only one major bank failure since World War I, and where there were no bank failures during the Great Depression. In Canada, by 1996 five of the eight chartered banks (with extensive nationwide branching) held 90% of bank assets. In fact, countries with more concentrated banking systems are less likely to have crises. Canada calls into question simple notions of "too-big-to-fail," which are discussed later. This model does not always work, though, as there have certainly been crises in countries with a small number of large banks.

The National Bank Acts and federal deposit insurance illustrate a number of key points about the production of bank money. The conundrum of the market economy is that there is a need for bank money, but the private sector cannot create riskless collateral to back the money. Collateral must be real assets, or claims on real assets (like loans or bonds), but these are of uncertain value. The uncertainty of their value is due to the fact that the length of time it takes to produce output in the economy is longer than the time intervals at which transactions with money are made. The National Bank Acts resulted in money trading at par, something we take for granted today. And deposit insurance is largely responsible for the Quiet Period.

These successes are worth dwelling on. In both cases the private sector's attempts at money creation—first private banknotes and then demand deposits—were plagued by difficulties rooted in the inability of the private sector to create riskless collateral to back money issuance. This is the gist of the problem: in order for bank debt to be used as money, to be liquid, it must not trade at a fluctuating discount and it must not be vulnerable to the fear of a sudden discount from par if information about a coming recession arrives. To meet demands for "money," the private sector persisted in its attempts to create new means for transactions and inevitably relied on risky collateral. If the world never changed, the Quiet Period—the Great Moderation—would have continued forever, as economists predicted.

III. FINANCIAL CRISES

Since 1793 panics have occurred [in the United States] in the following years: 1797, 1811, 1813, 1816, 1819, 1825, 1837, 1847, 1857, 1866, 1873, 1884, 1890, and 1893. The true name for a system with this record is the panic system.

—Theodore Gilman, *Federal Clearing Houses*, 1899

Financial crises in market economies are common, and relatively frequent. They occur much more often than people think and are not unique to certain historical periods or to emerging market economies. Only during the Quiet Period in the United States did the idea that financial crises are rare take hold. And, in the case of the United States, crises were viewed as having become extinct.

The history of market economies in every country includes crises—China before the Communists came to power, Japan in 1927, Argentina in 1890, and Australia in 1893, to name just a handful. Some of the more recent crises include Argentina in 1980 and 1995, Korea in 1997, Sweden in 1991, the Czech Republic in 1996–97, Hungary in 1997, Latvia in 1995, Uruguay in 2002, and so on. England had bank panics in 1819, 1825, 1847, 1857, 1866, 1890, 1974, 1984, 1991, and 2007–8. Table 3.1 lists crises in some selected developed countries.

The map in figure 3.1 shows crises around the world over the period 1970–2005. Countries in white had no systemic financial crisis during this period. The darkest countries had three or four crises, and the lighter

Table 3.1   Financial Crises, 1870–2008, Selected Countries

Country	Financial Crisis (first year)
Australia	1893, 1989
Canada	1873, 1906, 1923, 1983
Denmark	1877, 1885, 1902, 1907, 1921, 1931, 1987
France	1882, 1889, 1904, 1930, 2008
Germany	1880, 1891, 1901, 1931, 2008
Italy	1887, 1891, 1901, 1930, 1931, 1935, 1990, 2008
Japan	1882, 1907, 1927, 1992
Netherlands	1897, 1921, 1931, 1988
Norway	1899, 1921, 1931, 1988
Spain	1920, 1924, 1931, 1978, 2008
Sweden	1876, 1897, 1907, 1922, 1931, 1991, 2008
Switzerland	1870, 1910, 1931, 2008,
United Kingdom	1890, 1974, 1984, 1991, 2007
United States	1873, 1884, 1893, 1907, 1929, 1984, 2007

Source: Schularick and Taylor (2009, Appendix Table 1)

ones had one or two. The map also shows the output losses as a percentage of GDP.

What is a financial crisis? Is there something common to financial crises, or is each somehow different? If you have not thought about crises, the financial crisis of 2007–8 seems different. A common reaction of economists to the recent crisis is that it is special because it appears to be related to financial innovations that they were unfamiliar with. I am reminded of the words of William N. Parker (1986, 9),[1] a famous Yale economic historian, in discussing the problems an economist will have when he or she has no knowledge of economic history: "Such an economist becomes a shallower, narrower analyst with feeble capabilities for adapting the theory and statistics he has mastered to new and strange social environments. All problems strike such a one as new." When an event, a financial crisis, is repeated over and over again, it should seem natural for economists to seek a structural explanation, some common feature of crises that causes this repetition. It would seem obvious that each crisis is not due to coincidental bad events or unique institutional features.

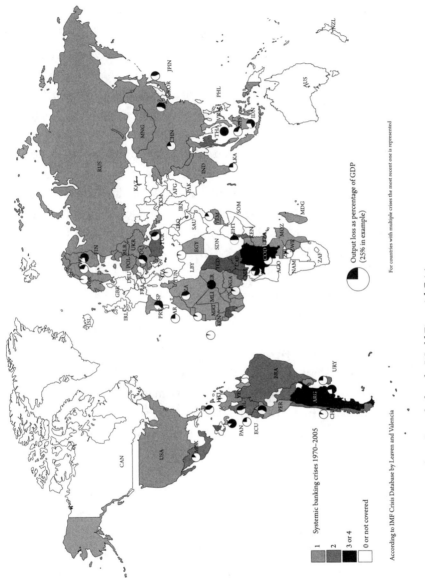

Figure 3.1 Systemic Banking Crises before the World Financial Crisis

Systemic banking crises 1970–2005

1

2

3 or 4

0 or not covered

According to IMF Crisis Database by Leaven and Valencia

 Output loss as percentage of GDP (25% in example)

For countries with multiple crises the most recent one is represented

Although every crisis is different in significant ways (and this is especially so in the modern era when central banks and governments are more actively involved, as we will see later), crises have the same root cause. Prior to the existence of central banks, financial crises were always bank runs. And in financial crises around the world since 1970, most (62%) involved bank runs and sharp reductions in demand deposits in the banking system. A financial crisis is about bank debt; it occurs when market participants come to mistrust the value of bank debt. Eventually I will come to the question of what I mean by "mistrust" and "bank debt," but first I will focus on defining a financial crisis.

A financial crisis can be understood most clearly if there is an observable, widespread bank run, as in the pre–Federal Reserve period in the United States. Then, a financial crisis was a more or less simultaneous run on *all* the banks in the banking system, with bank liability holders demanding cash. In the pre–Civil War Era in the United States this occurred with private banknotes, starting as early as the Panic of 1819, and then with demand deposits starting with the Panic of 1857 and continuing through the Great Depression. These panics were publicly observable: crowds of people lined up at their banks. They were *systemic* because *all* banks faced runs.

Once a central bank exists, crises are more complicated. But at root crises are the same: sudden large demands for cash from financial institutions in exchange for short-term debt obligations. The commonality of crises is one of the points that the Panic of 2007–8 should have made clear—the crisis mechanism was the same. In the Panic of 2007–8, it was sale and repurchase agreements (repo), commercial paper, and prime broker balances that were run on. This panic was not observable to most people because it involved wholesale markets where firms ran on other firms.

A defining feature of a run is that a large number of consumers or firms act at more or less the same time, making such large-scale demands for cash that the banking system cannot meet their demands for legal tender. In this sense, the banking system is insolvent; it cannot honor contractual debt obligations. Then banks either suspend convertibility—they simply do not pay out cash— or they are bailed out by the government or the central bank. In the Panic of 2007–8 firms tried to sell assets to raise the cash that was needed to repay repo depositors. But in doing so they just drove asset prices down, and eventually the Federal Reserve had to buy the assets, and the U.S. Congress passed the Emergency Economic Stabilization Act of 2008, which included an allocation of $700 billion dollars for the Troubled Asset Relief Program (TARP) to bail out firms. The alternative would have been to cash in all debts and obligations for the entire banking system—to liquidate the banking system. That alternative has never (intentionally) been chosen.

Two points are worth emphasizing and repeating. The first is the scale of the financial crisis. Typically, a large part of the banking system is involved—many or most banks. This is why these crises are called "systemic." Second, the event is one in which bank liability holders demand cash, rather than holding the bank debt. A large amount of short-term bank debt is turned in for cash at the same time. The scale of the cash demands is so large that banks cannot meet the cash demands. People who were on trading floors at investment banks and other financial firms in August 2007 through 2008 understand the scale of the event. In that case, the panic did not involve depository institutions or the checking accounts of households but the short-term debt issued to firms and institutions depositing in the old investment banks in the form of repurchase agreements or asset-backed commercial paper.

I have the feeling that experience counts for something, that living through a panic firsthand, as an eyewitness, allows one to understand these two points, the scale of the event and the demands for cash. But it is hard to convey the experience of a panic to those who were not there. The panics of the Great Depression were not experienced by most Americans alive now. And the Panic of 2007–8 was not seen or directly experienced by most people.[2] Firms and institutional investors did not line up at their banks to withdraw money, as people did in the film *It's a Wonderful Life*, in which there is a bank run on the Bailey Building and Loan Association (not a systemic event since it was the only bank that was run). When Frank Capra made the film in 1946, most Americans could remember the bank runs of the Great Depression and so the film would echo their experiences. In the Walt Disney film *Mary Poppins*, made in 1964, there is also a bank run scene, though it is shorter and not crucial to the plot. The memory of the Great Depression has faded in the United States, though many people in most other countries have had the unfortunate experience of being part of a bank run.

Getting a visceral sense of the event of a panic is, I think, crucial to thinking about the issues involved in addressing panics through policy. Having watched the events unfold on the AIG Financial Products trading floor, I think that no amount of empirical evidence, even if it could be produced, is a substitute for being an eyewitness. One eyewitness to the Panic of 1907, Charles Glover, president of Riggs National Bank of Washington, DC, said the same thing in testimony before Congress:

> I have been forty years a banker, and I have passed through all of the panics during that time. We went through a condition here in November [1907] that you gentlemen could hardly appreciate, unless you were in the banking business. I saw the suspension of the entire business of the United States. (Testimony to the Committee on Banking and Currency of the House of Representatives, April 13, 1908)

To try to convey the nature of the event of a financial crisis, here are some descriptions of panics, starting with the Panic of 1837, which started just after Martin Van Buren was elected the eighth president of the United States:

> Mr. Van Buren had taken his inaugural oath on the fourth of March preceding [1837]. On the tenth of May the great financial earthquake of the Suspension, breaking out at its commercial metropolis, rolled rapidly over the entire Union, in every direction, to the farthest extent of its limits. The whole banking system of the country strewed the ground with its ruins. All the great interests of production and commerce, of which the currency of a country is the life-blood, and of which the banks were accustomed channels and vehicles of circulation, lay likewise stunned and paralyzed by the shock. From every quarter a universal cry of agony arose from the land.... The catastrophe was so new—so appalling—so overwhelming; it fell so heavily up all interests and all parties; the explosion of the swollen credit bubble bore so ruinously.... A feeling of discouragement and despair seemed to chill and unnerve many of the truest and stoutest. ("Mr. Van Buren's Title to Re-election," *The United States Magazine and Democratic Review*, 7 (28–29) (April–May, 1840): 290)

This description could easily also apply to President Franklin Roosevelt, who took office in March 1933 at the height of the banking crisis of the Great Depression, or to President Obama, who took office in the midst of the recent financial crisis. The crises repeat and repeat. The descriptions are similar. Here are some more descriptions, this time of the Panic of 1857:

Imagine Lombard-street [in London] expanded to twice its length, and its trottoir [sidewalk] enlarged to more than twice the present width, and every third house a bank, with depositors or bill-holders bent upon obtaining gold for their debts—and you will have a real idea of the condition of Wall-street yesterday. New York was in a state of convulsion. A financial earthquake was rocking its moneyed institutions to their centre. One fell after another; shock followed shock; and in the panic no one felt sure that, at the day's close, anything would be left to tell the tale of the wealth, the commercial credit, and the mercantile honour of this community. This morning, the partial suspension of yesterday has become general, and New York is now doing business on currency. ("The Crisis and Its Causes," *Times* [London], October 27, 1857, quoted in the *Westminster Review* 69 [January 1858], 89)

And, from the same article:

The final blow was... as rapid, and apparently as unpremeditated, as the blow that brought about the French Revolution of 1848; like that, there was a concealed power that excited and directed the popular feeling.

The first run yesterday was made upon the smaller banks outside of Wall-street, that afford accommodation and circulation for the tradespeople, artisans, shopkeepers, hotelkeepers, &c.; these institutions were naturally in a less strong position than the banks doing business with the mercantile classes, and less able to stand a run. They opened at ten, and before twelve had fallen. Up to one o'clock everything was quiet in Wall-street; as quiet, that is, as it has been any day for the past three weeks. There was a steady payment of specie over the counter to depositors, but nothing indicating a general alarm. Almost in an instant the street was crowded, and a run began upon the American Exchange Bank, the weakest of the large institutions. I had passed the Exchange a few minutes before; there was no appearance of unusual commotion. When I looked from my window, there was a crowd of some hundreds (or thousands rather) gathered in front, and a long line of bill-holders and depositors formed *en queue*. Mr. David Leavitt (of North American Trust and Banking Company fame) mounted a step, and treated the crowd to the universal Anglo-Saxon panacea—a speech; and the crowd partially dispersed, but the bill-holders kept up the run. From every direction men now poured into Wall-street. The marble steps of the Custom-house, the classic entrances to the banks, the noble spaces around the Exchange, the ugly stoops (an inheritance from the architects of Amsterdam), that gave a ladder-like entrance to the offices, were alike covered with curious spectators.... The stream of the anxious in-goers steadily increased.... The banking community of New York was called upon to liquidate in less than two hours. No bank could have stood the pressure. Last night those that had gone safely through the day met in council. The session lasted until eleven o'clock, and resulted in a unanimous agreement to suspend specie payments over the counter. (89–90)

Like the recent financial crisis, there are always problems as well in the inter-bank markets. A letter from the secretary of the Treasury:

The suspension was preceded by a desperate struggle between all the banks themselves, and distrust and fear of currency was more apparent among them than with the public generally.... The fact that about the first of October a list of more than thirty failed banks, located in this State, was to be seen daily in our newspapers, began to tell fearfully among the public generally. The merchant, the mechanic, the grocer, and the butcher began business in the morning by examining what broken banks had been added to the list of yesterday; and their customers found that the bank note that passed freely yesterday was rejected this morning. It is not to be wondered at that a feeling of distrust and alarm began to prevail throughout the State in relation to our banks. ("Condition of the Banks throughout the United States," April 22, 1858, in *Executive Documents*, House of Representatives, during the first session of the thirty-fifth Congress, 1857–58 [Washington, DC: James B. Steedman], 114–15)

The Panic of 1857 involved both private banknotes and demand deposits, since it occurred at the end of the Free Banking Era. Again, on the Panic of 1857:

At ten o'clock a strong guard of detective police was placed at the gates of the Pennsylvania Bank, and a written notice posed on the railings, stating that the Bank had resolved to suspend payment in specie. Since that time, however, the excitement has been most intense. Gold-street, alongside the Bank, became thronged, and all ingress to the Bank was stopped, except to the clerks. The Girard Bank, in Third-street, was the next source of excitement. At this Bank the crowd of depositors was immense, and, at the time I now write, the most intense excitement prevails, in consequence of the approach of the hour (1 o'clock) to which the Girard Bank postponed payment of checks. All the other banks in the city are being run upon.... Every avenue of the city is crowded, as if for the celebration of some extraordinary event. ("The Financial Troubles, Bank Suspensions in Philadelphia, Baltimore, and Elsewhere," *New York Times*, September 26, 1857)

Bankers Magazine, November 1857, p. 412:

The banks of the city of New York, by their officers, assembled at the Clearing-House, Tuesday, October 13th, resolved to suspend specie payments.... Never... in the financial history of New York, was there a more trying and exciting time than [October 1857]. For weeks the merchants of New York had fallen in numbers, like so many sacrifices, at the threshold of the banks, beyond whose iron doors came no response to their appeals.... Each one sees the picture, though he may not have in Wall-street or in the neighborhood of the up-town banks—a street crowded with two distinct classes, the one thirsting for gold, crowding in hundreds the doors of the banks, and forming long lines up the steps and through the halls, with anxious faces, and hands nervously clutched over their checks and drafts, crowding and jostling; and the other, the lookers-on, crowding the sidewalks, joking and wondering how long the banks could stand the run—such was the picture. Between the distresses of the merchants who have been called upon to pay, *when they had nothing to pay with*, and the total destruction of confidence among the poorer classes of the people, there were chaos and confusion throughout the city. Early in the day there was a simultaneous run upon the several banks of the city, we believe without a single exception.

After the Panic of 1857 came the panics of 1873, 1884, and 1893, and then, fifty years after the Panic of 1857, the United States experienced the Panic of 1907:

When the bankers of Oklahoma reached their offices Monday morning, October 28, 1907, they found that over Sunday the banks of St. Louis and Kansas City, following the example of New York and Chicago, had suspended cash payments, except in small amounts; and that the Governor of Oklahoma, to give the banks time to meet the situation, had declared a legal holiday of a week. The panic was on. The principal correspondents of the banks were in St. Louis and Kansas City. Currency could not be obtained from either city except in driblets. An order for $5000 in currency might bring $500.00, if so much. The Oklahoma banks had no place to get currency to pay depositors in the panic evidently sweeping over the country.

The paralysis of trade the country over exceeded anything that had been seen in a generation, and the course of events was the same in Oklahoma as in the other states. Farmers would not sell hogs and grain and cotton because the buyers could not pay in actual money. The movement of commodities stopped; long trains of idle freight cars filled the city yards and cumbered the country sidings. The railroads bought little coal and the output of the mines fell off. Many railroad men, miners, mechanics, and laborers were idle and money to pay others could be scraped together only by the severest of expedients, and at great expense. Values melted away, and business was dead. (Cooke 1909, 86–87)

What do these descriptions of historical U.S. banking panics have to do with the modern era, with the recent financial crisis? Is it just a bygone era, irrelevant to modern policy questions? No; this time the "banks" were the old investment banks and the bank debt was sale and repurchase agreements (repo), commercial paper, and prime broker balances.

Repos are like demand deposits. One party deposits (lends) money in a bank, usually overnight, and will receive interest. To make the deposit safe, the depositor is provided with collateral in the form of a bond. So, for example, if an institutional investor deposits $100 million, then a bond with a market value of $100 million is given to the institutional investor as collateral. If the bank fails, then the institutional investor can sell the bond, without going into a bankruptcy procedure. The next morning the bond collateral is returned in exchange for the cash plus interest. Often, the transaction is "rolled over"—that is, extended for another night. The institutional investor can always withdraw the money, so to speak, by not rolling the repo.

Commercial paper is short-term debt issued by firms, but also by asset-backed commercial paper (ABCP) conduits, managed vehicles that buy asset-backed securities (bonds backed by pools of loans) using commercial paper. ABCP conduits are limited-purpose operating companies that purchase mostly highly-rated, medium- and long-term asset-backed securities and fund themselves with cheaper, mostly short-term, highly-rated commercial paper and medium-term notes. ABCP conduits peaked at just over one trillion dollars outstanding right before the financial crisis.

Prime brokerage is a type of banking provided to hedge funds and other large investors. Prime brokers, typically large banks, clear trades, provide leverage, and issue credit lines to hedge funds and other investors. Hedge funds typically use a prime broker to back their trades, so counterparties face the prime broker, not the hedge fund. The prime broker banks also provide financing to the hedge funds to allow them to obtain leverage, a higher ratio of debt to total capital. The amount of leverage a hedge fund can obtain with respect to an asset is determined through their margin requirements and the collateral risk-management policies of the prime broker. The prime brokers manage the risk incurred by lending to clients and taking their counterparty risk in trades by using margins calls, and possibly the liquidation of positions based on risk triggers. Most importantly, clients keep money at their prime brokers (prime broker balances). These are essentially like checking accounts for hedge funds.

The financial crisis of 2007–8 was a run on repo, prime broker balances, and asset-backed commercial paper. Paul Friedman, who oversaw the repo desk at Bear Stearns, testified:

> From approximately August 2007 to the beginning of 2008... the fixed income repo markets started experiencing instability, in which fixed income repo lenders began shortening the duration of their loans and asking all borrowers to post higher quality collateral to support those loans. Although the firm was successful in obtaining some long-term fixed income repo facilities, by late 2007 many lenders, both traditional and non-traditional, were showing a diminished willingness to enter into such facilities. During the week of March 10, 2008, Bear Stearns suffered from a run on the bank that resulted, in my view, from an unwarranted loss of confidence in the firm by certain of its customers, lenders and counterparties.... The loss of confidence had three related

consequences: prime brokerage clients withdrew their cash and unencumbered securities at a rapid and increasing rate; repo market lenders declined to roll over or renew repo loans, even when the loans were supported by high-quality collateral such as agency securities; and counterparties to non-simultaneous settlements of foreign exchange trades refused to pay until Bear Stearns paid first. ("Testimony of Paul Friedman before the Financial Crisis Inquiry Commission," May 5, 2010, 3)

Sam Molinaro, former chief operating officer and chief financial officer of Bear Stearns, testified:

In this panic, an increasing number of prime brokerage clients began to request that their available cash and securities be moved to other brokers. Moreover, late on Thursday [March 6, 2008], a significant proportion of our repo counterparties informed us that they would no longer lend to us, even on the basis of secured collateral. As a result of these conditions we experienced a significant cash outflow which reduced our liquidity pool. ("Testimony of Samuel Molinaro before the Financial Crisis Inquiry Commission," May 5, 2010)

Richard S. Fuld, Jr., chief executive officer of Lehman Brothers, stated in a written statement before the Financial Crisis Inquiry Commission, September 1, 2010:

The run on the bank then started. Lehman's principal clearing banks demanded that Lehman post additional collateral. Counterparties to the numerous repurchase transactions that Lehman conducted on a daily basis began to withdraw business and to demand increased collateral to consummate trades. Liquidity was frozen by those clearing banks, and hedge fund customers began migrating to other firms.

The Board of Governors of the Federal Reserve System reported that the vote was unanimous to act under section 13(3) of the Federal Reserve Act to extend credit to JPMorgan Chase to assist in purchasing Bear Stearns:

The senior management of Bear Stearns notified the Federal Reserve on the evening of Thursday, March 13, that it anticipated that many of its counterparties would on Friday not agree to roll over their repurchase agreements and, therefore, that Bear Stearns would be required on Friday to repay a significant portion of its repurchase agreement liabilities. Bear Stearns expected that it would not have sufficient funds or liquid assets to repay these obligations as they came due and would not be able during the short period before the markets opened on Friday to find a private-sector source of alternative financing. Bear Stearns reported that it would likely have to file for bankruptcy protection on Friday unless the Federal Reserve were willing to provide Bear Stearns with liquidity. (Federal Reserve Board, *Report Pursuant to Section 129 of the Emergency Economic Stabilization Act of 2008: Bridge Loan to The Bear Stearns Companies Inc. Through JPMorgan Chase Bank, N.A.*, 2)

Hector Sants, head of England's Financial Services Authority, said of the run on the British bank Northern Rock:

I think that the set of circumstances that transpired in the market were highly unusual and was not, I think, in fairness, anticipated by any regulators around the world; nor, indeed, if you look at the individual commentators. Some, of course, or a number, may have been pointing out the share price was too high; there was nobody really anticipating that set of circumstances. It is not just a question of the securitisation market being closed to [Northern Rock] for a prolonged period, it is also a question of other mechanisms of wholesale funding, in particular the repo market being closed. As we indicated, they had high quality assets—there is no suggestion here this is an organisation taking on poor quality assets—and it really is *an extraordinary set of circumstances which lead to them being unable to repo those assets for a period of six weeks or so as well as the combined closure of the securitisation.* (House of Commons 2008, 2:25; emphasis added)

There are many, many such descriptions, from around the world and through history. It is worth reading the descriptions to understand some basic points:

- Crises have happened throughout the history of market economies.
- Financial crises are about demands for cash in exchange for bank debt, which takes many different forms.

- The demands for cash are on such a scale—often the whole banking system is run on—that it is not possible to meet these demands because the assets of the banking system cannot be sold en masse without their prices plummeting.
- Crises are sudden, unpredictable events, although the level of fragility may be observable.

The crises described above involve different kinds of bank money. In 1857 customers of banks demanded gold and silver in exchange for their banknotes and demand deposits. In the panics of the National Banking Era, like the Panic of 1907, depositors demanded National Bank Notes in exchange for their checking accounts. In the Panic of 2007–8, depositors did not want the bonds as collateral for repo anymore. I will say more about the Panic of 2007–8 later. But at this point note that the run on repo involves the same vulnerability of bank debt that occurred with private banknotes and demand deposits. With repo, the backing collateral received by the depositor was not always U.S. Treasuries but sometimes risky bonds. The Panic of 2007–8 was structurally the same as the earlier panics.

The descriptions convey a sense of the suddenness of crises—"as rapid, and apparently as unpremeditated, as the blow that brought about the French Revolution of 1848." There is an abrupt change, like going over a cliff, or a sudden switch, a plunge. Economists like the term "regime switch" or "breakpoint." Also, the descriptions emphasize the scale of the event. It is systemic. Many institutions are run on at more or less the same time, such that the demands for cash cannot be met *by the system*. These crises are systemic, which—to repeat—means that the demands for cash in exchange for bank liabilities are of such a magnitude that the demands cannot be honored. Prior to the existence of the Federal Reserve System, the banks would suspend convertibility rather than try to honor the demands for cash. During the Great Depression, state governors and then President Roosevelt declared banking holidays to keep banks from having to pay out cash. These two characteristics—scale and demands for cash—are canonical features of systemic financial crises.

The banking system cannot possibly turn all, or significant amounts of, their liabilities into cash in a short period of time. This is because the backing assets can't be sold fast enough without pushing their prices down. But if banks don't have to sell assets, as in a suspension of convertibility, then it turns out the losses are minimal—or at least were during the National Banking Era.

There is a very important difference between the earlier runs, when there was no central bank and when the government did not intervene (and was not expected to intervene) and the later period, when the Federal Reserve System or other central bank existed, and later still, when deposit insurance was in place, or when the government was expected to intervene. With regard to the earlier, pre-Fed period, it is clear that a financial crisis is a system-wide bank run. Mass bank runs don't necessarily occur in the modern era, due to explicit or implicit government actions, or expectations of such actions. In the modern era, we can say that:

> A financial crisis is an event where holders of short-term debt issued by financial intermediaries withdraw en masse or refuse to renew their loans—*or would have engaged in such a mass run had not explicit or implicit government intervention been in place or been expected.*

While most crises involve bank runs, the definition is expanded because a clear-cut run may not occur because of expected government action. Instead of a straightforward panic, what happens depends critically on the private sector's expectations or beliefs about the policies of the central bank or government. The lack of a bank run because of these expectations or indeed of the government's actions creates the impression that financial crises are not related to the vulnerability of bank debt, but are about other factors, like shocks to bank capital and so on, as will be discussed below.

I readily concede that the phrase "*or would have engaged in such a mass run had not explicit or implicit government intervention been in place or been expected*" is tricky because it poses a counterfactual. Later, I will show concretely what this means when asking *what would have happened* in the 1920s and 1930s in the United States had the Federal Reserve System not been in existence. The key is that the expectations and beliefs of people in the economy must be understood in a concrete, practical way so that the counterfactual can be constructed. And later I will argue that this is an example of what economists need to do more generally.

Financial crises are not uncommon, and they occur in all market economies. They are sudden, unpredictable events, although the level of systemic fragility may be observable. They involve all or a significant number of banks (or other financial firms). A crisis may involve runs on banks, a sudden demand for cash on a scale that cannot be met by banks (although "banks" are not necessarily the firms that bank regulators think are banks). Bank runs may not occur if action by a government or central bank is expected, but there can still be a crisis in which the banking system is massively impaired.

IV. LIQUIDITY AND SECRETS

> Bank credit is an elemental thing consisting of purchasing power
> which a bank manufactures. This credit manifests itself in two forms,
> namely, bank notes and bank deposits.
>
> —Thomas Bruce Robb, *The Guaranty of Bank Deposits*, 1921

Financial crises are about bank debt. Debt is a financial contract under which the borrower promises to repay a fixed amount (known as par value, principal, or face value) at an agreed future date, the maturity date. Between the date when the money is borrowed and the date when it is to be repaid, the borrower may also pay interest to the lender. If the borrower does not repay the principal or interest, then there are consequences. For nonbanks, the consequence may be bankruptcy, a legal procedure for allocating ownership of corporate assets. For banks it is different: bank regulators intervene, and ultimately there may still be bankruptcy. Bank debt is short-term, giving the lender/depositor the right to get the cash back quickly. With banknotes or checking accounts, the bank customer has the right to demand cash at any time the bank is open. With repo and commercial paper, the maturity can be overnight, a few days, a week, or a month.

Banks and bank debt were at the root of every one of the 124 systemic crises around the world from 1970 to 2007 (some also involved currency crises in which the value of the domestic currency declined precipitously). Indeed, there cannot be systemic crises without bank debt.[1] But bank debt is needed for conducting transactions and is necessary for an economy to function. There is a demand for debt for transactions by households and firms, and banks supply the debt. This is an elemental feature of market economies. Debt is the technology for conducting trade. It is short-term and designed to be "safe." Bank debt is essential to transacting because it provides liquidity.

For example, if you had to sell a Van Gogh painting (lucky you to own one!) quickly, you would lose money. You don't really know what the painting is worth unless you are an art expert. And few people would believe that it was a Van Gogh. Anyone who actually knew the painting's worth could claim it was fake and try to buy it at a very low price. So you would take the painting to an auction house, and they would research its provenance, put out a catalogue, and after a year or so hold an auction. You would realize more of the value of the painting. You could not realize the value of the painting at short notice unless you were willing to take a great loss. On the other hand, a Treasury bill can be sold easily without loss of value. There is no need to determine the provenance of a U.S. Treasury bill—its value is known by all. Bank debt attempts to privately create this property of a Treasury bill, and this property is called liquidity.

Liquidity is a slippery and elusive idea. John Maynard Keynes wrote that an asset is liquid if its value is "more certainly realizable at short notice without loss" (Keynes 1930, 67). To trade easily, with liquidity, participants should not need to be concerned about whether the price of the "money" is right. The usual cause for concern, however, is the possibility that one side to the transaction knows more about the value of the money than the other side. In fact, just the possibility of one side knowing more than the other lowers the possible value of the transaction, even if no one really knows anything.

Let's take a concrete example. Richard Levin, president of Yale University, lives in New Haven, Connecticut. Suppose he goes to New York City to see a show, and before the show he wants to buy lunch at Belushi's Samurai Deli. Suppose President Levin offers a ten-dollar free banknote from the Bank of New Haven to Mr. Belushi to buy a sandwich. The following questions come up: First, what is the ten-dollar bill worth in terms of gold or silver—what is the discount from par? Second, does either party secretly know more than the other party about the value of the banknote? If there is a supposed discount from par, known from the secondary note market, there can still be a question of whether one party secretly knows that this discount is too high or too low. A party that knows a secret is said to have private information, and the situation between the two parties is then said to be one of asymmetric information.

The problem is that if one party suspects that the other party knows a secret about the value of the money, he may suspect that he will be taken advantage of and may not trade. Then President Levin won't get his sandwich and will go to the show hungry. To get him his sandwich, we are interested in knowing how the problem of secrets can be minimized. Minimizing the problem of secrets is the same as creating liquidity.

If there is no information to learn secretly, there can be no secrets, as with a Treasury bill. To minimize the problem of secrets, money must be backed with collateral that is riskless, or near-riskless. As we have seen, the problem is that the private sector cannot create riskless—secret-free—collateral. This was exactly the problem we saw earlier with the Free Banking Era, the National Banking Era, and with federal deposit insurance. In other words, if the collateral is riskless, and everyone knows the collateral is riskless, then there is no problem. And if it is costly to produce secret information, it may not pay to bother learning a secret if the collateral is near-riskless.

Let's go back to President Levin and Mr. Belushi. Suppose President Levin secretly knew that the Bank of New Haven backed their notes with risky collateral, and imagine that he knew the secret information that the note is only worth seven dollars. President Levin can benefit from this secret knowledge if he can use it to buy a sandwich worth more than seven dollars. Mr. Belushi then loses.

Of course, it could be that Mr. Belushi knows the secret that the note is only worth seven dollars. He could then claim that the note is only worth five dollars. President Levin can accept that statement and lose two dollars (if it's really worth seven dollars), or he can forego the sandwich and go to the show on an empty stomach.

If President Levin and Mr. Belushi thought that there were no secrets, and they each knew that the other thought the same way, then the note would be worth ten dollars, and a ten-dollar sandwich would be exchanged for the ten-dollar bill. That's the world of believing that there are no secrets. There's another world; let's call it the transparent world. In this world, they both know the secret that the note is worth seven dollars. Then only a seven-dollar sandwich could be exchanged. *They are better off if they think that neither knows a secret than they would be if the secret information were revealed.* If they are both ignorant, a ten-dollar sandwich can be exchanged. If they are both informed, then only the seven-dollar sandwich can be exchanged. If one of the two knows the secret and the other was aware of this, then the uninformed party might not trade at all, or accept that he will be taken advantage of. And if the sandwich is all the transactions in the entire economy, then there is a big difference between a ten-dollar club sandwich and a seven-dollar baloney sandwich.

The transaction technology is not just about prices—ten dollars versus seven dollars—because the actual amount and the quality traded are different. In one case a ten-dollar club sandwich is traded, in the other a seven-dollar baloney sandwich. These are different goods, one more desirable than the other. Perhaps an analogy will help to make the point that this is a technology. To get from New Haven to New York City, President Levin would have to take some means of transportation. In the early part of the 19th century he would have traveled by stagecoach. The trip would have taken the better part of a day, so President Levin wouldn't have gone very often. Thus trade between New Haven and New York City was infrequent compared to a decade or so later when there was a train line between New Haven and New York City (later this the famous "New Haven," a legendary railroad that operated from 1872 to 1969). With the railroad line in place, the transaction costs were reduced. In the same sense, if the money is secret-free, the transaction costs are reduced.

Markets are liquid when all parties to a transaction know that there are probably not any secrets to be known: no one knows anything about the collateral value and everyone knows that no one knows anything. In that situation it is very easy to transact. The situation where there is nothing to know or nothing worth knowing—no secrets—is desirable and allows for efficient transactions.

The idea that knowing nothing is desirable may seem counterintuitive. The whole idea of "efficient markets" is that asset prices contain information. But the stock market is much different from interbank and money markets. Bank debt is a senior claim on the collateral: debt holders are paid first and stock or equity is paid last. Since stockholders are paid last, all information about the collateral is relevant for them, so they have a big incentive to learn secrets— legally or otherwise. So in the end, there are no secrets (in theory), which is why the price reflects the information. With bank debt it is the opposite. The goal is to have no information revealed, and no possibility of any party wanting to learn, because of the overall cost of learning the secret.

Here's another example. A money market fund (MMF) is a kind of bank. Such a fund typically invests in high-quality, near-riskless securities, like U.S. Treasuries, bank certificates of deposit, and commercial paper. Their investors/depositors own shares in the fund and can write checks on their deposits. Money market funds are concerned with not "breaking the buck." This refers to a fund's net asset value (NAV) per share always being one. If the fund has $100 million in assets and investors own 100 million fund shares, then the fund's per share NAV is one dollar. If the assets go up in value, MMFs change the interest rates and keep the share value at one dollar. If the assets go down in value, an MMF may break the buck. This happened during the recent financial crisis. The Reserve Primary Fund, one of the oldest MMFs, broke the buck after it suffered losses due to the failure of Lehman Brothers on September 15, 2008. As a result, on September 19, 2008, the U.S. government announced that it would insure the MMFs to maintain the buck.

Some have proposed that MMFs float—that is, trade at whatever the NAV per share is, which may be less than one. This is tantamount to proposing that we go back to the world of free banking, where people and firms tried to trade with banknotes that continuously broke the buck. Pre–Civil War banknote markets functioned regularly with monies that traded with discounts. But the idea of all money is to avoid breaking the buck. Fears of breaking the buck can result in a panic. If the buck might be broken, then there is the possibility that someone other than you knows a secret and will take advantage of you. It's like the old saying—sometimes attributed to Warren Buffet—that if you do not know who the patsy is in a game of poker, it's you. Fear of being the patsy keeps people from trading.

Most of us are familiar with demand deposits (checks) and money market funds, which also can use checks, and previously I discussed banknotes, the pre–Civil War currency. There are also other forms of bank money. These other forms are called "money market instruments" and are used by companies, institutional investors, pension funds, hedge funds, states and municipalities, and central banks. These forms of money are like checking accounts for these large entities.

An important misunderstanding revealed by the crisis is that regulators and economists did not know what firms were banks, or what debt was "money." They thought that banks were only the firms that had bank charters, and that money was only in currency and demand deposits. They did not realize that repo and asset-backed commercial paper (ABCP) are also money, indeed, the two most important money market instruments—the two forms of money that suffered runs during the financial crisis of 2007–8.

Repo and ABCP were backed to a large extent by privately produced collateral in the form of asset-backed securities (ABS). As we have learned, it is impossible for the private sector to produce riskless collateral, and very hard for it to produce near-riskless collateral. There is a conflict between real investment in the economy, which is long-term, and consumption and transaction demands, which are short-term. Real investments are uncertain, particularly as they have longer horizons than the horizon over which consumption takes place. Think of making a submarine, which takes about a year, versus buying lunch.

Before the recent financial crisis, repo and ABCP often used collateral that was produced by the private sector. The collateral was often asset-backed securities, which are the outcome of securitization. Securitization is the process of moving long-term bank loans off balance sheets by selling them to a special purpose vehicle (a legal entity), which in turn finances the purchase of the portfolio of loans by packaging and selling the loans in the capital markets. Securitization markets are some of the largest markets in the world. In 2002 in the United States, the amount of securitized bonds issued ($662.4 billion) first exceeded corporate bond issuance ($636.7 billion). In 2005 issuance exceeded U.S. corporate bond issuance, even excluding mortgage-related securitization. The ABS issued was overwhelmingly rated AAA/Aaa.

Securitization creates high-grade debt that is used as collateral—collateral that can be used to back repo and ABCP. So one kind of long-term debt, ABS, becomes the backing for the short-term debt. The structure of asset-backed securities can be very complicated and opaque. The idea is that they make good collateral because of their lack of secrets. The problem with privately produced collateral is that it is not riskless, however, and there might be secrets worth learning sometimes.

The problem is if we start in a situation where there are no secrets because the backing collateral for the money is known to be high-grade, then a shock or bad event might raise the possibility that there could be a secret. Maybe there is no secret to learn, but maybe there is—we don't know. Someone might actually learn a secret, or we may just fear that someone has. The way to prevent being taken advantage of is to avoid using bank debt and get cash. This is called a "flight-to-quality." All the bank money was secret-free initially, but afterward all the bank money can be vulnerable to secrets, or information-sensitive, when there is bad news.

The vulnerability of bank debt to mass runs is due to its design. Invulnerability to secrets is by design, but an event can happen that causes all parties to worry that others are learning secrets. To determine the value of the backing collateral, show me the money.

The banks don't have the money, since it has been lent out, and they suspend convertibility—that is, the banks just say no to the demands for cash. The bank debt is contaminated by the secrets problem. This was a major problem during the suspension periods prior to the Federal Reserve System. There was a shortage of acceptable money.

Before the Federal Reserve came about in the United States, banks tried to reduce the possibility of anyone finding secrets by creating stronger backing of demand deposits. The principal way they did this was by organizing themselves into clearinghouses. These were organizations that "cleared" checks. Originally, checks drawn on different banks had to be settled—taken back to the bank and exchanged for cash. Now when someone writes me a check, I take it to my bank and deposit it. The bank then takes the check to the clearinghouse and asks for the money. In that way, the person who wrote me the check has the amount of the check subtracted from their account in their bank (through the clearinghouse) and I have it added to my account (assuming the check doesn't bounce). If there are many, many such checks on many banks, the process of clearing can become very complicated.

The Supreme Court of Pennsylvania described a clearinghouse as follows:

> It is an ingenious device to simplify and facilitate the work of the banks in reaching an adjustment and payment of the daily balances due to and from each other at one time and in one place on each day. In practical operation it is a place where all the representatives of the banks in a given city meet, and, under the supervision of a competent committee or officer selected by the associated banks, settle their accounts with each other and make or receive payment of balances and so "clear" the transaction for the day for which the settlement is made. (quoted by J. Cannon [1910a], 1)

Before clearinghouses, each bank would send a clerk to carry checks to each of the other banks and present them for payment. So during any business day clerks from each bank would visit each other bank, crossing paths all day. As was bound to happen, the clerks would see each other going to and from the banks, and often clerks from several banks would be at the same bank presenting checks at the same time. In this way the clerks got to know each other and eventually would stop at the street corners where they met and exchanged checks without actually going to the banks. It wasn't long before they were meeting regularly by appointment in a public house (bar). This of course saved a lot of time, and when it was discovered by their bosses it became the clearinghouse. Sometimes this story is told about the banks in Edinburgh, but most historians cite documents to the effect that London had the first official clearinghouse in 1775.

By 1889 fifty-one U.S. cities throughout the country had clearinghouses.

By the nineteenth century, clearinghouses performed a large variety of functions beyond mere check clearing. A manager of the New York City Clearing House Association, William Sherer, explained in a speech at the New York State Bankers' Association on June 22, 1901:

> The clearing-house, as one writer puts it, has become the "conservator of sound banking." The requirement of weekly statements from member and non-member banks gives all business interests an opportunity to judge of each bank's condition. The clearing-house committee, the executive committee of the association, composed of men of large experience and of ability as bankers equal to any in the world, keep informed as the affairs of the banks through the weekly statements and records of their daily transactions at the clearing-house, and are thus enabled to judge whether a bank is being managed in a way detrimental to the safety of the banking and business interests.
>
> This committee has power to examine any bank or trust company making exchanges at the clearing-house and to suspend an institution from its privileges, if in the judgment of the committee, that be the proper step to take. (New York State Bankers' Association 1901, 51)

Mr. Sherer describes one way in which clearinghouses acted like a central bank—monitoring and examination of member banks—but there were others. In response to a panic, toward the end of the nineteenth century, clearinghouses issued their own money, called clearinghouse loan certificates. There were two uses for this new credit instrument. First, these instruments

Table 4.1 U.S. Clearinghouses in 1889

City	Date Established	Number of Member Banks
New England		
New York	1853	65
Boston	1855	54
Providence	1866	34
Hartford	1872	15
New Haven	1873	10
Springfield, MA	1872	10
Worcester	1861	8
Portland, ME	1865	7
Lowell	1876	7
Mid-Atlantic Region		
Philadelphia	1858	41
Pittsburgh	1866	19
Baltimore	1858	23
Syracuse	1874	8
Wilmington, DE	1887	6
Buffalo	1889	12
Middle		
Chicago	1865	20
Cincinnati	1866	17
Milwaukee	1868	11
Detroit	1883	17
Cleveland	1858	11
Columbus	1868	14
Indianapolis	1871	7
Peoria	1880	10
Grand Rapids	1885	7
Other Western		
Kansas City	1873	11
Minneapolis	1881	16

(continued)

Table 4.1   Continued

City	Date Established	Number of Member Banks
St. Paul	1874	14
Omaha	1884	8
Denver	1885	10
Duluth	1887	7
St. Joseph	1877	7
Wichita	1888	8
Topeka	1887	6
Des Moines	1887	9
Sioux City	1889	11
Western		
San Francisco	1876	17
Los Angeles	1887	8
Portland	1889	10
Seattle	1889	12
Tacoma	1889	7
The South		
St. Louis	1868	17
New Orleans	1872	15
Louisville	1876	22
Memphis	1879	8
Richmond	—	—
Galveston	1885	—
Dallas	—	7
Fort Worth	1888	—
Norfolk	1871	6
Nashville	1889	10
Birmingham	1889	9

Source: Bailey (1890)

No._____

LOAN COMMITTEE OF THE

Detroit Clearing House Association.

*Detroit, Mich.*_____

*This certifies that*_____ *has deposited with the committee securities in accordance with the proceedings of a meeting of the association held*_____*upon which this certificate is issued. This certificate will be received in lieu of balances at the Clearing House for the sum of five thousand dollars from any member of the Clearing House Association.*

On surrender of this certificate by the depositing bank above named. The committee will endorse the amount as payment on the obligation of said bank held by them and surrender up a proportionate part of the collateral securities held therefor.

FIVE THOUSAND DOLLARS.

Committee.

Figure 4.1 Detroit Clearing House Association Clearing House Loan Certificate

were used only among members of the clearinghouse as a substitute for cash in the clearing process. Later, as their use evolved, clearinghouse loan certificates were issued directly to the public as money. Clearinghouse loan certificates were a way of creating safe collateral by bank coalitions—the clearinghouses—during crises. These credit instruments were liabilities of the clearinghouse members *jointly*, rather than of any individual member.

The first issue of loan certificates occurred in 1860, though the origins were in the response of New York City banks to the Panic of 1857. In 1860, just after the election of Abraham Lincoln as president, the economic situation in the country was deteriorating. Banks were hesitant to loan, and some of the best banks could not finance themselves, even offering high interest rates. George S. Coe (1817–96), who was for many years the president of the American Exchange National Bank of New York, had the idea of a new credit instrument. The proceedings of the New York Clearing House Association of November 21, 1860, explained Coe's proposals (see *Bankers Magazine* 15 [1860–61]: 500; also quoted by Redlich [1968, 161]):

In order to enable the Banks of the City of New York to expand their loans and discounts, and also for the purpose of facilitating the settlement of exchanges between the Banks, it is proposed that any Bank in the Clearing House Association may, at its option, deposit with a Committee of five persons—to be appointed for that purpose—an amount of its bills receivable, United States stocks, Treasury notes, or stocks of the State of New York, to be approved by said Committee, who shall be authorized to issue thereupon to said depositing Bank, certificates of deposit, bearing interest at seven per cent, per annum, in denominations of five and a thousand dollars each, as may be desired, to an amount equal to seventy-five per cent. of such deposit. These certificates may be used in settlement of balances at the Clearing House, for a period of thirty days from the date hereof, and they shall be received by creditor Banks, during that period, daily, in the same proportion as they bear to the aggregate amount of the debtor balances paid at the Clearing House. The interest which may accrue upon these certificates shall at the expiration of thirty days, be apportioned among the Banks which shall have held them during the time.

The securities deposited with said Committee as above named shall be held by them in trust as a special deposit, pledged for the redemption of the certificates issued thereupon.

The Committee shall be authorized to exchange any portion of said securities for an equal amount of others, to be approved by them, at the request of the depositing Bank, and shall have power to demand additional security, either by an exchange or an increased amount, at their discretion.

The amount of certificates which the Committee may issue as above shall not exceed $5,000,000.

This agreement shall be binding upon the Clearing House Association when assented to by three-fourths of its members.

Resolved, that in order to accomplish the purpose set forth in this agreement, the specie belonging to the associated Banks shall be considered and treated as a common fund for mutual aid and protection, and the Committee shall have the power to equalize the same by assessment or otherwise.

For this purpose statements shall be made to the Committee of the condition of each Bank on the morning of every day, before commencement of business, which shall be sent with the exchanges to the Manager of the Clearing House, specifying the following items, viz:

Loans and discounts.
Deposits.
Loan certificates.
Specie.

This plan was the blueprint for the clearinghouse loan certificate, a new form of debt that could be used to settle clearinghouse balances. The plan also involved pooling and equalizing member banks' specie reserves as a way to avoid suspension. This meant that the member banks became a single entity for the period of suspension. As a result, the suspension of specie payments that seemed imminent was avoided.

Clearinghouse loan certificates were again issued during the Panic of 1873. On September 20, 1873, the process began when the president of the New York Clearing House announced the plan with virtually the same words that had been used in 1860. The system of issuing joint liabilities, backed by the clearinghouse itself (that is, all member banks), continued to evolve with successive crises until the Panic of 1893, when the certificates were issued in small denominations directly to the public for the first time. The total amount of clearinghouse hand-to-hand currency issued during the Panic of 1893 was

Table 4.2 Clearinghouse Loan Certificates Issued by the New York Clearinghouse ($millions)

Year	Date First Issued	Months until Redeemed	Maximum Amount Created	Bank Deposits
1860	November 23	3.5	$6.9	$99.6
1861	September 19	7.25	22	99.3
1863	November 6	2.75	9.6	159.5
1864	March 7	3.25	16.4	168.0
1873	September 22	3.75	22.4	174.8
1884	May 15	4.25	21.9	317.2
1890	November 12	2.75	15.2	386.5
1893	June 21	4.66	38.3	398.0
1907	October 26	5	88.4	1,023.7
1914	August 3	4	109.2	—

Sources: Report of the Comptroller of the Currency, 1907, 63; Dwyer and Gilbert (1989); Swanson 1908a, 1908b

around $100 million, about 2.5% of the money stock. During the Panic of 1907, about $500 million was issued, around 4.5% of the money stock.

The intent of the clearinghouse loan certificate was to minimize the likelihood of there being a secret about any individual bank, since, by pooling all the banks' assets, diversification would minimize this chance. Nevertheless, the certificates would trade at a discount for a while. So even though they came close, clearinghouse loan certificates are not an example of the private sector successfully creating riskless debt.

During the recent financial crisis the Federal Reserve, using the Term Securities Lending Facility (TSLF), introduced in March 2008, allowed banks to exchange asset-backed securities for U.S. Treasury bonds. The TSLF was unique in that U.S. Treasuries entered the economy in a very specific way—they were exchanged for private asset-backed securities (ABS). The ABS were secret-prone, but the treasuries were not, and the collateral behind bank repo was improved. The evidence suggests that TSLF was uniquely effective for this reason. In the end, there were no secrets to be learned.

Debt exists because it minimizes secrets. Bank debt is designed to be secret-proof, and thus liquid; that is, debt that can be traded easily, at par, without worrying about a loss to a counterparty that has private information. But a small shock to the economy can cause market participants to think that others know secrets, and they lose confidence in the debt's invulnerability to secrets. This creates a crisis when much of the banking system is leveraged with debt that is thought to be liquid but turns out not to be. Clearinghouse loan certificates were a response to such crises, to try to engineer secret-proof bank debt.

V. CREDIT BOOMS
AND MANIAS

> Prosperity breeds credit, and credit stimulates enterprise, and enterprise embarks in labors which, about every ten years in England, and every twenty years in this country, it is found that the world is not ready to pay for. Panics have recurred in England in 1797, 1807, 1817, 1826, 1837, 1847, 1857 and there was very nearly one in 1866. In this country we have had them in 1815, 1836, and 1857, and by panics we do not mean such local whirlwinds as have desolated Wall Street, but widespread commercial crises, affecting all branches of business.
>
> —*The Nation*, September 25, 1873

Financial crises are often preceded by credit booms, extended periods during which the amount of credit granted—through loans, bond issuance, and mortgages—rises. Because there are potentially more defaults if there is a shock to the financial system (through people learning secrets), a credit boom increases the fragility of the system. This does not mean that credit booms are bad, but to start with we must get a sense of how they happen.

In the modern era a lending boom can be defined as a period when private credit grows abnormally faster than private gross domestic product (GDP)—simply a high-percentage increase in credit granted over some years. If we look for average growth in the ratio of private credit to GDP in excess of 10% per year over the three years prior to a crisis, then about a third of the crises in

1970–2007 had credit booms. Strong credit growth was observed before many famous crises, such as those in Argentina in 1980, Chile in 1982 (where it was 34.1%), Sweden, Norway, and Finland in 1992, Mexico in 1994 (the Tequila Crisis), and Thailand, Indonesia, and Korea in 1997 (the Asian Crisis). In fact, the most useful indicators of the likelihood of a financial crisis is a measure of credit creation. It is the canary in the coal mine.

Figure 5.1 provides a sense of the credit growth in the five years prior to financial crises. As the figure shows, strong credit growth preceded most banking crises.

Let's look at an example. One of the most important emerging-markets crises was the Tequila Crisis of 1994–95, which started in Mexico. Prior to the crisis, Mexico seemed healthy. It was growing again after the 1980s, called the "lost decade." The proximate shock that triggered the Tequila Crisis was a sudden devaluation of the Mexican peso. In December 1994, the Mexican Central Bank widened the exchange rate bands, which resulted in an immediate 15% devaluation of the peso, and sovereign default was imminent. Domestic interest rates also increased, causing losses in the Mexican banking system. There was also a political crisis: an armed insurrection, the assassination of the leading presidential candidate, kidnappings of prominent

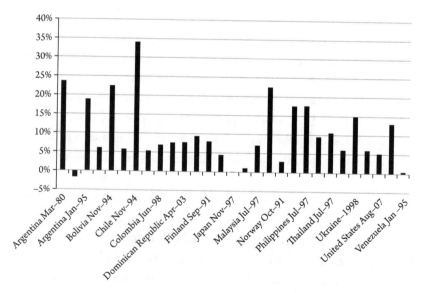

Figure 5.1 Annual Growth in Private Credit to GDP Ratio, Leading Up to a Crisis (t-4, t-1) (%)
Source: Laeven and Valencia (2008).

businessmen, and political scandals. The Tequila Crisis had large spillover effects on Brazil and Argentina. It showed how important international capital flows can be if a shock causes a drastic decline in the exchange rate.

There were unique and new aspects to the Tequila Crisis, but what was not new was the preceding credit boom. Francisco Gil-Diaz, the former vice-governor of the Bank of Mexico, described the boom:

> Mexico's credit expansion churned out impressive numbers. From December 1988 to November 1994, credit from local commercial banks to the private sector rose in real terms by 277 percent, or 25 percent per year. Some items provide a better understanding of the underlying trends: credit card liabilities rose at a rate of 31 percent per year, direct credit for consumer durables rose at a yearly rate of 67 percent, and mortgage loans at an annual rate of 47 percent, all in real terms. (Gil-Diaz 1998, 306–7)

Gil-Diaz attributed the credit boom to a number of factors: "The financial sector...underwent a substantial liberalization, which, when combined with other factors, encouraged an increase in the supply of credit of such magnitude and speed that it overwhelmed weak [bank] supervisors, the scant capital of some banks, and even borrowers" (see Gil-Diaz [1998, 303]). Figure 5.2 shows the growth in credit per capita in Mexico prior to the Tequila Crisis. The crisis date is the dark bold vertical line.

There was no bank run, because the depositors were rescued. Very soon after the 1994 devaluation, the Mexican government began rescue operations and a series of attempts to recapitalize the banks. The rescue effort prevented a systemic breakdown of the banking system but was very costly: about 15% of GDP. That there were no bank runs during the Mexican crisis is an example of a broader phenomenon. Expectations of being saved by government actions changed people's behavior. But the government was expected to act, because if they did not, there would be a bank run.

The same pattern of the credit boom in Mexico was present in the recent financial crisis, but the form of credit was different. Specifically, the boom was with a newer type of debt—asset-backed securities (ABS). Figure 5.3 shows the rise of *nonmortgage* asset-backed securities. Pictured is the outstanding amount.

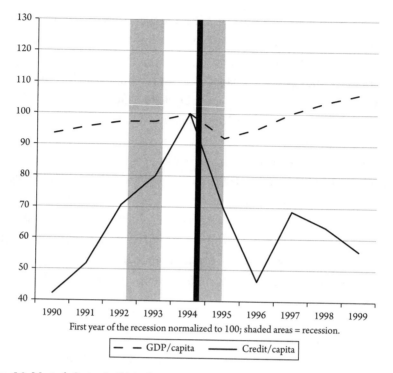

Figure 5.2 Mexico's Systemic Crisis, Starting December 1994 (peak-trough: 10/92–10/93 and 11/94–07/95)
Sources: Business cycle dating from Economic Cycle Research Institute (http://www.businesscycle. com/resources/cycles/); World Bank.

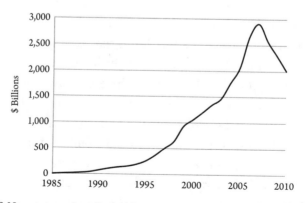

Figure 5.3 U.S. Nonmortgage Asset-Backed Securities Outstanding
Source: Securities Industry and Financial Markets Association.

Nonmortgage asset-backed securities largely finance types of consumer debt unrelated to home purchases—like credit card debt, automobile loans, and student loans—and a large fraction of general consumer credit in the United States is financed by securitization. Roughly, securitization has funded between 30% and 75% of lending in various consumer lending markets and about 64% of outstanding home mortgages. In total, securitization has provided over 25% of outstanding U.S. consumer credit. This rise of nonmortgage-related ABS is the most recent version of the traditional credit boom preceding crises. Securitization played an important role in the crisis because asset-backed securities were used as the collateral for repo and as assets for ABCP conduits. More generally, there was rise in private-credit-market debt outstanding, as shown in figure 5.4.

Figure 5.4 shows the rise in household and financial-sector borrowing. Borrowing is related to growth in the economy, so it is a good idea to scale the outstanding debt amounts by the gross domestic product, shown in figure 5.5.

Even scaled by gross domestic product, the increase in household and financial sector debt is apparent, starting in the 1990s. Also apparent is the financial crisis.

A credit boom means that households and firms are borrowing more and more, and the figures above suggest it was mostly households involved in the recent U.S. credit boom. What were they doing with the money? Although

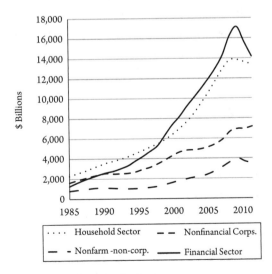

Figure 5.4 Credit Market Debt Outstanding by Sector
Source: Federal Reserve System, Flow of Funds.

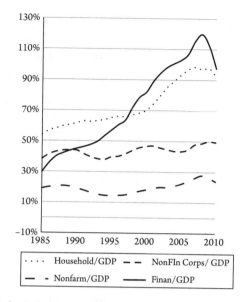

Figure 5.5 Credit Market Debt Outstanding by Sector, as a Percent of GDP
Source: Federal Reserve System, Flow of Funds; Bureau of Economic Analysis.

nonmortgage-related securitization increased, the answer appears to be that banks were lending to borrowers buying land or houses. In other words, banks were lending against real estate, which is the best collateral. Although there has been little research on this, there appears to be a connection between bank credit creation and increases in real-estate prices. And generally there are often increases in house prices with credit booms. This was true of the recent financial crisis. Mortgage-related securities also grew enormously. Figure 5.6 shows the outstanding amounts of mortgage-related securities per capita. In 1980 the per capita amount of mortgage-related securities outstanding was $487.78; it was $8,835.54 in 1995, $12,639 in 2000, and $25,839 in 2006. The figure shows mortgage-backed securities, which played a central role in the recent crisis.

The figure shows an upward trend, but keep in mind that it combines two trends. First, more and more people are getting mortgages, and second, more and more of those mortgages are being financed through mortgage-backed security issuance, rather than by banks simply holding the mortgages on their balance sheets. So the figure shows the combined effect of the credit boom in mortgages and a financial innovation used to facilitate the credit creation.

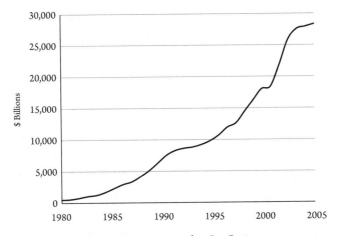

Figure 5.6 U.S. Mortgage-Related Securities Outstanding Per Capita
Source: SIFMA: Includes GNMA, FNMA, and FHLMC mortgage-backed securities and CMOs,
CMBS, and private-label MBS and CMOS.

The United States has seen many credit booms and associated land- and
house-price increases. They have been described as bubbles, manias, and
speculations. The observation that credit booms and real-estate-related price
rises are related is quite old. As we go back in history, the data become increasingly sparse, but many of the earliest booms were related to the sales of
public lands. One of the first credit booms in the United States was based on
land in Maine. It was described by Hugh McCulloch in his 1888 memoir *Men
and Measures of Half a Century*.[1]

> The wildest speculation that has ever prevailed in any part of the United
> States, was in the timber lands of Maine. In 1832, or about that time ... it
> became known to people in Massachusetts, that a good deal of money
> was being made by a few investors in the Maine timber lands. A large
> part of Maine was covered in a magnificent forest.... These lands were
> offered for sale by the State at very low prices, and those who bought
> early and judiciously did make what were then considered large for-
> tunes.... It was not long before reports of their gains went out ... until
> almost everybody in New England who heard them was seized with a
> desire to speculate in Maine lands. (215)
>
> *Purchases and sales of land were made chiefly upon credit. Very little money
> was handled in the transactions, whether large or small.* It was upon promis-
> sory notes that the gambling fabric rested, and when the explosion took

place, it was these promissory notes, for which nothing available for their payment had been received, that brought ruin to many hundreds of households. (217; emphasis added)

Another observer of early credit booms was Michael Chevalier, a Frenchman who had been sent to the United States in 1834 by the minister of the interior of France to inspect the public works in the United States. He toured the United States for two years and sent back twenty-three letters, totaling 440 pages, which were collected in his 1839 book *Society, Manners and Politics in the United States*. Although not as well-known as Alexis de Tocqueville, Chevalier was also a keen observer of American life. On August 4, 1835, he wrote (305): "Every body is speculating, and every thing has become an object of speculation.... The principal objects of speculation are...cotton, land, city and town lots, banks and railroads." This was just before the Panic of 1837, when there were large sales of public lands. Benjamin Horace Hibbard (1870–1955) an agricultural economist at the University of Wisconsin and author of the classic *A History of the Public Land Policies*, describes the rush for land:

> Thousands of men, with little or much money, had a vision of settlement, wheat, prosperity and profits. There was an undue amount of zeal in attempts to help the vision to come true. The condition of the currency was such as to greatly facilitate the speculation. (Hibbard 1965, 215)

The size of this rush for land is reflected in the receipts for public land sales. Aaron Sakolski (1880–1955) in *The Great American Land Bubble* (1932, 235) noted that:

> In 1825, receipts from public land sales amounted to but $1,216,090. They rose to $2,329, 356 in 1830, and then continued [in table 5.1]:

Land prices kept rising, which required buyers to borrow more and more. This was noted by Davis Rich Dewey, a scholar of financial history, who commented on the connection between credit booms and land prices in this period:[2]

Table 5.1   Sales of Public Lands Prior to the Panic of 1837

Year	Acres Sold	Receipts
1831	2,777,857	$3,557,064
1832	2,462,342	3,115,376
1833	3,856,227	4,972,285
1834	4,658,219	6,099,981
1835	12,564,479	15,999,804
1836	20,074,871	25,167,833
1837	5,601,103	7,007,523

As the market value of the land frequently rose too much above the government selling price, there was an eager contest on the part of those who could borrow money to buy for speedy sale at an advanced price or hold the land for future profit. Borrowers found ready accommodation at local banks, and with the loans thus secured made their purchases from the land receiver; the purchase money in many instances was thereupon re-deposited by the government in the bank whence it came, where it once more served as a loan to another or even the same land speculator. These local banks and the government surplus thus became involved in a common network of credits; banks were established to meet this temporary demand, so that the lender leaned upon the borrower. (Dewey 1918, 225)

Contemporary observers noted the growth in bank credit. For example, James Buchanan (1791–1868), senator from Pennsylvania and later the fifteenth president of the United States, in a speech in the United States Senate, noted:

Bank capital, bank notes, and bank loans, have increased with alarming rapidity for the last few years. The President, in his Message, states that between the commencement of the year 1834, and the first of January 1836, the bank capital of the country had increased from $200,000,000 to $251,000,000, the notes in circulation from $95,000,000 to $141,000,000, and their loans and discounts from $324,000,000 to $457,000,000. We know that since the first of January, 1836, the increase has still been proceeding at a rapid rate, and many new banks have been created.... Under any sudden revulsion of trade, these banks either sink under the weight they have heaped upon themselves... or, if they survive the shock, they greatly injure, or wholly ruin those members of the community around them who have unfortunately become their debtors. (Appendix to Cong. Globe, 25th Cong., 1st Sess. [1837], 100)

Hugh McCulloch also linked the credit booms to the banking crises.

The great expansion of 1835 and 1836, ending with the terrible financial collapse of 1837, from the effects of which the country did not rally for years, was the consequence of excessive bank circulation and discounts, and an abuse of the credit system, stimulated in the first place by Government deposits with the State banks, and swelled by currency and credits until, under the wild spirit of speculation which invaded the country, labor and production decreased to such an extent that the country, which should have been the great food-producing country of the world, became an importer of bread stuffs.

The financial crisis of 1857 was the result of a similar cause, namely, the unhealthy extension of the various forms of credit. (1888, 218)

McCulloch's view of the Panic of 1857 was the common view at the time. For example, the *Westminster Review* reported:

As the resources of the mercantile community were trenched upon, mortgages were called in, land lots found worthless, and high rents being no longer maintainable in an impoverished community, a great depreciation took place in real estate. With the thousands now out of employment, and the general pressure on the trading classes, rents in New York, Philadelphia, and Boston will largely recede, and outside lots remain unoccupied for a time. Thus the various securities of banks, note-brokers, merchants, and store-keepers have, by the reaction of the gigantic system of speculation which pervades the country, been reduced to nothingness, and large concerns, with an improving business and accumulating capital, brought to insolvency. ("The Crisis and Its Causes," *Westminster Review* 69 [1858]: 91, reprinted from the *Times* [London; 1857])

Sound familiar?

The pattern is repeated over and over. There was another credit boom and land-price rise in the period 1873–96, during which western agricultural prices and land prices rose and many mortgages were bought by banks around the country. Then came bad news for agriculture, followed by foreclosures, bankruptcies, and bank failures—and the Panic of 1893. Allan Bogue, in a classic study of this boom and bust, wrote:[3]

> Between 1888 and 1894 most of the mortgage companies failed. The causes of failure were closely interrelated. The officers of the mortgage agencies had misunderstood the climatic vagaries of the plains country. They had competed vigorously to finance the settlement areas beyond the ninety-eighth meridian (e.g., western Kansas and Nebraska). Beginning in 1887 the plains country was struck by a series of disastrously dry years. The effects of drought and short crops are sometimes alleviated by high prices, but in these years the prices of agricultural products were depressed. Many of the settlers along the middle border failed to meet their obligations. The real estate holdings of the companies grew to unmanageable size; operating capital was converted into land at a time when the bottom had dropped out of the land market. (1955, 267)

Such booms did not end well, as is attested in a rhyme that tells the sad story of one borrower:

> Just about three years ago,
> I bought a lot and bought it low;
> The man that sold it told me so,
> And he's the one that ought to know.
>
> Fifteen thousand was the price,
> He didn't have to ask me twice;
> I paid it half in one big slice,
> And felt as rich as Calvin Brice.[4]
>
> And for the rest I gave my note;
> And as my name I glibly wrote,

I had no thought, no more'n a goat,
How big the load I'd have to tote.

Now I sit in silent gloom,
Thinking of my awful doom;
I want to lie in my tomb
Before we hit another boom.

(William S. Witham, *Bankers' Magazine* 57 (1898): 506)

Earlier in American history, credit booms were not only related to land. Chevalier noted that "Speculations in railroads have hardly been less wild than those in land" (1839, 307). This is not surprising. The railroad was a major innovation, and building it required enormous amounts of capital. In 1830 there were only twenty-three miles of railroads in the United States. But by 1893 there were 173,433 miles (Wright 1886, 19). Figure 5.7 shows the enormous growth of railroad construction during the nineteenth century.

This enormous growth had to be financed—in advance of any revenue being earned (the railroad track had to be built before it could carry passengers).

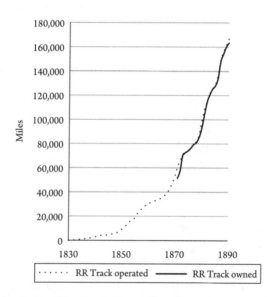

Figure 5.7 Growth of Railroad Track in the United States during the Nineteenth Century
Source: Susan B. Carter, Scott Sigmund Gartner, Michael R. Haines, and Alan L. Olmstead, eds., *Historical Statistics of the United States, Earliest Times to the Present* (Cambridge, UK: Cambridge University Press, 2006), series Df 874, Df 875.

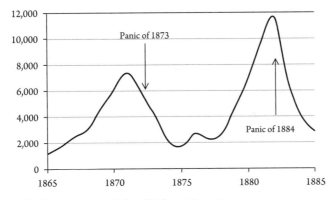

Figure 5.8 Year-by-Year Increase in Railroad Miles in Operation
Source: Wright (1886)

According to Jenks (1944, 8): "In the final analysis, the funds for railway construction came from the extension of credit by American banks and from foreign exchange supplied by European investors."[5]

The view at the time was that railroad-related credit booms were related to
crises. For example, Myron T. Herrick (1854–1929), chairman of the board
of the Society for Savings, Cleveland, Ohio (and also the forty-second governor of Ohio and ambassador to France), discussing the lessons of the Panic of
1907, observed, "In recent times railroads and railroad finance have played an
important part in every economic crisis" (Herrick 1908, 14). Another observer also noted the connection in a famous book, *Industrial Depressions*:
"The statistics of railroad building... show that just prior to periods of depression, especially in later periods, there has been an enormous extension of railroad building, a large part of which must be considered as speculative"
(Wright 1886, 242).[6] The data that Wright refers to—"the statistics of railroad building"—are shown in figure 5.8 to which I have added arrows indicating the panic dates.

There are many other modern examples of land- and house-price booms
that were alleged to be linked to credit booms based on bank lending. A
famous example was the Florida real-estate boom. In popular culture, the
1920s real-estate boom is remembered in the Marx Brothers' 1925 musical
The Cocoanuts, which became the 1929 movie of the same name. In one scene
in the film, Groucho Marx is an auctioneer selling Florida land of questionable value. Indeed, the Roaring Twenties was very much about a housing

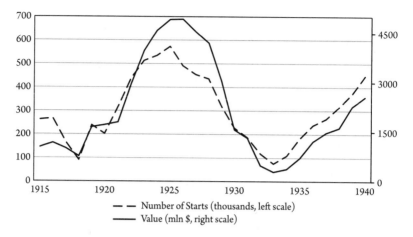

Figure 5.9 Single-Family Housing Starts and the Value of New Units, 1915–1940
Source: Susan B. Carter, Scott Sigmund Gartner, Michael R. Haines, and Alan L. Olmstead, eds., *Historical Statistics of the United States, Earliest Times to the Present* (Cambridge, UK: Cambridge University Press, 2006), series Dc511 and Dc257.

boom. Figure 5.9 shows the bulge in housing starts (the number of houses on which construction began) and the value of new housing units in the 1920s. In addition to Florida there were similar housing booms in Southern California in the 1880s. My Yale colleague Robert Shiller discusses these in his book *Irrational Exuberance*. There are many other examples.

The key point here is that an increase in credit, possibly fueling housing booms, creates fragility in the financial sector. This is hardly a new observation. The *Times* of London reported in 1857:

> It is not that the land and town speculations of themselves create panics, but that they greatly increase the effect of panics, while they promote the spirit of speculation, gambling, and greed after sudden wealth.... In conjunction with this vast land speculation, the United States have been the scene of various great operations, which being simultaneously wound up, have aggravated the severity of the crisis and constituted a panic. The railway system has been enormously extended in the United States, because each community knows the advantages of it, and is desirous of enjoying them by all means, believing that the pecuniary results may in time be sufficient to repay the outlay....
>
> In these operations the spirit of land speculation is to be clearly traced, for many of the companies are as much land as railway speculations,

endowed with large grants of alternate sections of the public lands, relying upon the sale of these at an improved price for the supply of funds, rather than on existing traffic....

The banks have had the great hand in feeding railway enterprises, in supplying manufacturing operations. ("The Crisis and Its Causes," *Westminster Review* 69 [1858]: 87, 88, reprinted from the *Times* [London; 1857])

Everyone can see increases in land and house prices. And policymakers can see credit booms, even if people can't. Credit booms clearly raise issues for policymakers:

What is the harm of expanding credit? It will be asked. Credit stimulates business and lively business means good times and prosperity. Yes, but credit also means speculation and an ultimate collapse followed by years of depression and hard times. Too much credit is like a dose of morphine, the effect of which is fine while it lasts but it is followed by the inevitable reaction. Bank-credit is purchasing power the same as money; increased purchasing power means additional demand and higher values. When values are going up, everybody thinks he can make a fortune by becoming a bull. The market goes up and up regardless of intrinsic values until the limit of credit is reached or until something causes it to contract, somebody has to sell in order to pay his debts, the selling movement is started and values decline as rapidly and unreasonably as before they rose. (Earl Dean Howard, "What Currency Reform Means to the Businessman," *Business World*, September 15, 1906, 726)

What should policymakers do when they see a credit boom? Today we don't talk about going off morphine, as Mr. Howard's metaphor suggests. Rather, we talk about whether the central bank should "take the punch bowl away just when the party is getting good," a line originally uttered by then–Federal Reserve chairman William McChesney Martin.

VI. THE TIMING
OF CRISES

Just before the panic [of 1857] most of the banks were enjoying good business and were riding on the high tide of success. Many were constructing substantial banking houses and looking forward with hope for a long period of prosperity.

—W. Harrison Bayles, 1916

Financial crises are an integral part of business cycles. As the economy nears a business-cycle peak, it is weak and there may be imminent problems with banks. And a credit boom may have exacerbated the situation by endangering more banks, which are most vulnerable when the economy is near a business-cycle peak. If new information signals an imminent downturn, bank-debt holders, fearing possible losses, will run on the banks. When everyone receives the same new information at the same time and sees the same implications, everyone runs on the banks.

During the National Banking Era, panics occurred at or near business-cycle peaks, when unanticipated information (a news shock) arrived forecasting a recession. As we have seen, the actual number of banks that failed during and after the panics in the National Banking Era was very low. But some banks did fail. The possibility of a bank failure was of concern because a household would have its life savings in one bank. So, the chance—even if small—that that bank would fail was a big risk. On top of that, with secrets about certain banks more likely, checks were not likely to trade at par, so you would lose money buying goods. To avoid being taken advantage of, your best bet was to avoid bank debt and go get cash. Before the information shock, all money was secret-free, but when there was bad news it became secret-sensitive. To examine the connection between financial crises and business cycles, it is best to start with the National Banking Era, before the founding of the Federal Reserve System, since it is a period that is simpler in important respects. With a central bank or the possibility of government intervention, the situation becomes much more complicated.

THE PRE-FED PERIOD

During the National Banking Era, every major business-cycle downturn was accompanied by a banking panic. As Wesley Mitchell put it, "When prosperity merges into crisis... heavy failures are likely to occur, and no one can tell what enterprises will be crippled by them. The one certainty is that the banks holding the paper of bankrupt firms will suffer delay and perhaps a serious loss on collection" (Mitchell 1941, 74). In our terminology, Mitchell is saying that at the peak of a business cycle, "when prosperity merges into crisis," there is the possibility of secrets, because some firms and banks will fail, and no one knows which ones.

Households and firms did know, through new information—a news shock—that prosperity was merging into crisis. News about the macroeconomy—about the failures and liabilities of nonfinancial corporations that was published in newspapers read by everyone—coincided with panics and was a leading indicator of a recession. Every time the news shock exceeded a certain threshold there was a banking panic, and there were no instances where the shock threshold was exceeded and there was no panic. Households and firms that learned information about the liabilities, or debt, of failed nonfinancial firms knew that a recession was coming and withdrew from their banks. Their behavior was rational.

The larger the information shock, portending a recession and possible problems with banks, the higher the perceived risk of demand deposits in banks, the higher the losses on deposits during the recession, and the higher the currency-deposit ratio as households switched from bank deposits to currency—and the more severe the recession. Despite the small sample of panics, all of these correlations are present in the data to a significant degree. There is nothing mysterious.

A leading indicator of the state of the economy is the liabilities of failed businesses.[1] Victor Zarnowitz and Lionel J. Lerner studied lengthy historical records of firm failures back to 1875.[2] Their study provides some help in understanding the dynamics of firm failures. They found that "the tendency for turns in liabilities to anticipate general business reversals reflects the early timing of failures of larger companies" (Zarnowitz and Lerner 1961, 358). As they describe it:

> First, there is the little known but well-established fact that liabilities tend to lead the numbers of failures cyclically. This implies that failures increase among larger businesses before they do among small ones, which on the surface seems rather strange. One might expect small concerns to show greater and earlier vulnerability to worsening business conditions than bigger companies. Second, the number of failing concerns that are relatively large in terms of liabilities tend to lead at the peaks and troughs of the business cycle. This can be inferred from the National Bureau studies of statistical indicators of business cycle turns. (350)

This may help explain why there is a lot of attention devoted to the failures of large firms and large banks.

The liabilities of failed businesses were widely reported and discussed in the press. The opening paragraph of each issue of *Dun's Review* often contained this information. For example, the issue of January 4, 1896:

> The commercial failures during the complete year 1895 number 13,197, against 13,885 in 1894, but the aggregate of liabilities is slightly greater, $173,196,060 against $172,992,856, so that the average per failure is $13,124, against $12,458 in 1894....Classified returns made only by R. G. Dun & Co. disclose the meaning of the change, showing a heavy increase, 66 per cent., in liabilities of manufacturing failures for the past quarter, while in trading liabilities a small decrease appears. In seven States the increase in manufacturing failures for the year was $18,570,586, or 62.6 per cent., while in all other States there was a decrease of 31.9 per cent. The effects of unreasonable speculation in materials, rapid advances in prices of goods, heavy purchases ahead of distribution, and enormous increase in production, clearly appear in returns.

Discussing the causes of the Panic of 1893, W. Jett Lauck gave an example of how such data was thought of in relation to crises:[3]

Table 6.1   Mercantile and Industrial Failures, 1892–93

	First Quarter	Second Quarter	Third Quarter	Fourth Quarter	Total
1893					
Number	3,202	3,199	4,015	4,826	15,242
Liabilities ($)	47,338,300	121,586,539	82,470,040	95,389,010	346,779,889
1892					
Number	3,384	2,119	1,984	2,857	10,344
Liabilities ($)	39,284,349	22,989,331	18,659,235	33,111,252	114,044,167

The mercantile and industrial failures throughout the year [1893] were phenomenal. The aggregate liabilities of mercantile and industrial establishments which failed in 1893 were three times as great as the liabilities embraced in the failures of 1891, and almost twice as great as those of the panic year of 1890. The total number of failures during 1893, and the liabilities involved, exclusive of railroads and banks, is given below. For purposes of comparison the returns for 1892 are also added:

An examination of these figures reveals two interesting facts relative to the disastrous conditions which prevailed during 1893. *In the first place they show that the mercantile and industrial failures began to increase before 1893....* The weaker industrial and mercantile concerns experienced difficulty in maintaining their solvency, and as a consequence the amount of failures during the last quarter of 1892 and the first quarter of 1893 showed a decided increase. (Lauck 1907, 105–6; emphasis added)

The problem is that firms' liabilities were bank loans. As Mitchell put it, discussing the situation just prior to the Panic of 1893:

The most dangerous element in the situation was probably the doubtful character of many bank loans.... The banks seem to have thrown not a little good money after the bad. When the hour of need came they found it impossible to realize upon a considerable portion of their nominal loans. On paper they were reasonably strong; in reality many banks were very weak. (Mitchell 1913, 55)

There is no other explanation as to why households and firms ran to their banks to withdraw their deposits at more or less the same time. They all received the same information shock reading their newspapers.

THE POST-FED PERIOD

In the era of central banks, there have been fewer bank runs, but the timing of the panics is different. Financial crises in this era are empirically associated with a weakening macroeconomy, low GDP growth, credit growth, and with currency crises. The difference between this and the prior period is that in the post-Fed period the central bank or government may try to prevent secrets from mattering.

The presence of such a large actor on the stage—like an eight-hundred-pound gorilla—changes the expectations of firms and households in the economy. News shocks about the future come with expectations about how the central bank and the government will act. The effect of expectations on current actions is one of the central lessons of modern macroeconomics—it is what "rational expectations" is all about.

Determining just how the introduction of the Federal Reserve System in 1914 fundamentally altered depositor behavior will give us a clue about economists' inference problems about financial crises. We can do this by measuring the size of the news shock necessary to cause a panic. Since the unanticipated liabilities of failed businesses can be measured, it can be used as a proxy for people's expectations, and we can then link an empirical measure of beliefs to actions.

An information signal in June 1920, based on the unanticipated liabilities of failed non-financial firms, that would have would have been large enough to result in a panic in the National Banking Era didn't cause a panic in 1920. National Bureau of Economic Research business-cycle dating puts the peak of the cycle at January 1920 and the trough at July 1921, a recession during which GNP fell 8% from 1919 to 1920 and 7% from 1920 to 1921. Another signal also would have caused a panic in December 1929.[4] Both shocks follow the business-cycle timing pattern of the National Banking Era, coming just after business-cycle peaks. However, the panics of the Great Depression happened in October 1930, March 1931, and January 1933—well after the information signal and the business-cycle peak.

Using data from the National Banking Era—estimating the relationship between the size of the information shock and the percentage of banks failing

Table 6.2 Actual and Predicted Losses on Deposits and Bank Failures during the 1920s and 1930s

	Bank Failures		
Date	Predicted % of National Banks Failing	Actual % of National Banks Failing	Actual % of All Banks Failing
June 1920	1.137	0.27	0.91
December 1929	0.77	26.24; 13.36	36.08; 30.76

	Losses on Deposits	
Date	Predicted Losses at National Banks	Actual Losses at National Banks
June 1920	7.14	0.42
December 1929	4.84	18.41

Source: Gorton (1988)

and percentage loss on deposits—we can predict the bank failures and losses that would have occurred had the Federal Reserve System not been introduced in 1914. The results are shown in table 6.2.[5]

The results show that in June 1920 there would have been many more bank failures and losses on deposits. There was, in fact, no panic, and actual bank failures and losses were lower. This was commented upon at the time. The *American Review of Reviews* wrote:

> The admirable workings of the Federal Reserve system is one of the matters to be proud of in the troublous times of the past decade.... There can be no doubt that we should have had within the past six months a terrible panic and unprecedented financial and industrial distress but for the help of the Reserve system in giving a true emergency elasticity to credit and currency. The current reports of the condition of banks in the Reserve system reflect clearly how we are emerging from the financial danger zone. ("The Progress of the World," *American Review of Reviews* 63 (May 1921): 470)

Indeed, seemingly everyone thought that the Federal Reserve's existence provided a cure for panics. Toward the end of 1921, then–Commerce Secretary Herbert Hoover noted that although bank panics were considered inevitable, "we know now that we have cured it through the Federal Reserve System" (quoted in Ginzberg [2004, 33]). Magnus W. Alexander, the president of the National Industrial Conference Board, asserted that "there is no reason why there should be any more panics" (quoted in Angly [1931, 12]). Irving Bush, a Progressive and successful businessman announced, "We are only at the beginning of a period that will go down in history as a golden age" (quoted in Angly [1931, 12]). Academics agreed: Wesley Mitchell (1922) wrote, "We have learned how to prevent crises from degenerating into panics" (22).

Charles O. Peple, director-general of the Federal Reserve Bank, Richmond, said:

> [The Federal Reserve Act] made many panics, that is currency panics, absolutely impossible. It made any sort of panic very much more improbable that it has ever been in the history of this country. (*Proceedings of the Twenty-Third Annual Convention of the Maryland Bankers' Association, May 29 and 30, 1918* [Baltimore: Maryland Bankers' Association 1918], 75)

In an address delivered before the Democracy of New Hampshire, at Concord, NH, March 16, 1916, Senator Robert L. Owen of Oklahoma (one of the Senate sponsors of the Federal Reserve Act of 1913) said:

> [The Federal Reserve System] made a future financial panic or currency panic impossible. It made stable for the first time in the history of the Untied States the credit system of the people of the United States. (*Senate Documents*, 64th Cong., 1st Sess., December 6, 1915–September 8, 1916)

All in all the mood resembled the Great Moderation assertions of our own era—that the problem of crises had been solved. No wonder that Milton Friedman, winner of the Nobel Prize in 1976, and Anna Schwartz called the 1920s "the high tide of the Reserve System," suggesting that this was a period during which the Federal Reserve became confident in its use of the new tools of policy (1963).

Households did not panic in 1920 because they expected the Federal Reserve System to act, and during the Great Depression their reaction was delayed as they waited for the Federal Reserve System to act. Households' and firms' behavior depends on expectations of action by the central bank and the government. While expectations of intervention to prevent losses on deposits should prevent bank runs, in fact they just change the dynamics of runs.

QUIET RUNS AND WHOLESALE RUNS

One outcome of the change in behavior due to expectations of rescues is a "quiet run"—a slow and steady drain of cash from banks, rather than a sudden demand for cash by all depositors. The drain is slow and steady, because government policies are uncertain.

In January 1932, during the Great Depression and the administration of President Herbert Hoover, an act of Congress established the Reconstruction Finance Corporation (RFC). By June and July of 1932 the RFC was making loans, secured by collateral, to banks. Initially these loans were secret—no one knew if a bank had received a loan from the RFC. The secrecy created a stir, and subsequently the clerk of the House of Representatives interpreted the law as requiring him to publish the names of all borrowers. The list showed no improprieties, but it had the disadvantage of making depositors nervous. As Nadler and Bogen (1933) explain:

> A quiet run set in on a number of institutions. So long as they had collateral available to pledge as security for additional loans from the Reconstruction Finance Corporation, they would obtain new cash to meet the run, but sooner or later either the collateral gave out or the Reconstruction Finance Corporation realized that it was impossible to stem the run, and the banks once again began to fail in large numbers. During October, 1932, 103 banks failed, with far-reaching effect. They destroyed again the belief of a large number of people in the United States, revived after the Chicago episode [in which the RFC stemmed a panic with its loans] was past that with the Reconstruction Finance Corporation in operation large failures were impossible. (132)

The episode illustrates several points. First, the RFC was successful when its loans could be kept secret—that is, when the identities of the banks were secret. Second, the quiet run was motivated by concerns about the condition of banks that were identified by the government as weak. In other cases of quiet runs, there are concerns about the extent of government support for banks or the banking system. Quiet runs are caused by or distorted by government actions.

The RFC example shows the vulnerability of the financial system to information during a crisis. The episode illustrates why the Federal Reserve's discount window is not effective during crises. Individual banks simply do not want to step up to the window, because this is taken as a sign of weakness. There is a danger that a bank asking for help would face a run. Note that it is not public information when a bank goes to the discount window. But it seems that the market learns this information. Brian Madigan, director of the Division of Monetary Affairs of the Federal Reserve said (2009):

> The problem of discount window stigma is real and serious. The intense caution that banks displayed in managing their liquidity beginning in early August 2007 was partly a result of their extreme reluctance to rely on standard discount mechanisms. Absent such reluctance, conditions in interbank funding markets may have been significantly less stressed, with less contagion to financial markets more generally. Central banks eventually were able to take measures to partially circumvent this stigma by designing additional lending facilities for depository institutions; but analyzing the problem, developing these programs, and gathering the evidence to support a conclusion that they were necessary took valuable time. Going forward, central banks and other policymakers need to avoid measures that could further exacerbate the stigma of using central bank lending facilities.

In the financial crisis of 2007–8 one study showed that banks were willing to pay thirty-seven basis points more than the discount rate to avoid using the discount window.

The clearinghouses had avoided this problem of "stigma" by keeping the identities of loan certificate users secret. This problem of stigma is why on October 13, 2008, then-U.S. Treasury secretary Hank Paulson, at a meeting with nine banks, including the U.S. dealer banks, gave them no choice but to take TARP money.[6] The government took $250 billion in equity stakes. In Secretary Paulson's "CEO Talking Points" it says:

> To encourage wide participation [in TARP], the program is designed to provide an attractive source of capital, on identical terms, to all qualifying financial institutions. We plan to announce the program tomorrow—and—*that your nine firms will be the initial participants.* (emphasis added)[7]

Here is another example of a quiet or slow run, caused by the government, which led to a full-blown panic: Argentina in 2001. This description is from a summary of a talk by Mario Blejer, an Argentine economist and former central banker, summarized by the World Bank:

> The banking crisis occurred after more than a year of declining deposits, something Blejer called unprecedented. So it was not a traditional bank run. He said the reason was government abuse of the banking sector. People took their money out of the banks, he said, because they feared government policies would make the banks insolvent and the government would confiscate the money. The fear developed because he believes the public was observing the government undermining the private sector in the bank portfolios. This was occurring during 2001. The government began forcing the sector to take on more and more government bonds. The interest rates were high, so the initial reaction from the banks was positive, but eventually they realized the government might default on the bonds, so they began to refuse the deposits, which the government continued to force upon the banks. Interest rates began to rise and the price of the bonds fell. By the end of 2001, the banks implemented withdrawal restrictions as investors began to panic. The panic resulted in public riots and the fall of the government by the start of 2002. Currency was converted to pesos, which created more debt for the banks. To avoid a total collapse of the sector, the government sought to stabilize the banks by providing further issuances of bonds. At that point, Blejer was appointed Director of the Central Bank. The run was continuing despite restrictions the banks were placing on withdrawals. A run began on the peso as well, as the exchange rate began to climb. The Central Bank sought to maintain liquidity in the banking system in order to defuse a bank run. Such an effort would create hyperinflation, one of the tradeoffs he and colleagues had to consider: either have hyperinflation or allow the banking sector to collapse. To avoid either scenario meant slowing the bank run and providing some liquidity. [It was important] to get investors to buy Central Bank assets rather than government bonds. Also critical was to slow the devaluation and chaos of the currency market.[8]

The problem of quiet runs induced by government policies continues in Argentina. The *Financial Times* reported on October 31, 2011, that

Argentines, whose favoured mode of saving in a crisis-prone country has been to buy dollars, from today face tighter foreign exchange controls designed to clamp down on capital flight, which Buenos Aires is struggling to contain.... One banker...said his customers had pulled 500m pesos ($118m...) out of savings accounts last month.... He said that the clamps could backfire and prompt an "enormous shock" in the banking system if people suspected a crisis was brewing and rushed to withdraw cash.

The recent situation in Greece is similar. As one media source reported:

Greece, in the middle of its own financial crisis, is teetering on the brink of a default. Many of its wealthier citizens are also uneasy about what lies ahead for their cash. According to estimates from private bankers in Greece and Cyprus, as much as 10 billion Euros have left the country for Greek-owned bank subsidiaries in Switzerland and Cyprus in the last couple of months.[9]

Related to quiet runs are wholesale runs, which are usually quiet, and involve corporate and institutional depositors rather than households. In the 1970s and 1980s firms and institutional investors often bought large, uninsured certificates of deposits and commercial paper with fairly short maturities. If they refused to renew these loans to the bank, then the bank had to honor this by repaying cash. There were important examples of this before the recent financial crisis.

The first is the failure of Penn Central Railroad, a private company, and concerns commercial paper. The Federal Reserve intervened to prevent the realization of systemic risks when Penn Central Railroad became bankrupt in June 1970. Initially the Fed had refused to lend to Penn Central, although the Nixon administration had requested it. But the Fed was concerned about the effect the Penn Central bankruptcy would have on the commercial paper (CP) market, thinking that it would be difficult for other issuers to roll over their commercial paper. In the end, the Fed eased access to its discount window, suspended the ceiling on large-denomination bank CDs (to allow money from maturing CP to be invested there), and engaged in aggressive open market operations.

The Penn Central default caught the market by surprise; it was the first default of an investment-grade company in the postwar period. Between

June 24 and July 15, 1970 outstanding commercial paper dropped almost 10%. The episode is important for two reasons. First, it was the first instance where the debt involved was not traditional bank debt, demand deposits, or bank notes; it was commercial paper. Second, the lenders refusing to renew their loans, by refusing to accept newly issued commercial paper to replace their maturing paper, were not households but institutional investors, like insurance companies. This was an early sign that the financial structure was changing. It was lucky that this did not grow into a systemic crisis.

About fifteen years later, a second wholesale run occurred at Continental Illinois National Bank and Trust Company. The FDIC described the run:

> Large foreign depositors became nervous after hearing rumors of Continental's imminent failure, and, in May 1984, began a high-speed electronic deposit run on the bank. The run may have been triggered by U.S. investment banking firms, acting on their own, making inquiries in Japan to see if there were any banks interested in taking over Continental. What is certain is that banks in the Netherlands, West Germany, Switzerland, and Japan had increased their rates on loans to Continental. Reuters, the British news agency, picked up that information and put it on its news wire on Tuesday, May 8, 1984. When a second news story came out on Wednesday, May 9, from Commodity News Service that a Japanese bank was considering buying Continental, Japanese and European money was quickly withdrawn. Foreign bankers withdrew more than $6 billion before May 19. In the U.S., the Chicago Board of Trade Clearing Corporation withdrew $50 million on or about May 9; word of the withdrawal hit the wire services, and a deposit run ensued. (Federal Deposit Insurance Corporation 1997, 547)

The following description appeared in an article in the *American Banker*:

> The old-fashioned run on a bank by retail depositors has, on the whole, become a phenomenon of the past because of the safeguards erected over the last half-century. However, the phenomenon of a run on a bank in the Euromarkets is a new challenge for banks, supervisors, and central banks as lenders of last resort. (Mendelsohn 1984, 548)

Bank runs are not irrational events. They are caused by the arrival of bad news about the economy. The news, if bad enough, causes a loss of invulnerability to secrets of bank debt. Holders of the debt want cash.

Banking panics—mass runs—are less frequent these days, as firms and consumers have deposit insurance and expect the government to intervene. Expectations of government actions to save the value of deposits change the behavior of depositors. So bank runs either do not occur at all, or they occur later when the events reveal that the central authorities have made mistakes and deposits might not be saved.

This does not change the fact that systemic financial crises are due to the vulnerability of bank debt, which by design is intended to prevent secrets. A shock can cause the fear that it will not trade at par. Then there are very large demands for cash from the banking system. It is the fact that all bank debt becomes information-sensitive at the same time that causes this problem. The demands for cash are so large that they cannot be met—assets cannot be sold fast enough without crushing the prices—and a systemic crisis ensues.

VII. ECONOMIC THEORY WITHOUT HISTORY

> The phenomena of a volcanic eruption or of a great earthquake are eagerly investigated by the men of science for what light they may cast upon the workings of the laws of nature. Not less reasonable may it be for the student of economics to avail himself of periodic financial upheavals for acquiring a broader judgment upon the laws of finance.
>
> —Henry Clews, 1891[1]

Despite the frequency of financial crises in U.S. history and elsewhere, economists thought that the era of financial crises in the United States was over. So crises are not central to modern macroeconomics or financial economics. It is not that economists ignored crises, but they largely studied the Quiet Period, because they thought it was the most relevant period and, importantly, that because it is the most recent period, it provided the most data.

Economists did not see that the economy had changed, and they misunderstood the vulnerability of bank debt. So the markets that were central to the recent financial crisis went unnoticed. Since the development of these markets was below the surface, it seemed the Quiet Period would last forever. When the financial crisis did occur, the explanations were superficial and

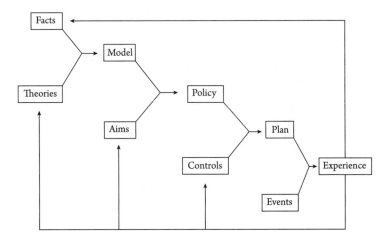

Figure 7.1
Source: Stone (1997).

dismissive, reflecting a lack of institutional and historical knowledge, and focusing on the outward details of the crisis.

The diagram in figure 7.1, from Richard Stone's 1984 Nobel Prize lecture, shows how the production of economic knowledge is supposed to work.[2] The arrows suggest the interaction between models, policy, experience, facts, and theories.

The diagram begins with the production of Facts, which is informed by the Experience of using previously produced Facts combined with Theories to create new Models. Facts are combined with Theories, leading to Models (depending on Aims) and then to Policy. Finally, Events occur and there is the Experience of Policy, which then feeds back to the process of producing new Facts and Theories. Economists inhabit some of the boxes and not others. Economists mostly engage in producing Models. Rarely do they have direct Experience, which means using economic plans and models while working in a private firm or the government. Experience counts for something—living through a panic as a firsthand eyewitness is different than reading about it in the newspaper. Some economists are involved in policymaking through stints in government positions, though these are usually temporary. In Stone's case, he worked at the Ministry of Economic Warfare in England during World War II, and later joined the Central Economic Information Service of the War Cabinet, where he worked with James Meade (winner of the Nobel Prize in 1977).

Stone's diagram emphasizes the interaction of events with policies, and the experience of that interaction as the driving stimulus of new ideas. It is not necessarily the case that the production of economic knowledge follows the orderly progression in Stone's diagram. While the arrow from Experience goes back to Facts, the production of new information or new data plays a much greater role in the diagram than it does in the current actual practice of macroeconomics. It is also noteworthy that Stone, perhaps unintentionally, did not include the notion of the testability of a theory or formal tests of a hypothesis. The implication is that the persuasiveness of a theory, its ability to fit the world, does not depend on tests, though tests can provide interesting provocations.

Let's briefly look at Stone's knowledge process at work in one of the most important examples in modern macroeconomics. The Phillips curve, which describes a negative relationship between wage changes and unemployment, was taken as a fact in the early 1960s. William Phillips observed this over the period 1861–1957 in the English economy, and similar patterns were later found in other countries. There was a great deal of empirical support for the Phillips curve, so it was regarded as one of the more stable relations in economics. It was a Fact.

The greatest weakness of the original Phillips curve was that it lacked any theoretical explanation—a Model—underpinning it. In Stone's diagram, this Fact went straight to Policy. It was interpreted as an option for government authorities to increase employment by pursuing an expansionary monetary policy, which would raise wages and inflation. So an expansionary monetary policy, it was thought, could lower unemployment. But Events and Experience intervened in the 1970s. Figure 7.2 shows the high inflation—shown in the federal funds rate—and high unemployment of the period. It is a shocking violation of the Phillips Curve.

Robert Lucas (Nobel Prize winner in 1995) argued that it made no sense to think of the Phillips Curve as a policy device, because the expectations of the public would incorporate the fact that the government was behaving this way, and the benefits of increased employment would not materialize. This could explain the observed experience of the 1970s. Lucas noted:

> If it was in fact the conjunction of real world shifts in the questions to which people wanted answers together with technical improvements in economic theory which led to the major rethinking of business cycle

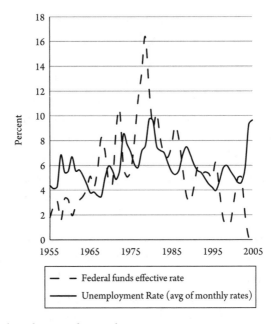

Figure 7.2 U.S. Federal Funds Rate and Unemployment, 1955–2010
Source: Federal funds from Federal Reserve H.15 release; Bureau of Labor Statistics.

theory that I have been calling the neoclassical synthesis, then it is not unlikely that more recent developments can be similarly attributed to forces to these two categories.

The real world event from the recent past which first comes to mind is the combination of inflation with higher than average unemployment that characterized the 1970s.... These events were badly misforecast with 1960s vintage econometric models. (Lucas 1980, 705)

The breakdown of the Phillips Curve in the 1970s was the formative experience for a generation of macroeconomists. The generation of macroeconomists prior to those of the 1970s and 1980s had focused on the issue of Capitalism versus Socialism, and produced (1974 Nobel Prize winner) Friedrich von Hayek's *The Road to Serfdom* and (1978 Nobel Prize winner) Milton Friedman's *Capitalism and Freedom*, reflecting the Cold War. Before that was the Great Depression, and the advent of Keynesian economics. Throughout these trends, there was the overarching project of building macroeconomic models, starting with Leon Walras (1834–1910) and Yale economist Irving Fisher (1867–1947). The breakdown of the Phillips Curve led to the next step in that project. With the interaction of the experience of the 1970s and the inability of the existing theory to explain it, economists began to incorporate expectations of the future into models of the private decisions of firms and households, especially expectations about government actions.

But how do we incorporate a policy's own effects into the policy itself? Robert Lucas argued that, using traditional models, we can't. This is now known as the Lucas critique. In a famous paper in 1976, he wrote that the behavior of people and firms is a function of the economic environment, which includes the current set of policies. Describing that behavior with an econometric model cannot provide the basis for considering the effects of different policies because people and firms would behave differently under those policies. Or, in the language of economics, "Given that the structure of an econometric model consists of optimal decision rules of economic agents, and that optimal decision rules vary systematically with changes in the structure of series relevant to the decision maker, it follows that any change in policy will systematically alter the structure of econometric models" (Lucas 1976, 41).

Here's a simple example. Some time ago, the state police of a U.S. state were considering buying radar guns—what were the costs and benefits? The state hired a consulting firm, which experimented with radar guns on various highways and estimated how many extra speeders would be caught and how much additional money the state would make from the extra speeding tickets. The estimated revenue was far higher than the cost of the radar guns, so the state bought them. But when state troopers used them, the extra revenue from the speeding tickets issued was far less than estimated. The problem was that the behavior of drivers changed. Speeders bought radar detectors and slowed down near the radar guns. The estimation of how many additional speeders would be caught was based on the assumption that people would drive in the same way after the radar guns were in use.

How could the consultants have taken into account the change in behavior that occurred once the radar guns were in use? In practice, there is no good way to answer this question. In principle, one could imagine building a model of driving behavior that is based on a model of why people speed in the first place, and how they respond to getting tickets. Do people get a thrill from speeding? Are they always late? Would they make use of technology that would allow them to avoid getting tickets? A model would need to answer questions like these. For radar guns it probably doesn't make sense to even bother. But for questions of macroeconomic policy—like how taxes would change behavior, what the inflation rate should be, or what the effects of various unemployment insurance programs would be—it might.

So economists took the Lucas critique very seriously. In giving policy advice, it is an important problem. To work, an estimated model would have to be at a deeper level, at the level of preferences, technology, and information: (1) how consumers and firms make decisions, (2) what technology is available to produce goods, and (3) what the economy has available to use as productive inputs. Rational expectations are also part of the model. People in the model economy form their expectations about the future in such a way that they do not systematically make mistakes. They are forward looking and understand how the world works—they can't be fooled by policies.

Finn Kydland and Edward Prescott (Nobel Prize winners in 2004) demonstrated that such a model could be built, a model that mimicked the behavior of the macroeconomy. The basic idea was to specify a model economy with deep parameters about how decisions are made, what technology was available for production, and so on, and then show that when shocks hit this economy ("technology shocks") that the resulting behavior of the model economy mimicked that of the actual economy. Such a model enabled policy experiments to allow for people and firms changing their behavior, because the changes would occur in the model.

The germ of this idea came from a famous paper by Irma Adelman (born in 1930) and Frank L. Adelman (1917–2002) published in 1959. In this paper the Adelmans simulated a model of the U.S. economy that two other economists, Lawrence Klein (1980 Nobel Prize winner) and Arthur Goldberger, had estimated. The Klein-Goldberger model of the U.S. economy had twenty-five equations that described the evolution of twenty-five macroeconomic variables for the U.S. economy. The Adelmans asked whether the Klein-Goldberger model could generate business cycles. First, they simulated the model on a computer to see if it displayed inherently cyclical behavior. They found that:

> when random shocks of a realistic order of magnitude are superimposed upon the original form of the Klein-Goldberger equations, the cyclical fluctuations which result are remarkably similar to those described by the NBER as characterizing the United States economy. The average duration of a cycle, the mean length of the expansion and contraction phases, and the degree of clustering of individual peaks and troughs around reference dates all agree with the corresponding data for the

United States economy. Furthermore, the lead-lag relationships of the endogenous variables included in the model and the indices of conformity of the specific series to the overall business cycle also resemble closely the analogous features of our society. All in all, it would appear that the shocked Klein-Goldberger model approximates the behavior of the United States economy rather well. (620)

To understand the importance of the Adelmans' paper, we can use the Turing test, a test proposed by Alan Turing to determine whether computers can think.[3] The essence of the test is that a judge asks questions of two participants who cannot be seen or heard, and one of them is a computer. If, by looking at the answers, the judge cannot identify which participant is the computer, then the computer has passed the Turing test. The question with the development of modern macroeconomics is that if the judge receives two sets of output, one generated by an economic model, the other the actual data from the economy—can the judge determine which set of data is generated by the model?

To show the mimicking behavior of the model, the model needed to be calibrated with real data, reflecting deep parameters of the economy. However, macroeconomists used short time series. In a famous 1990 paper establishing the stylized facts of business cycles, Kydland and Prescott analyzed quarterly U.S. data for just thirty-five years, 1954–89. Table 7.1 shows a list of the business cycles selected in bold.

The short period of time used is astounding. Since there were no crises in the United States during these periods—the Quiet Period—financial crises did not make the list of stylized facts to be incorporated into macro models. Instead, macroeconomics focused on real factors as the cause of business cycle fluctuations.

Because there were no financial crises during the Quiet Period, no one thought that the deep parameters needed to include a technology for conducting transactions or financial intermediaries.[4] Instead, the workhorse model was the neoclassical growth model of Robert Solow (Nobel Prize winner in 1987), which focused on the diminishing returns to capital in the production process.

Macroeconomists were not trying to explain systemic crises prior to the Panic of 2007–8, and did not include them in models, because they thought they would not recur. As Thomas Sargent (Nobel Prize winner in 2011) put it: "[Macroeconomic] models were designed to describe aggregate eco-

Table 7.1 U.S. Business Cycle Chronology

Peak	Trough
	December 1854
June 1857	December 1858
October 1860	June 1861
April 1865	December 1867
June 1869	December 1870
October 1873	March 1879
March 1882	May 1885
March 1887	April 1888
July 1890	May 1891
January 1893	June 1894
December 1895	June 1897
June 1899	December 1900
September 1902	August 1904
May 1907	June 1908
January 1910	January 1912
January 1913	December 1914
August 1918	March 1919
January 1920	July 1921
May 1923	July 1924
October 1926	November 1927
August 1929	March 1933
May 1937	June 1938
February 1945	October 1945
November 1948	October 1949
July 1953	*May 1954*
August 1957	*April 1958*
April 1960	*February 1961*
December 1969	*November 1970*
November 1973	*March 1975*
January 1980	*July 1980*
July 1981	*November 1982*
July 1990	March 1991
March 2001	November 2001
December 2007	June 2009

Source: National Bureau of Economic Research

nomic fluctuations during normal times when markets can bring borrowers and lenders together in orderly ways, not during financial crises and market breakdowns." This was not a conscious choice, as if there were in fact other models designed to explain fluctuations during abnormal times, and a decision was made to have models for "normal" times and other models for abnormal times. And even if one claimed that, why would there be two separate types of models? Models were designed without incorporating anything that would explain crises, because economists thought they were irrelevant. Older papers with models that included the financial sector are now commonly cited as evidence that macroeconomists were thinking about crises. But these models were not mainstream models, and in any case they cannot display crises. If they could, why not incorporate them into the "normal" models?

According to Kydland and Prescott:

One way to test a theory is to determine whether model economies constructed according to the instruction of that theory mimic certain aspects of reality. Perhaps the ultimate test of a theory is whether its predictions are confirmed—that is, did the actual economy behave as predicted by the model economy, given the policy rule selected? (1996, 84–85)

This is a reasonable criterion. We know now that the current versions of these models cannot mimic what just happened—the financial crisis.

Macro econometrics and calibration methods need data, and abundant data is readily available only for the post–World War II era. The Quiet Period was convenient because it was the most recent period, unlike the more distant past, where data was scant. It would have been difficult to build data sets for the past that are as rich as the modern data needed for macroeconomic models. But not impossible—many have devoted their careers to just this. It was a choice that was made—to not use the past.

Economists tend to dismiss the past as different and therefore irrelevant. This is not based on serious testing or study, but on casual observation with limited knowledge. The set of "Facts" is limited by this blindness. The view is that history comes from a different structure, that the economic environment of, say, the nineteenth century was so different from today that little can be learned from the past. Deirdre (Donald) McCloskey, an economic historian, in a well-known paper noted—thirty-five years ago—that "forty years of investment in mathematizing economics has made it less acceptable among economists to admit ignorance of mathematics than to admit ignorance of history" (1976, 439).

The relevant past is the history of market economies, not an arbitrary recent period that is largely determined by data availability. But it is not only an issue concerning past data. Macroeconomics is framed by what is measured even in the current period. Once national accounts had been conceptualized and put into practice, as a result of the work of Richard Stone and Simon Kuznets (1901–85, Nobel Prize winner in 1971), macroeconomists had a set of stylized facts to work with. Solow was quite explicit about this. Kydland and Prescott essentially used the same growth framework (the neoclassical growth model of Solow) for their work.

Without a historical perspective, economists are myopic. The period of the Great Moderation, when there were substantial declines in macroeconomic volatility, is basically a twenty-year period that began in the mid-1980s. The irony is that there was a growing credit boom in the United States, and the so-called shadow banking system was developing during this period.

With different data, macroeconomics might well look at the world very differently. A very big problem in understanding what happened in the recent crisis has to do with measurement. Risks are not measured. Certain kinds of money are not measured. Measurement systems in an economy with financial derivatives cannot be based on cash. New Facts need to be produced.

The achievements of modern macroeconomics are powerful insights into the role of expectations about the future and the effects of that on policy. The 2011 Nobel Prize in economics, shared by Thomas Sargent and Christopher Sims, confirmed these achievements. But these achievements were forged during a period when the Phillips curve did not describe reality, and the data requirements for macro models were such that history could not be incorporated into the models. This was acceptable because of the unspoken view that crises were a thing of the past in the United States. But the models could not display crises.

Looking back at Richard Stone's figure, it is easy to see where we are now. Real world developments forcefully intervened. The Experience of the financial crisis places us on two arrows, one pointing to Facts and the other pointing to Theories. The past, a rich laboratory for understanding the present, lacks data richness, which is needed for some models, but we need to add economic history to the Facts. Sophisticated econometric methods come at a large cost; the data requirements narrow our field of vision. In this trade-off the loser has been economic history, although there have been consistent complaints about this.

One notable complaint came in December 1984, at the annual meetings of the American Economic Association, held that year in Dallas, Texas. There was a session at those meetings called "Economic History: A Necessary though Not Sufficient Condition for an Economist." The session was planned by the then president of the American Economic Association, Charles Kindleberger of MIT, and included the following participants: Kenneth Arrow, Paul David, and Gavin Wright (all from Stanford University); Charles Kindleberger, Robert Solow, and Peter Temin (all from MIT); Donald McCloskey (University of Iowa); William N. Parker (Yale); and W. W. Rostow (University of Texas). This lineup included two of the world's best theorists—Arrow (1972 Nobel Prize winner) and Solow—and the best economic historians of that time. The papers were subsequently published as a book, edited by Yale professor William N. Parker, and included a comment from Kindleberger (1986). While there was little disagreement about the importance of economic history, the trends pointed out at that time have not changed. Kindleberger noted that "economic history is losing its place in economic curricula" (84). It used to be that economics PhD programs required at least one term of economic history, but this has disappeared. Many top economics programs that previously had two or three economic historians now have none. In 1984, Kindleberger was in a bit of a foul mood: "I have lately suggested that much of the field today is bankrupt" (85).

VIII. DEBT DURING CRISES

The complicated credit economy of our day is built on a foundation of public confidence, the cement of which is the system of legal rules relating to private rights. When the foundation is shaken by doubts of the economic soundness of the structure, the cement of legal rules loses its strengthening force. On the contrary, it becomes a source of weakness, binding the structure so rigidly that danger of collapse is imminent unless the system is loosened. A principle of elasticity, which in normal times may hamper the free flow of credit, becomes a necessity in times of crisis. For some 1400 years Western civilization has made use of extraordinary devices for saving the credit structure, devices generically known as moratoria. The moratorium is a postponement of fulfillment of obligations decreed by the state through the medium of the courts or the legislature. Its essence is the application of the sovereign power.

—A. H. Feller

Typically, when holders of bank debt demand payment in fixed amounts, borrowing banks must legally honor these demands. But historically, during financial crises, debt contracts have not been enforced. Banks would suspend convertibility—refusing to honor demands for cash—and the government would help banks by upholding suspensions of convertibility and declaring bank holidays. Courts have ruled that failure to honor bank-debt contracts in a crisis did not mean banks were insolvent, so bank-debt holders simply couldn't collect what they were owed. And it wasn't only bank debt.

Facing the burdens of crushing debt during crises, debt moratoria and stay laws erased or reduced the mortgage obligations of households. Debt during crises is not the debt of noncrisis times.

This idea is anathema to many people, including many economists, who argue that the failure to enforce this obligation creates "moral hazard," in the form of the increased risk borrowers take because they know they'll have the option to renege on their obligations. But this in an option only when everyone, the whole economy, is in trouble. That event is not predictable.

Another way to say this is that the *banking system* has always been viewed as too big to fail. When the demands for cash during a crisis cannot be met, there are two choices: either don't enforce debt contracts or liquidate the banking system. No society with a market economy has ever (intentionally) chosen to liquidate its banking system.

BANKS AND DEBT BEFORE THE NATIONAL BANK ACTS

Early in American history the enforceability of the obligation of banks to pay their debt was generally established. An early interesting example is when the Suffolk Bank of Boston "disciplined" a country bank by demanding note redemption in specie. The Suffolk Bank was a quasi-central bank; it accumulated private banknotes of country banks outside Boston as people and firms spent the money in Boston. Those who received the notes in Boston deposited them in the Suffolk Bank, which could then take the notes back to each country bank and demand specie. The Suffolk Bank made the country banks hold sufficient reserves to redeem their notes under threat that the Suffolk Bank would show up and redeem large quantities of notes. The issue came up in a legal case decided in May 1821. In the case, *Suffolk Bank v. Lincoln Bank*, the circuit justice, charging the jury, said:

> The act of Massachusetts (St. 1809, c. 38) under which this suit is brought, declares, that, "if any incorporated bank shall refuse or neglect to pay on demand, any bill or bills by such bank issued, such bank shall be liable to pay to the holder of such bill or bills after the rate of two per cent. per month on the amount thereof, from the time of such neglect or refusal, to be recovered as additional damages in any action against the bank for the recovery of the said bill or bills." It is the duty of every

bank to pay its bills in specie on demand, if such demand is made at the bank within the usual banking hours, and the omission of pay under such circumstances, is a neglect or refusal within the meaning of the act. (23 Cas. 346; 1821 U.S. App. LEXIS 364)

In this case the Lincoln Bank delayed payment, claiming that the specie coins had to be counted and weighed. The judgment was for Suffolk. However, the courts did not always enforce debt claims. In some states if a bank refused to honor a banknote, the head cashier was obligated to sign the note and date it, so that the noteholder could earn a penalty interest rate during a grace period. In *State of New York v. Bank of Washington and Warren*, Justice John Wood-worth wrote:

> The facts stated … are not a cause of forfeiture [of the bank's charter] in the act of April 7, 1817, by which the defendants were incorporated. … The 10th section declares that on refusal to redeem in specie, the defendants should, on pain of forfeiture, discontinue and close their banking operations, until such time as they should resume the redemption of their bills. It further allows 10 per cent damages on all notes, which shall have been demanded and not paid. …
>
> It will be seen by this specification, that the time for resuming operations is not limited in terms, nor was it intended to be. I think it manifest the legislature did not intend that the refusal to pay on demand should be a ground of forfeiture, whatever may have been the cause of refusal; but on the contrary, intended that the business of the bank might be again commenced at an indefinite period, whenever the defendants should resume payment of their bills. If this be the construction, of which I have no doubt, it follows, that, whether the suspension was six months, or six years, there was no cause of forfeiture. (Supreme Court of New York, August Term, 1826 [6 Cow. 211])

Some clarity was to come. On May 10, 1837, the banks of New York City suspended convertibility in response to bank runs, and within a few days all the banks in the United States suspended as well:

> In the first three weeks of that month, two hundred and fifty firms went down, with losses of over a hundred million; cotton fell fifty percent,

and New Orleans contributed failures of $27,000,000 in two days; the State [New York] advertised a loan of half a million at six percent without receiving a single bid; a general run started; after consultation among themselves, the New York banks suspended specie payments on May 10, and those throughout the country which had not gone under followed their example. (Lanier 1922, 205)[1]

Suspension of convertibility was a violation of banks' charters, however, which would be forfeited if such contracts were not honored after a grace period. John Quincy Adams (later the sixth U.S. president) put it this way:

We are now told that all the banks in the United States have suspended specie payments—and what is the suspension of specie payments but setting the laws of property at defiance? If the president and directors of a bank have issued a million bills promising to pay five dollars to the holder of each and every one of them, the suspension of specie payments is, by one act, the breach of one million promises. What is this but fraud upon every holder of their bills? (Letter to *The Financial Register of the United States*, July 1, 1837, 2:59)

As the grace period ran out, and the banks worried about losing their charters, they appealed to the state legislature. Richard Hildreth reported the events:[2]

The suspension was everywhere acquiesced in as an act of necessity, and was even hailed by many of the merchants as a sure relief to all their troubles. The Legislature of New York, which was in session at the time, passed an act legalizing the suspension for one year, but forbidding the banks to make dividends during its continuation. (1840, 97)

When the New York banks appealed to the state legislature for help, on May 16, 1837, the legislature passed "an act suspending for a limited time, certain provisions of law, and for other purposes." It stipulated that "every provision of law in force, requiring or authorizing proceedings against any bank in this State, with a view to forfeit its charter, &c.," was "suspended for one year."[3]

Similar acts were passed by the legislatures of other states as well. And in the remaining states, the state governments simply overlooked the suspension "as a thing rendered excusable by the circumstances of the times" (Hildreth 1840, 97). Courts interpreted state statutes and bank charters to mean that debt had to be honored in circumstances indicated by the bank charter, but that it did not have to be honored due to suspension, as long as a penalty rate was paid. In Ohio the court said:

> The legislatures of this state have nowhere declared, by express statute, that the act of suspension is a forfeiture of the franchises of banking. By the statute of February 25, 1839, certain acts *are* declared forfeitures, as refusing an inspection to the bank commissioners, refusing answers under oath, neglecting to furnish monthly statements....
>
> But that the legislature did not intend such forfeiture should ensue from a mere suspension, is plain, because they provided a different penalty.... The due payment of its notes is intended to be secured by creating a liability to pay twelve per cent. damages....
>
> We entertain no doubt that the suspension of specie payments may be continued long enough and be carried far enough to work an entire forfeiture of banking franchises and to authorize the sovereign to resume the powers it has conferred on a corporation. For a bank of circulation is created to provide by its credits a currency which may serve as money; whenever this currency becomes discredited, irredeemable, inconvertible, so that it no longer fulfills this end, there is a misuse of its powers, such as upon common law principles may work a failure. The end of its creation must be carried to be attended by this result, whether this consequence follows a mere refusal to pay its debts, or whether such omission to pay must be carried to the suspicion of insolvency, are points of difference among the judges of New York, as to which, perhaps, our legislature may properly furnish a rule, as the legislature of New York has done....
>
> The legislature, in the charter of this bank, looking to this event, have provided such a remedy, believing that it was better to secure to the holder of its notes twelve per cent. damages for a neglect to pay its debts, instead of the multiplied inconveniences and derangements involved in a liquidation and close of its business.[4]

In the case of *James Rockwell v. The State of Ohio, for the use of John Nevins* (1841), the court ruled that a bill be endorsed by the head cashier when the bank refused to pay only if there was a general suspension (11 Ohio 130, 1841 WL 59 [Ohio]). And the interest penalty provided by the act was only relevant during a general suspension, because its purpose was to provide an incentive not to suspend:

> The law, then, provides that if any banking institution in this state shall hereafter suspend payment of its notes in gold and silver, it shall be the duty of the cashier to indorse, etc. It is to guard against a general suspension, or the suspension of the payment of its notes generally by the bank, that the act confers upon the holders of its bills the authority to require this indorsement, and inflicts the penalty of non-compliance; it was never the intention of the law to give the penalty upon an *isolated controversy* between an officer of the bank and holder of a bill, which resulted in a demand of payment, and refusal to pay or indorse. Such a transaction would hardly be worthy of legislation and the bill holder is left to his remedy, by action, for the recovery of his debt. But to prevent a general suspension of the payment of its notes, which affects the whole community, the provision was made.

In this case, the Ohio court made the important distinction between periods of "general suspension" and other periods. Penalty interest during the grace period was only relevant during general suspension. The intention of the penalty was to provide an incentive not to suspend convertibility. This was also the logic of states that prohibited paying dividends during periods of suspension—to create an incentive to resume convertibility.

For other courts, the issue was not whether there was a general suspension but the length of the suspension period. Here is Mississippi chief justice William Sharkey writing in a case in 1846:

> How far a mere temporary suspension of specie payments by a bank will work a forfeiture of charter, and what is a *temporary* suspension? *Quaere?* [That is the question.]
>
> In the year 1840 the Commercial Bank of Natchez, chartered previously, being in a state of suspension of specie payments, the legislature passed a law that all the banks in the state by the first of April, thereafter, should pay specie on their notes of five dollars; by the first of July on their notes of ten dollars; by the first of October on their notes of twenty

dollars, and by the first of January, 1841, on all their notes, bills, and other liabilities: *Held,* that this act was constitutional and valid; and a failure on the part of the bank to comply with the provisions of the law would work a forfeiture of its charter....

Can the state create a bank and empower it to issue notes without requiring it to redeem them in specie? This question admits of none other than a negative answer. Can a bank, then, do what the legislature could not empower it to do, and still retain its franchises? On a careful examination of the authorities referred to, we find them correctly holding that conditions in a charter are to be construed as conditions in individual contracts, and to be construed most favorably to the grantee; that a substantial compliance is all that is required; that courts should incline against a forfeiture. From most of the authorities it is impossible to extract any precise rule, susceptible of a certain practical application. There is but little diversity of opinion when the suspension is what is called permanent, or continued. Then all agree, with perhaps a solitary exception in Alabama, that it is cause of forfeiture. This was admitted in New York under charters that sanctioned a suspension by requiring that during its continuance the banks should cease to do business. But the decisions do not define what they mean by a permanent or continued suspension or insolvency, and what by a temporary suspension. These terms have no definite legal meaning, and in common meaning they do not convey to the mind the idea of any precise rule by which to ascertain when a forfeiture has occurred. Nothing is permanent which may vary or change, and nothing can be said to be continued which does not remain in the same state....

But the law does not measure the precise time of suspension which is requisite to constitute forfeiture.[5]

It was "impossible to extract any precise rule" as to when suspension was temporary or permanent. In other words, there was no way to distinguish an event that would leave the banks solvent and whole from another event that would ultimately render them insolvent.

To settle the issue of suspension, New York State passed a constitutional amendment in 1846 that prevented suspension of convertibility by banks: "The legislature shall have no power to pass any law sanctioning in any manner, directly or indirectly, the suspension of specie payments by any person, association or corporation, issuing bank notes of any description" (Article VIII, Section 5).

The idea of the amendment was to prevent the New York State legislature from allowing banks to suspend convertibility as the legislature had done in 1837. But, in the next systemic event, the Panic of 1857, they again faced the possibility of liquidating the banking system. If they did not act, the courts had to enforce bank debt contracts and declare banks insolvent. If a bank could sell its assets, as in normal times, then the bank was solvent. But if it cannot get cash because markets are not functioning, was it insolvent or merely "illiquid"? Resolving these issues was just as difficult in the nineteenth century as it was during the recent financial crisis.

In 1858 the court determined:

An inability to pay, *arising from unexpected and unforeseen contingencies,* would not alone be evidence of insolvency within the statute under consideration, or any concerning bankruptcies or insolvencies. A merchant or trader who should be driven to protest, by the failure to receive an expected remittance, or the bankruptcy of a debtor, upon whom he had relied, would not for that reason be deemed insolvent, and yet would have failed to fulfill his obligations according to his undertaking. If, from taking a reasonable view of his situation and the surrounding circumstances at the time, it could fairly be seen that he was able not only ultimately to pay his debts, but could at once recover from the temporary embarrassment and derangement of his business, by a proper application of his means, and carry on his business and meet his engagements in the ordinary course, and as persons in the same business usually do, he would properly be called solvent. *So, too, if the present inability to pay was the result of a crisis, a peculiar stringency in the monetary affairs of the country, instead of the failure of one individual, and one source of supply, and by which he was cut off temporarily from the resources upon which he was accustomed to rely, and upon which traders in like circumstances are accustomed to rely, the effect would be the same on the general question of insolvency.* It is no evidence of insolvency that a trader habitually relies upon anticipating the payment of his bills receivable, by procuring them to be discounted to meet his engagements, or procuring loans upon his own credit, relying upon collections to repay the loans.

This usual reliance may fail him, and he be left unable to meet his engagements, and yet be far from insolvent within any definition of the term. *The same principle applies to banking corporations and associations. The liabilities of these institutions, payable presently, always exceed very largely the present absolute ability to pay. Every dollar of their circulation and the entire deposits is subject to call, and may be demanded in a single day, and yet it is well known that no bank keeps on hand, either in coin or bills of solvent banks, an amount equal to one tenth of the obligations which they are legally bound to answer on demand. The law recognizes this fact in the provision which it makes for giving fifteen days for redemption of bills transmitted under protest to the banking department, and ten days for the repayment of demands presented, before proceedings can be had for the dissolution of corporations and association on account of such non-payment.* (Ferry v. Bank of Central New York [1858], 15 How. Pr. [N.Y.] 445; emphasis added)

The court argued that if the failure to pay occurs during a crisis—"unexpected and unforeseen contingencies"—then this is not a normal situation. But what is a "crisis"? These questions were answered in 1857 in *Livingston v. Bank of New York*, in which the court held that insolvency of a bank cannot be inferred from its suspension of specie payments when suspension was general and nearly universal throughout the state and every other section of the country:

We are left, then, to the mere legal inference of insolvency, resulting from the suspension of specie payments by a bank of issue.

Is such the necessary inference from suspension, no matter what the bank's assets may amount to, in cases where suspension is general, and nearly universal, throughout the state and every other section of the union? It seems to me that it is not....

The mere fact of suspension of specie payments (when it is general) is not of itself sufficient proof of fraud or injustice to authorize such injunction. ([1857] 26 Barb. [N.Y.] 304)

The *Livingston* ruling meant that New York banks would not be liquidated during the Panic of 1857. The response to the *Livingston* ruling at the time was much different than it would be today. John A. King, the governor of

New York, in his annual message to the Senate and Assembly of January 5, 1858, said:

> A judicial opinion [*Livingston v. Bank of New York*] from the supreme court, promulgated in the city of New York, quieted the immediate apprehension of the banks of being forced into liquidation. And the whole business community pledged themselves to stand by and aid, instead of crippling or annoying them. It is, therefore, with the deepest satisfaction I have found my confidence in the will and in the ability of the banks to effect an early resumption. (Lincoln 1909)

Yale professor William Graham Sumner, speaking of the *Livingston* case fifty years later, wrote:

> It was nothing less than a *coup d'etat*. The [New York State] Constitution had explicitly provided against any suspension of specie payments, on any pretext whatever, and this constitutional provision now proved as ineffective as all the old legislative enactments. The situation was somewhat paradoxical. It had been hoped that the severe constitutional prohibition would prevent banks from ever putting themselves in a position to suspend. They had come into that position. It was said that the terror of forfeiture was what made them adopt their policy of self-protection, to the ruin of the mercantile world, although the construction of the bankers was that the public was in a panic lest the banks should all be wound up in case they suspended. This was the knot which the Judges cut, and everybody was forced to acquiesce in their action. It was a most conspicuous failure of legal regulation of banks, and illustrated that dilemma of legislation in which a restriction to be effective must be intensely severe, and if it is intensely severe, proves impracticable when it is needed. (1896, 427)

The *Livingston* decision, which I call the Livingston doctrine, reverberated through American history, finding its way into standard law books, established the general idea that crises were exceptional circumstances that exempted debt from enforcement, and eventually gave the Federal Reserve System the power to lend $29 billion to JPMorgan Chase to buy Bear Stearns during the Panic of 2007–8.

BANKS AND DEBT IN THE NATIONAL BANKING ERA

As you may recall, the Panic of 1873 was a rude awakening to the fact that financial crises had not been ended by the National Bank Acts. Banks suspended convertibility in 1873, this time refusing to convert demand deposits into National Bank notes. By then the popular press had internalized the Livingston doctrine:

> We distinctly emphasize the point that these are not [bank] failures, but only enforced temporary suspensions. When a firm has good and ample assets but is obliged to cease paying out cash because the cash is exhausted by compliance with unreasonable demands, to call the suspension a failure is a misuse of language.... The suspended companies and firms have no more "failed" than banks have, and their suspension should not be in the least reckoned against their credit.... Far from criticizing the course of the banks, we applaud its wisdom. *Financier*, September 27, 1873

Suspension was never questioned or legally challenged during the National Banking Era. Although it was illegal, banks continued to suspend during each crisis of that era (1863–1914). Along with suspension came the use of clearinghouse loan certificates, which were eventually issued to the public as hand-to-hand currency. The legality of clearinghouse loan certificates was also questionable. Washington Augustus Clark described how this was addressed:

> During the past half century we have experienced severe panics, when the cast iron rule of the national banking law afforded little or no relief, and other expedients had to be resorted to in order to relieve the situation. The national banks, therefore, falling back upon the old proverb "Necessity is the mother of invention," have resorted, from time to time, to the issuance of "clearing house certificates," which have been used in severe panics, not only to pay balances between respective banks, but, in smaller communities, have been even put in circulation and passed as currency. Under these trying circumstances the Comptroller of the Currency and the Secretary of the Treasury, both realizing the unparalleled condition encountered by the banks have, at least, *winked at this violation of law and permitted the banks the use of this unusual currency*

until normal times were restored. That was just the view taken by Judge Butler in holding that suspension at such a time as 1837 was not unreasonable but intended for the benefit and protection of both the bank and community. (Clark 1922, 154; emphasis added)

The Livingston doctrine appeared again, as regulators "winked at this violation of the law and permitted banks to use this unusual currency until normal times were restored." Once more there is the distinction between "normal" times and times of crisis.

The possible violation of the law in issuing clearinghouse loan certificates concerned the provision in the National Bank Acts that adopted a tax on private banknotes. Banknotes were not banned but taxed out of existence; it became too expensive to issue them. The question later was whether clearinghouse loan certificates were private bank money that should be taxed. In the tradition of finding ways to avoid liquidating the banking system, the U.S. attorney general ruled that the tax on private banknotes did not apply to clearinghouse loan certificates. According to the attorney general, "the tax on State

---

BOX 8.1 Albany Clearing-House Certificate, $10. Albany, Georgia

No. ___.]

ALBANY, GA., *August 29, 1893*

This certifies that the First National Bank of Albany, Ga., has deposited with the undersigned offices of the Albany clearing house securities of the value of twenty dollars for the payment of the sum of ten dollars to said bank or bearer in lawful money of the United States, at six months from date, or earlier, at option of said bank. But no certificate is to be issued bearing date later than January 1, 1894. This certificate will be received on deposit by any bank or banker belonging to the Clearing House Association of Albany at par at any time before its maturity.

_____, *President*

_____, *Secretary.*

Indorsed: The following banks compose the Albany Clearing House Association: First National Bank, Commercial Bank, Exchange Bank.

banks imposed by the act of February 8, 1875, chapter 36, section 19, applies only to promissory notes and not to other negotiable or quasi negotiable paper. If there is any doubt as to the meaning of a statute imposing this tax, the doubt must be resolved in favor of exemption." Further, according to the attorney general:

> Three of the instruments submitted by you are plainly not notes, but checks, and may be left out of consideration. The two other papers are substantially alike, one of them being as follows:
>
> ...In my opinion...the paper is not a note within the meaning of the statute. (20 U.S. Atty. Gen. 681, 1893 WL 259 [U.S.A.G.])

While the attorney general refused to act against clearinghouse loan certificates, the banks still faced the problem that courts might not recognize and uphold the legal status of the certificates. Fortunately, the courts played ball. For example, in *Philler et al. v. Patterson* in 1895, Justice Williams wrote:

> The clearing-house association is nothing more nor less than an agreement among 38 national banks [of Philadelphia] to make their daily settlements at a fixed time and place each day.... We come now to consider the [clearinghouse loan] committee and the position in the general scheme occupied by it.... The banks agreed that they would deposit in the hands of certain persons, to be selected by them, and to be called the "clearing-house committee," a sum of money, or its equivalent in good securities, at a fixed ratio upon their capital stock, to be used for payment of balances against them....
>
> On the 24th day of September, 1873, the associated banks entered into another agreement with each other, by which, "for the purpose of enabling the banks, members of the Philadelphia Clearing-House Association, to afford proper assistance to the mercantile and manufacturing community, and also to facilitate the inter-bank settlements resulting from the daily exchanges," they authorized the committee to receive from any member of the association additional deposits of bills receivable and other securities, and issue certificates therefore "in such amount and to such percentage thereof as may, in their

judgment, be advisable." The additional certificates, if issued, they agreed to accept in payment of daily balances at the clearing house.... When a bank to which certificates had been issued under the original plan or the contract of 1873 failed to redeem them when their redemption became necessary, it was the duty of the committee to collect the securities in their hands, and apply the proceeds to the payment of the holders of the certificates.... We are unable to... see in what respect these banks have violated the statutes of the United States relating to national banks.... This same method, or one identical in general outline, has been adopted by the banks in every great city in the United States, and by many in other lands; and, as far as I am aware, it has nowhere been held that the method it illegal. (May 29, 1895 [168 Pa. 468, 32 A. 26])

By the end of the National Banking Era the legal history and banking institutions incorporated almost a century of experience of banking panics and had successfully avoided liquidating the banking system. Clearinghouses were increasingly innovative in creating private money during crises. But crises persisted.

BANKS AND DEBT DURING THE FEDERAL RESERVE PERIOD

The role of the clearinghouses as lenders of last resort ended with the start of the Federal Reserve System in 1914. But the same problem of whether to liquidate the banking system would arise again during the Great Depression. Franklin Delano Roosevelt, the thirty-second president of the United States, faced the same problem that the eighth president, Martin Van Buren, had faced almost a century earlier. Van Buren, the first president born after the American Revolution, took office in March 1837, shortly before the onset of the Panic of 1837. When President Roosevelt took office on March 4, 1933, a crisis was already underway (just as there was when Barack Obama, the forty-fourth president, did seventy-five years later). On the night of Sunday, March 5, 1933, Roosevelt closed all the banks of the country from March 6 to March 9 and placed an embargo on gold exports. This was not a usual bank holiday. It was a federal order that all banks were to close, including state banks. Roosevelt's Executive Order no. 6260 says:

Now, therefore, I, Franklin D. Roosevelt, President of the United States of America, in view of such national emergency and by virtue of the authority vested in me by said Act and in order to prevent the export, hoarding, or earmarking of gold or silver coin or bullion currency, do hereby proclaim, order, direct and declare that from Monday, the sixth day of March, to Thursday, the ninth day of March, Nineteen Hundred and Thirty Three, both dates inclusive, there shall be maintained and observed by all banking institutions and all branches thereof located in the United States of America, including the territories and insular possessions, a bank holiday, and that during said period all banking transactions shall be suspended. During such holiday, excepting as hereafter provided, no such banking institution or branch shall pay out, export, earmark, or permit the withdrawal or transfer in any manner or by any device whatsoever, of any gold or silver or bullion or currency or transact any other banking business whatsoever.

To do this, Roosevelt claimed authority under the Trading with the Enemy Act (TWEA). This seems like a farfetched interpretation. The Trading with the Enemy Act was passed on October 6, 1917, six months after the United States had entered World War I, and regulated the affairs of foreign-national noncitizens. It was modeled after the British Trading with the Enemy Act, and was intended to prevent an enemy foreign national from using property that he owned or controlled in the United States, and to allow the U.S. government to control that property (thus it could "freeze assets"). Roosevelt's decree applied not only to foreigners but to American citizens and banks.

Almost thirty years after Roosevelt's 1933 proclamation, it was effectively still in place, and people were arrested for possession of gold bullion. In one such instance in 1962 the United States District Court for the Southern District of California in the United States, *Plaintiff v. James Briddle, Harold Mitchell, Defendants*, wrote:

In an obviously strained effort to find legal support for such drastic and unprecedented control of the banking business of the nation, the President made reference to the "national emergency" and to authority claimed under the above-quoted provisions of the Trading with the Enemy Act of 1917 (40 Stat. sec. 411). Although this action was cheerfully accepted, and even welcomed, at the time, it was clearly unauthorized, since nowhere in the Constitution is the President given authority to act in an "emergency" as such, and the requisite war conditions which might have been called into play his granted power as Commander-in-Chief or his delegated power under the Trading with the Enemy Act of 1917 did not obtain. (22 F. Supp. 584)

But in 1933 the constitutionality of President Roosevelt's order was not challenged, most likely because of the passage four days later of the Emergency Banking Relief Act. Consisting of nine pages, it was introduced, passed, and signed on a single day, March 9, 1933.

The act has five parts, called "Titles." Title I amended the Trading with the Enemy Act of 1917 to confirm and approve the orders and regulations the president or secretary of the Treasury had given since March 4, 1933. It also amended the TWEA to allow the president the authority to declare a national emergency and have absolute control over the national finances and foreign exchange of the United States in the event of such an emergency. Section 11 of the Federal Reserve Act was amended to authorize the secretary of the Treasury to order any individual or organization in the United States to deliver any gold that they possessed or had custody of to the Treasury in return for "any other form of coin or currency coined or issued under the laws of the United States." Basically, the president was given broad power over the operations of banks that were members of the Federal Reserve System during an emergency.

Title II authorized the comptroller of the currency to seize control of and operate any bank in the United States or its territories and to establish the terms and conditions under which the bank was administered and reopened or liquidated. Title III allowed banks to issue preferred stock that could then be bought by the Reconstruction Finance Corporation. Issuance of preferred stock was new to bank capital structures at this time. Title IV gave broader power to the Federal Reserve banks to issue notes, and made all direct obligations of the United States eligible as collateral for Federal Reserve banknotes. Finally, Title V appropriated $2,000,000 to the president to carry out this legislation, and stated: "If any provision of this Act, or the application thereof to any person or circumstances, is held invalid, the remainder of the Act, and the application of such provision to other persons or circumstances, shall not be affected thereby."[6]

Here the Livingston doctrine again came into play. Thus in the *American Law Reports*: "A bank is not required to keep sufficient money on hand to pay all of its depositors on demand, and is not insolvent if, because of an emergency, or crisis, it is unable to pay all demands made on it" (85 A.L.R. 811, originally published 1933). With the banks facing massive demands for currency, President Roosevelt declared the bank holiday as a device for preventing creditors from collecting from the borrowing banks, a way to prevent debt contracts from being enforced. This had already started in various states that had declared bank holidays.

Roosevelt's extraordinary action of declaring a national banking holiday on flimsy legal grounds, was within the tradition of avoiding liquidating the banking system. To justify this action, President Roosevelt

---

BOX 8.2 Chronology of Banking Holidays during the Great Depression, 1933

February 14: Michigan eight-day bank holiday decreed by Governor Comstock.

February 24: Governor of Maryland decrees a three-day holiday.

February 25: Indianapolis banks limit withdrawals to 5 percent of deposits.

February 27: Pennsylvania, Ohio, and Delaware enact legislation permitting individual banks to restrict deposit withdrawals.

March 1: Five states, including California, declare banking moratoria.

March 2: Seven additional states in the West decree bank holidays.

March 3: New York Federal Reserve Bank raises rediscount rate from 2½ to 3½ percent. Announces money in circulation rose $732,000,000 for week ended March 1, a record rise.

March 4: New York and Illinois banks close, as well as Federal Reserve Banks. Other states follow suit, as well as security and commodity exchanges.

March 5: President Roosevelt decrees four-day bank holiday and embargo on gold shipments. Congress called in special session for March 9.

March 7: [Treasury] Secretary Woodin promulgates rules authorizing banks to make payments to cover needs for foods and medicines.

Source: Nadler and Bogen (1933, 201)

gave the most important speech by a U.S. president during a financial crisis. The speech, on March 12, 1933, was Roosevelt's first fireside chat. Called "The Banking Crisis," the speech was carried by radio to all parts of the nation. It is an extraordinary example of managing expectations (later formalized by rational expectations) by means of Roosevelt's stentorian tones, the clarity of the narrative, the credibility of the actions of the banking holiday declaration, and the explanation of how banks would reopen.

Roosevelt started by clearly explaining the problem—that is, he provided a narrative of what happened:

> First of all, let me state the simple fact that when you deposit money in a bank, the bank does not put the money into a safe deposit vault. It invests your money in many different forms of credit—in bonds, in commercial paper, in mortgages and in many other kinds of loans. In other words, the bank puts your money to work to keep the wheels of industry and of agriculture turning around. A comparatively small part of the money that you put into the bank is kept in currency—an amount which in normal times is wholly sufficient to cover the cash needs of the average citizen. In other words, the total amount of all the currency in the country is only a comparatively small proportion of the total deposits in all the banks of the country.
>
> What, then, happened during the last few days of February and the first few days of March? Because of undermined confidence on the part of the public, there was a general rush by a large portion of our population to turn bank deposits into currency or gold—a rush so great that the soundest banks couldn't get enough currency to meet the demand. The reason for this was that on the spur of the moment it was, of course, impossible to sell perfectly sound assets of a bank and convert them into cash, except at panic prices far below their real value. By the afternoon of March third, a week ago last Friday, scarcely a bank in the country was open to do business. Proclamations closing them, in whole or in part, had been issued by the Governors in almost all the states. It was then that I issued the proclamation providing for the national bank holiday, and this was the first step in the Government's reconstruction of our financial and economic fabric.

Then President Roosevelt explained how the problem was being addressed:

> The second step, last Thursday, was the legislation promptly and patri-
> otically passed by the Congress confirming my proclamation and broad-
> ening my powers so that it became possible in view of the requirement
> of time to extend the holiday and lift the ban of that holiday gradually in
> the days to come. This law also gave authority to develop a program of
> rehabilitation of our banking facilities. And I want to tell our citizens in
> every part of the Nation that the national Congress—Republicans and
> Democrats alike—showed by this action a devotion to public welfare
> and a realization of the emergency and the necessity for speed that it is
> difficult to match in all our history....
>
> We start tomorrow, Monday, with the opening of banks in the twelve
> Federal Reserve Bank cities—those banks, which on first examination
> by the Treasury, have already been found to be all right. That will be fol-
> lowed on Tuesday by the resumption of all other functions by banks
> already found to be sound in cities where there are recognized clearing
> houses. That means about two hundred and fifty cities of the United
> States. In other words, we are moving as fast as the mechanics of the
> situation will allow us.
>
> On Wednesday and succeeding days, banks in smaller places all
> through the country will resume business, subject, of course, to the
> Government's physical ability to complete its survey. It is necessary that
> the reopening of banks be extended over a period in order to permit the
> banks to make applications for the necessary loans, to obtain currency
> needed to meet their requirements, and to enable the Government to
> make common sense checkups.

Roosevelt was careful not to blame the bankers:[7]

> Some of our bankers had shown themselves either incompetent or dis-
> honest in their handling of the people's funds. They had used the money
> entrusted to them in speculations and unwise loans. This was, of course,
> not true in the vast majority of our banks, but it was true in enough of
> them to shock the people of the United States, for a time, into a sense of
> insecurity and to put them into a frame of mind where they did not dif-
> ferentiate, but seemed to assume that the acts of a comparative few had

tainted them all. And so it became the Government's job to straighten out this situation and do it as quickly as possible. And that job is being performed.

President Roosevelt ended with a call for confidence:

> After all, there is an element in the readjustment of our financial system more important than currency, more important than gold, and that is the confidence of the people themselves. Confidence and courage are the essentials of success in carrying out our plan. You people must have faith; you must not be stampeded by rumors or guesses. Let us unite in banishing fear. We have provided the machinery to restore our financial system, and it is up to you to support and make it work.
>
> It is your problem, my friends, your problem no less than it is mine. Together we cannot fail.

It was a remarkable speech.[8] The next day depositors lined up to redeposit their money in the banks. The Emergency Banking Act was passed with alacrity, and there was no legal challenge to the bank holiday.

The contrast with the events of 2007–8 is stark. Neither the Bush nor the Obama administration offered a clear narrative of the financial crisis of 2007–8.[9] There was no speech akin to President Roosevelt's. President Roosevelt's declaration of a bank holiday had little legal foundation. But the history of not liquidating the banking system was ingrained, and his speech was successful in articulating a coherent explanation for his actions.

The tool of the bank holiday has since entered the arsenal of anticrisis weaponry around the world. For example, after months of runs of dollar deposits, and substantial liquidity support from the government, Uruguay declared a banking holiday on July 30, 2002. In Ecuador, in the midst of a currency crisis and a lack of confidence in the banking system, the government declared a bank holiday in March 1999. But not all of the examples of modern bank holidays were successful.

BANK INSOLVENCY

The history of coping with financial crises has consistently been one of avoiding liquidation of the banking system, whether by allowing suspension of

---

BOX 8.3 Chronology of the Passage of the Emergency Banking Act of 1933

12:04 a.m. President and Congressional leaders end conference at White House.

10:30 a.m. Roosevelt makes final revision of message to Congress.

11:30 a.m. Congressional and banking leaders [meet] at Capitol after bill details.

12:00 noon Congress' extra session called to order.

12:30 p.m. Roosevelt message calling for immediate action delivered.

12:37 p.m. Message read to Senate.

1:40 p.m. Bank bill introduced in Senate, referred to Committee.

2:55 p.m. House begins consideration of bank bill.

4:05 p.m. House passes bill without dissent.

4:10 p.m. Senate banking committee approves bill.

4:30 p.m. Senate begins its consideration.

7:23 p.m. Senate passes bill by 73 to 7 vote.

7:40 p.m. Speaker Rainey calls House to order and signs bill.

7:55 p.m. Vice President Garner signs bill and messenger leaves with it for White House.

8:36 p.m. President Roosevelt signs the emergency bank bill, making it law.

10:10 p.m. President Roosevelt issues proclamation extending banking holiday indefinitely.

Source: Federal Reserve Bank of Boston (n.d.)

---

convertibility, declaring that banks were not insolvent if they did not pay their debt during such a suspension period, or by declaring bank holidays. Bank insolvency is not a clearly defined term. It has been interpreted to mean not honoring debt contracts in normal times, not in crises. So for all banks to credibly suspend convertibility (and not be declared insolvent), they must agree that there is a crisis. After the Federal Reserve came into being, the mechanism for doing this has not existed. Bank regulators and the central bank must decide what a crisis is or wait until it becomes obvious. This is clearly a difficult problem. On the one hand, deciding to act early means that there may be government action before there is a consensus that there is a crisis. But waiting to act means much larger costs—as we will see.

The leading example of this problem is the 1982 failure of Penn Square, the small bank failure that ultimately doomed the much larger Continental Illinois Bank, which failed in 1984. Irvine Sprague, the chairman of the Federal Deposit Insurance Corporation at that time, discussed the closing of Penn Square:

> Recalling the tense drama more than three years later, [Comptroller of the Currency Todd] Conover told me: "I was new on the job. I was under a lot of pressure to close Penn Square. I kept asking people in the agency to tell me what it took to make a finding of insolvency." He was told there is nothing in the law that defines insolvency. The law just says the comptroller shall close the bank whenever it becomes insolvent, "or something nondescript like that," Conover added. (I. Sprague 1986, 119–20)

The problem in this case was that it did *not* occur during a financial crisis. But later the regulators feared that the failure of Continental Illinois would *cause* such a crisis. One interpretation of the regulatory actions was that they prevented a crisis. But, as we will see, such counterfactuals are difficult to construct. A similar issue occurred with Lehman Brothers—was it insolvent?

> "What does solvent mean?" JP Morgan CEO Jamie Dimon responded when the FCIC [Financial Crisis Inquiry Commission] asked if Lehman had been solvent. "The answer is, I don't know. I still could not answer that question." JP Morgan's Chief Risk Officer Barry Zubrow testified before the FCIC that "from a pure accounting standpoint, it was solvent," although "it obviously was financing its assets on a very leveraged basis with a lot of short-term financing." (Financial Crisis Inquiry Commission 2011, 325)

The difficulty of determining bank insolvency explains why banks have never been part of the usual corporate bankruptcy procedure. Bank insolvency has always been determined at the discretion of the regulators, as Todd Conover quickly learned.

DEBT AND THE FEDERAL RESERVE: EXIGENCIES

In a crisis the Federal Reserve System is in a position to act decisively to save financial firms, and even nonfinancial firms. A paragraph added to the Federal Reserve Act by the passage of the Emergency Relief and Construction Act in July 1932,[10] Section 13(3), provides that:

> In *unusual and exigent circumstances,* the Board of Governors of the Federal Reserve System, *by the affirmative vote of not less than five members,* may authorize any Federal reserve bank, during such periods as the said board may determine, at rates established in accordance with the provisions of section 357 of this title, to *discount for any individual, partnership, or corporation, notes, drafts, and bills of exchange* when such notes, drafts, and bills of exchange are *indorsed or otherwise secured* to the satisfaction of the Federal reserve bank: *Provided,* that before discounting any such note, draft, or bill of exchange for an individual or a partnership or corporation the Federal reserve bank shall obtain evidence that such individual, partnership, or corporation is *unable to secure adequate credit accommodations from other banking institutions.* All such discounts for individuals, partnerships, or corporations shall be subject to such limitations, restrictions, and regulations as the Board of Governors of the Federal Reserve System may prescribe. (emphasis added)

"Unusual and exigent circumstances" is an echo of the Livingston doctrine's prerequisites for general suspension.

Federal Reserve chairman Ben Bernanke explained the use of Section 13(3) during the recent financial crisis in testimony before the Committee on Financial Services of the U.S. House of Representatives on February 10, 2009:

> Prior to 2008, credit had not been extended under [Section 13(3)] authority since the 1930s. However, responding to the extraordinarily stressed conditions in financial markets, the Board has used this authority on a number of occasions over the past year.

Following the Bear Stearns episode in March 2008, the Federal Reserve Board invoked Section 13(3) to make primary securities dealers, as well as banks, eligible to borrow on a short-term basis from the Fed. This decision was taken in support of financial stability, during a period in which the investment banks and other dealers faced intense liquidity pressures. The Fed has also made use of the Section 13(3) authority in its programs to support the functioning of key credit markets, including the commercial paper market and the market for asset-backed securities. In my view, the use of Section 13(3) in these contexts is well justified in light of the breakdowns of these critical markets and the serious implications of those breakdowns for the health of the broader economy.

HOUSEHOLDS AND DEBT

The same principle of not enforcing debt contracts during economic crises has also held with respect to home mortgages. During crises homeowners with mortgages have also been given relief from their debt obligations. There were debt moratoria, stay laws, and bank holidays that provided relief for mortgage holders. There is a long history of mortgage relief during crises.

Sometimes a moratorium amounted to closing the courts, or closing them for every kind of case other than criminal cases. Then foreclosures could not be ordered by courts. Bank holidays also prevented banks from collecting on debts. More common forms of relief included prohibition of lawsuits, the staying of action after suits are commenced, forbiddance of the service of process notifications, attachment, execution of judgment, foreclosure, the exercise of rights of entry, or extensions of the period for redemption of foreclosed property. Stay laws limited actions to collect on debts.

The ingenuity of our legislators is responsible for numerous novel devices for the relief of debtors. By far the most common method resorted to has been the creation of a new period of redemption or the alteration of an existing period. Other devices that have been attempted include the alteration of the interest rate on the debt, change in the remedy available to the mortgagee upon default, the imposition of new duties upon the mortgagee as a prerequisite to foreclosure, change in the procedure of foreclosure sales, alteration of court procedure for the enforcement of debts, change in the method of executing judgments for the payment of secured debts, and the creation of barriers to the collection of debts." (Rogers 1933–34, 329)

Of course, these actions were controversial. But, like *Livingston* and the subsequent history, courts distinguished between "normal times" and "times of public stress." For example, the New York Court of Appeals justified this as follows: "That the government may be required, in times of public stress, so to legislate as to nullify private contracts is an implied term of every contract, so that such legislation, if enacted, does not impair the obligation of the contract within the meaning of the limitation" (Sliosberg v. New York Life Ins. Co., 244 N. Y. 482, 497, I55 N. E. 749, 756 [1927]; cited by Feller [1933, 1074]).

The most famous case, with the widest implications, is the *Blaisdell* case from the Great Depression.[11] In it, the U.S. Supreme Court held that the Minnesota Mortgage Moratorium Act of 1933 was constitutional. This was the first case considered with regard to Great Depression debtor relief legislation. Daniel Rogers summarized the key provisions of the act:

1. The legislative declaration that an emergency exists, and that the enactment is made under the police power;
2. The abolition of the right of foreclosure by advertisement, where provided in the contract, and the requirement that all foreclosures be by action;
3. Determination of terms on which the extension will be granted, more or less according to equitable rules, such as requiring the mortgagor to pay a reasonable rental, etc.;
4. Prohibiting deficiency judgments until the expiration of the period of redemption;
5. Prescribing a definite limit of time for which the extension could be made. Thus it is apparent that the legislature endeavored to meet the constitutional objections to prior relief legislation on the ground of impairment of the obligation of contract. (Rogers 1933–34, 347)

Suspension of mortgage enforcement was discretionary, case-by-case, responding to individual debtors' relief applications.

The *Blaisdell* decision seemed to contradict the contract clause of the U.S. Constitution, which states that "no State shall enter into any Treaty, Alliance, or Confederation; grant Letters of Marque and Reprisal; coin Money; emit Bills of Credit; make any Thing but gold and silver Coin a Tender in Payment of Debts; pass any Bill of Attainder, ex post facto Law, or Law impairing the

Table 8.1 State Moratorium Legislation, 1932–34

States Passing Legislation	States Not Passing Legislation
Arizona	Alabama
California	Arkansas
Delaware	Colorado
Idaho	Connecticut
Illinois	Florida
Iowa	Georgia
Kansas	Indiana
Louisiana	Kentucky
Michigan	Maine
Minnesota	Maryland
Mississippi	Massachusetts
Montana	Missouri
Nebraska	New Jersey
New Hampshire	New Mexico
New York	Nevada
North Carolina	Oregon
North Dakota	Rhode Island
Ohio	Tennessee
Oklahoma	Utah
Pennsylvania	Virginia
South Carolina	Washington
South Dakota	West Virginia
Texas	Wyoming
Vermont	
Wisconsin	

Source: Alston (1984)

Obligation of Contracts, or grant any Title of Nobility" (article 1, section 10, clause 1). But the Supreme Court upheld the Minnesota legislation. Such state moratoria were widespread, especially in the states that were most in need of relief.

Like *Livingston*, *Blaisdell* echoes through history. On May 23, 1983, the Minnesota state legislature enacted moratorium legislation based on the 1933 Minnesota Act (Minn. Stat. § 583.03 [Supp. 1983]).

The *Blaisdell* and *Livingston* cases established the idea that debt contracts can be violated during economic crises. *Livingston* established the important principle that banks should not be liquidated during systemic crises, but should be liquidated if they cannot honor their debt in noncrisis periods. Banks can be liquidated after the crisis is clearly under control—as with the clearinghouse system.

Courts, legislatures, and Congress have gone to great lengths to avoid liquidating the banking system during crises. They have distinguished between normal times and times of crisis, and have not enforced bank-debt contracts in times of crisis. A crisis was considered to be occurring if there was a general suspension of convertibility, and suspension was never prohibited. After the Federal Reserve System came into existence, it was harder to establish whether there was a crisis, and when to declare banks insolvent. But the overriding theme, which Roosevelt used to justify his declaration of a nationwide bank holiday, is the tradition of refusing to liquidate the banking system, debt be damned.

IX. THE QUIET PERIOD AND ITS END

American bankers for decades operated by the 3-6-3 rule: pay depositors 3% interest, lend money at 6% and tee off at the golf course by 3 p.m. They could afford to be that precise because federal and state laws set the strict rules by which they operated and protected them from competitors. As a result, the power and prestige of bankers remained as secure as their vaults, while profits were steady and certain.

Suddenly, all that is gone. Bankers now face their most strenuous survival test since the Great Depression. Everywhere they turn, bankers are becoming mired in swamps of controversy and competition. Consumers, who in the past accorded bankers blind trust, are rebelling against skyrocketing fees, poor service and impersonal treatment. Such marketing powerhouses as Sears, Roebuck and Merrill Lynch are now financial bazaars that have attracted thousands of bank customers with lucrative new services. As they became free of much federal regulation, banks began engaging in suicidal price wars. Because of poor management, overzealous lending and some bad luck, commercial bank profits have been battered.

—William Blaylock, Christopher Redman, Adam Zagorin, and Stephen Koep, "Banking Takes a Beating," *Time*, December 3, 1984

Banking was a sleepy business during the Quiet Period. Banks had subsidized deposit insurance since 1934. And for most of that time, they were prohibited from paying interest on deposits. And they earned more than a competitive profit because of these protections. The value of these protections, guaranteed by a charter from either the federal or state government, is called a bank's "charter value."

Charter value reflected certain banks' monopoly power over the industry, and this created a tension that was recognized very early. John Jay Knox (1828–92) was the comptroller of the currency in 1872 and was later the president of the National Bank of the Republic in New York City. In his *History of Banking in the United States* he discussed this tension:

> The idea that the privilege of banking should be a monopoly to be exercised only by capitalists who were granted exclusive rights by the Government, was the [view] that prevailed [under the National Banking System]. This plan would doubtless have secured safety to the public if it could have been strictly carried out. It was, however, repugnant to the ideas of liberty which control under the institutions of the United States. The Federal Government and the governments of the several States all claimed and exercised the right of granting charters to banking corporations; and while the Federal Government granted but one, to be exercised at any time, most of the States were forced by the political parties which from time to time controlled them to extend the privilege, until from competition, a State banking charter became of very little value. As the system of chartered banks lost the feature of monopoly, it became less safe to the public, inasmuch as a legitimate banking business could not afford profit to all, and many of the banks were forced to adopt doubtful and dangerous, if not dishonest, methods in order to secure dividends for their stockholders. (1900, 92)

As Knox suggests, this created political issues as well, since the idea of monopoly is generally anathema, although with other industries, like public utilities, it is accepted. The banking monopolists, like the First and Second Banks of the United States, the Suffolk Bank, and even the New York Clearing House Association, and more recently the Federal Reserve System, have all been swept up in politics, even if their central banking functions may have been effective.

THE DECLINE IN CHARTER VALUES IN THE 1980s

The history of banking in the United States implicitly revolves around a conflict between charter value, which creates an incentive for banks not to become too risky, and competition, which creates risks. If a bank is deemed insolvent, it loses its charter and the protections that come with it, so the higher a bank's charter value, the higher the incentive it has to avoid risk. But as companies without bank charters compete with banks by offering the same services, the value to a bank of having a charter decreases, and to compete and stay afloat, a bank must take on more risk.

The traditional model of banking began to break down because of competition from outside the regulated banking sector in the early 1980s. Charter values started to decline, banking started to transform itself, and a credit boom began, all increasing system fragility. And this was all during the so-called Great Moderation.

Competition threatened both the liability side and the asset side of the balance sheet. On the liability side, banks faced ceilings on the interest rates they could pay on checking accounts. As long as there was no competing product and interest rates were low, consumers continued to rely on checks. But in the late 1970s as inflation rose, interest rates had to follow. The average annual inflation rate rose from less than 2% in 1950–65 to around 4.5% in 1966–73, and to almost 9.5% in 1974–81. Interest-rate ceilings meant that banks were paying rates far below market interest rates. So depositors became interested in other products.

The main new product was money market funds.[1] Money market funds (MMFs) grew from $2.2 billion in assets at the end of 1974 to $74.4 billion by the end of 1980. Then MMF growth truly skyrocketed—from $76.36 billion in 1980 to $1.85 trillion by 2000—an increase of over 2,000%. MMFs reached a peak of $3.8 trillion in 2008, making them one of the most significant financial product innovations of the last fifty years.

On the asset side of the balance sheet, in the 1980s junk bonds and commercial paper became substitutes for longer- and shorter-term bank loans, and represented an important step in the unbundling of the traditional intermediation process. This was a dramatic shift in corporate finance. Bank loans accounted for 36.6% of total credit-market debt raised in 1977–83, but only 18.2% of the total debt raised between 1984 and 1989. Borrowing via public debt markets increased from 30.5% to 54.2% over this period. The junk bond market grew from $10 billion in the early 1980s to over $200 billion by the end of the decade. This growth came at the expense of bank loans.

Another competitor with bank loans was commercial paper (CP), a short-term debt contract issued directly in the capital markets. This market grew in parallel with MMFs, as these funds needed an asset class to invest

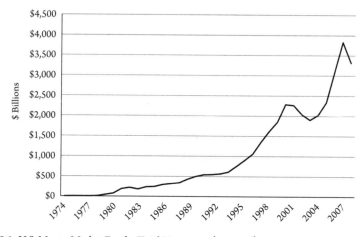

Figure 9.1 U.S. Money Market Funds: Total Net Assets (year-end)
Source: 2011 Investment Company Fact Book.

in. Over the 1980s, the CP market grew at a 17% average annual compound growth rate.

And as charter values declined in the face of all this competition, deregulation added to the ongoing transformation of the banking industry. Limited-entry protection disappeared. In 1994 the prohibition of branching across state lines was eliminated. Between 1980 and 1998 there were about eight thousand bank mergers involving about $2.4 trillion of acquired assets. It was a turbulent era.

Competition and deregulation hurt bank profits, and the effects are evident in bank interest expenses. In 1979 interest expenses were 5.17% of gross total assets, or 5.48 percentage points below the one-year Treasury note rate (10.65%). In 1986, the same measure was only 1.32 percentage points below the Treasury benchmark. Banks responded to these changes, and their rates of return did go back to pre-deregulation levels in the early 1990s. In order to stay competitive with nonbanks and their products, banks had to restore their profitability levels.

The deterioration of the traditional banking business model is summarized by the decline in the value of banks' charter values. A valuable bank charter provided an incentive for banks to self-regulate, to internalize risk management. Thus banks do not appear to have engaged in the moral hazard allegedly created by the protection of government deposit insurance. The competition from junk bonds and MMFs and the deregulation of limited entry and interest rate ceilings caused bank charter values to decline, which in turn caused banks to increase risk and reduce capital. The end of the Quiet Period meant that the traditional business model of banking had to be transformed. And indeed it was, through financial innovation.

INNOVATION

Innovation eroded the profitability of the traditional bank business model. In the face of competition from new products like money market funds and junk bonds, banks needed to innovate in order to survive as profitable companies. The most important bank innovation was securitization.

Securitization involves financing loans by selling them. It works like this: Since a loan or mortgage is a legal commitment of the borrower to repay the loan over some years, the loan contract is a legal commitment of cash coming in over a future period. Securitization is the process of selling a portfolio of such loans to a new company called a "special purpose vehicle" (SPV). The

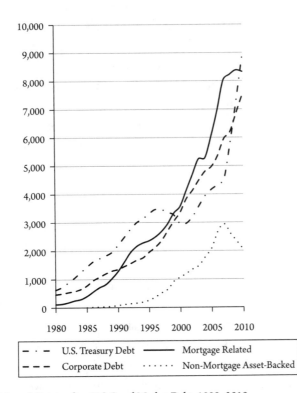

Figure 9.2 Selected Outstanding U.S. Bond Market Debt, 1980–2010
Sources: U.S. Department of Treasury, Federal Reserve System, Federal agencies, Dealogic, Thomson Reuters, Bloomberg, Loan Performance, and SIFMA.

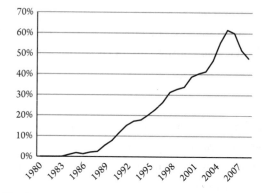

Figure 9.3 Ratio of Total Private Securitization to Total Bank Loans
Source: Federal Reserve Flow of Funds

SPV issues securities in capital markets to finance the purchase of the portfolio of loans. These securities are called asset-backed securities (ABS). If the pool of loan purchases is residential mortgages, then the securities are called mortgage-backed securities. Other important ABS categories are credit card receivables (that is, the amounts that people have run up on their credit cards and must repay), auto loans, and student loans.

Since 1980, securitization became an enormous banking activity. Figure 9.2 shows the outstanding amounts over time.[2]

When a bank sells its loans, the loans move off of the bank's balance sheet. An indication of the shift from on-balance sheet loan financing, where a loan is not sold, to off-balance sheet financing is given by the ratio of securitized loans to bank loans held on balance sheet.

When a bank makes the credit decision to grant a loan, and the obligation is accepted by the borrower, the borrower legally accepts the obligation to repay the loan over time. In the traditional banking model, the bank waits for the money to be repaid. With securitization, the bank sells the promise to repay and receives the present value of the promised cash flows that will come in the future.

There are several important sources of value in securitization. First, an SPV cannot go into bankruptcy or financial distress. If the underlying loans do not pay enough to honor the asset-backed security obligations of the SPV, due to defaults, then the asset-backed securities go into early amortization rather than default. This means that however much money is paid to the SPV—not enough to pay the promised amounts—is paid out as "principal" early.

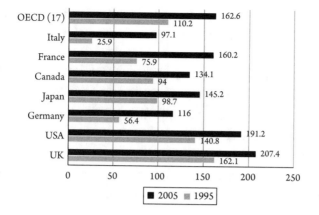

Figure 9.4 Financial Assets of Institutional Investors, 1995 and 2005 (percent of GDP)
Source: Gonnard, Kim, and Ynesta (2008, 4)

Thereafter, the principal just keeps paying down. Early amortization means that the SPV avoids costly bankruptcy proceedings.

A second source of value comes from the fact that an SPV involves no managerial discretion; it is simply a repository of claims on future cash flows. The credit decision has already been made by the sponsoring bank. A normal firm is long-lived, and its existence depends on managerial and strategic decisions made by the board of directors and the management. The associated risks are much more complicated than those of a large portfolio of car loans, for example. Separating the car loans from the more complicated risks makes the portfolio easier to value.

Finally, at the same time that the amount, or supply, of securitization developed, demand for it also rose. One source of demand was money market funds, which need short-term assets to invest in. MMFs became lenders in the repo market, and could accept asset-backed securities as collateral. Another category of investors was also growing: institutional investors and pension funds.

In addition, nonfinancial firms also increased the amounts of cash their treasury departments held. From 1980 to 2006, the ratio of cash to assets for U.S. industrial firms more than doubled from 10.5% to 23.2%. Firms, pension funds, and institutional investors hold large amounts of cash because they need to invest large amounts of cash for short periods to earn interest. But they also need it to be safe. Since there are no insured demand deposit accounts large enough to accommodate these customers, they end up using repo and commercial paper as their checking accounts.

Repo is of particular interest. In repo, a pension fund, for example, goes to a financial institution and "deposits" $100 million overnight. The pension fund will earn interest on this loan—say, 3%. To make this deposit safe, the financial institution provides the pension fund with collateral, which the pension fund takes possession of. The collateral, which might be an asset-backed security, earns, say, 6% interest for the financial institution. So the financial institution is borrowing at 3% and earning 6%, just like a traditional bank. It is spread banking in a new form.

This is the "shadow banking system," a new depository banking system that arose to meet the needs of the large depositors. And the "banks" involved were the old investment banks and large commercial banks. The size of the repo market is not known, because the government did not measure all of it, only part of it. Economists at the Bank for International Settlements reported that repo markets had doubled in size since 2002, "with gross amounts outstanding at year-end 2007 of roughly $10 trillion in each of the U.S. and Euro markets, and another $1 trillion in the UK repo market" (Bank for International Settlements 2009, 37). They reported that the U.S. repo market exceeded $10 trillion in mid-2008. The European repo market, generally viewed as smaller than the U.S. market, was EUR 4.87 trillion in June 2009, having peaked at EUR 6.78 trillion in June 2007, according to a survey by the International Capital Markets Association (International Capital Market Association, 2007). According to the same survey the year before, the global repo market grew at an average rate of 19% per year between 2001 and 2007.

The financial innovation in the early 1980s, money market funds in particular, was due to the high inflation of the 1970s. That inflation led to the collapse of the thrift industry as well. It was the period when the Phillips curve got the attention of macroeconomists. But they missed the beginnings of the start of the transformation of the banking system. Junk bonds were an innovation that seems unrelated to inflation. The decline of the traditional banking business model and the rise of institutional investors led to securitization. But it wasn't only these innovations that mattered.

There are many other important financial innovations that occurred during this period. The changes to the bankruptcy law that provided that repurchase agreements would not be settled in a Chapter 11 bankruptcy proceeding allowed repo to become an important money system. The innovation of General Collateral Finance (GCF) repo by the Depository Trust and Clearing Corporation (DTCC) was important. In this system a division of DTCC becomes the legal counterparty to all GCF repos, eliminating counterparty risk. And there were many more innovations. These innovations, mostly hidden from the public eye, are part of a long history of innovation, including the development of checks, clearinghouses, clearinghouse loan certificates, electronic rather than paper registration of securities, and the development of safe and efficient payment and settlement systems. During the financial crisis of 2007–8 some of these innovations became the focus of attention during the recent financial crisis. And then there were the innovative responses to the financial crisis that the Federal Reserve System implemented.

There was no financial crisis between 1934 and 2007 because the Quiet Period was an era in which banks were earning monopoly profits, based on high charter values and a lack of invasive innovation. They did not want to jeopardize their charters by taking risk, and there was no reason for the banks to innovate, because they were profitable. Eventually, however, the world changed, and bank charters lost value.

One response was securitization. The supply of securitization met the demand from new large investors: pension funds, institutional investors, and nonfinancial firms. And these large entities also needed checking accounts, so the demand for repo and commercial paper grew. This new banking system followed the 3-6-3 paradigm, but it was not in the old banking tradition. So their liabilities were not insured and they were vulnerable to panic.

X. MORAL HAZARD AND TOO-BIG-TO-FAIL

Last month we had a group of economics and banking professors at the Corporation for lunch and during the discussion they were adamant in their position that "big banks never close." By their definition, anything over $10 million in deposits would be beyond the small category.

—Irvine Sprague, former chairman of the Federal Deposit Insurance Corporation, 1986

The U.S. savings and loan fiasco during the 1980s and 1990s and the Latin American debt crisis in the early 1980s foreshadowed the end of the Quiet Period. But regulators and economists were conceptually trapped, and the discussion about banking focused increasingly on two ideas: moral hazard and too-big-to-fail. These notions highlight the role of the government in banking, in particular the idea that the government causes problems. Because of the vulnerability of bank debt, governments and central banks use tools like deposit insurance and bailouts to prevent bank runs. But often we do not observe the bank runs that would have happened had the government not intervened.

Moral hazard and too-big-to-fail assume that because of the protection of deposit insurance or the implicit promise of a bailout due to a bank's size, banks take risks they would not otherwise. This extra risk taking is now often assumed to make the financial system more fragile or even to cause crises.

However, moral hazard and too-big-to-fail are not the causes of the problem—they are side effects of attempted government remedies for financial crises. Importantly, we have seen that before these notions existed, prior to the Federal Reserve or deposit insurance, financial crises occurred regularly. And what prevented crises during the Quiet Period, between 1934 and 2007, after the founding of the Fed and deposit insurance?

Deposit insurance and bank bailouts are government responses, for better or worse, to bank runs. By looking at how these policies have succeeded in the past, even if their success was limited in important ways, we can address the problem of bank runs without creating problems of moral hazard and too-big-to-fail.

MORAL HAZARD

In one context, moral hazard is the idea that when a business's legal structure provides limited liability for the shareholders, they can lose no more than the value of their shares, and there is a conflict of incentives between shareholders and bondholders. Shareholders can take risks that benefit them at the potential expense of the bondholders. Shareholders get the upside and don't have to worry about the downside. Bondholders understand this problem and act to prevent it through bond covenants, rules that prohibit or require certain practices by management. This conflict always exists when there is limited liability; it is a general problem.

Modern banks also have limited liability. The problem with banks is debt, which is vulnerable to runs. Banks try to create liabilities that do not reflect information about the backing collateral, whatever it is. The debt is designed to trade at par, so no one has an incentive to find secret information that can be profitable but cause the debt not to trade at par. The whole point is that the debt price does not change to reflect changes in the risk of the backing collateral. But the private sector cannot do this perfectly, because the backing collateral is not, in fact, riskless. With deposit insurance, depositors do not have an incentive to question the value of the backing collateral, and there should not be banking panics. But to prevent risk taking the government must examine and monitor banks, and provide incentives to shareholders to prevent risk taking, much like bond covenants for limited liability corporations. If regulation and incentives do not work, then there is a problem. As economist T. Bruce Robb put it in 1934, "If there is a real demand for bank-deposit insurance, does anyone seriously believe that adequate safeguards cannot be devised to control the moral hazard this insurance may foster?" (1934, 62). It may be possible to design such a system, as Robb suggests, although experience shows that it is not easy. But after deposit insurance was adopted in 1934, the Quiet Period followed, so we know it is somehow possible.

A few U.S. states first experimented with insurance systems for bank liabilities prior to the Civil War, but they were not used again until the Panic of 1907. A. Piatt Andrew, a Harvard economics professor, assistant secretary of the Treasury, and later member of Congress, explains:

> The idea [of deposit insurance] was born in Oklahoma in the very throes of the panic of 1907, after the shortest possible period of gestation. The panic, it will be remembered, began October 28, 1907; and it was not until three weeks later, on November 16, that Oklahoma became a State, and that its first legislature began its session. Nevertheless the panic was not yet over, currency was still at a premium, and clearing house certificates were still outstanding throughout the country when the Oklahoma legislature passed its famous law. This first legislature of a new State had been in session only four weeks when, on December 17, it adopted with scarcely any debate a law without precedent in any other country, and with only a dimly remembered, unsuccessful precedent in the United States—a law which nevertheless presented what was probably the most far-reaching and drastic experiment in banking legislation that had been made anywhere in the world for at least two generations. (Andrew 1913, 600)

Robb later wrote:

> It will be remembered that Oklahoma presented bank guaranty to the world as a panacea for panics. Being twelve years removed from the panic it is difficult to realize the appeal which this argument made at the time. The newspapers and periodicals of that day abound with the expressions of both bankers and individuals who implicitly believed that panics would be impossible if people had the assurance that their deposits were safe. (Robb 1921, 180)

This was an outcome of the Populist movement, the largest mass movement in U.S. history. The Populist roots of deposit insurance would eventually carry the day during the Great Depression, when Congress passed federal deposit insurance. People wanted deposit insurance because they did not want panics. During the debates over federal deposit insurance, the issue of moral hazard arose, but it was already an old argument. Robb offered an early discussion of it before the FDIC. His book is about various early-twentieth-century state deposit insurance schemes, some of which worked and others of which did not.

> Bank-deposit insurance will have a tendency to relax the vigilance of the depositing public. But this is of little consequence. The theory assumes that the public has perfect knowledge of all the complex ramifications of the modern banking business, and consequently can govern itself accordingly. It has been pointed out repeatedly that this is far from the truth. The truth is that the average depositor knows very little regarding the operation of the modern bank, and that effective state supervision is not the great palladium of public safety.
>
> But there remains the contention that under a guaranty law a reputation for foresight and prudence in handling funds has lost most of its significance to a banker as a business-getter. Ancillary to this is the inference that a reckless straining after abnormal profits will tend to replace conservative banking. This is one phase of the moral hazard in insurance. The attempt will now be made to ascertain whether the practice comports with this theory, and to what extent the operation of the laws tends to set in motion social forces that counteract this moral hazard. (1921, 189)

Robb's first point is essentially that since depositors could never really keep track of which banks were riskier in the first place, it doesn't really matter if deposit insurance removes the incentive for them to do so. Even without deposit insurance, the rates on deposits do not vary according to risk, because depositors cannot effectively know which banks are riskier, since bank debt is designed to be opaque and information-insensitive. Seemingly, depositors would want to know which banks were riskier, but the whole point of bank debt is to eliminate the incentive to do so. So if there is no incentive to learn information, or secrets, about certain banks in the first place, it is illogical to argue that deposit insurance removes it. Before deposit insurance, the only effective monitoring of banks was by other banks in a clearinghouse where banks monitored each other. But this did not prevent panics.

When depositors received information that a recession was coming, they were unsure which banks might be in trouble, so they tried to withdraw from all banks. If depositors could determine which banks were riskier, then only those banks would have faced runs.

This suggests that, whether banks have insurance or not, there is already moral hazard relative to the ideal world where all risk is priced correctly. In the pre-Fed period, private bank clearinghouses mutually monitored members for this reason. But not all banks belonged to clearinghouses.

Notably, the states that adopted deposit insurance in the early 20th century (Oklahoma, Kansas, Nebraska, Texas, South Dakota, Mississippi, and North Dakota) were largely rural states without supervisory clearinghouses. There were clearinghouses that cleared checks in these states, but they did not supervise banks.

Robb goes on to look at the different experiences of the above seven states. The evidence "is conflicting," but in the end, he concludes:

> While it is true that insurance relaxes the vigilance of the party insured, it is also true that it sets in operation powerful social forces working in the opposite direction. Thus, paradoxical as it may seem, fire insurance is probably the most potent factor in the world in working toward fire prevention. It is extremely significant that the same principle is found operating in bank-deposit insurance. Every state that has adopted such laws has raised its banking standards. Ten years ago Oklahoma had about the lowest banking standards in the country; today wholly because of the pressure of the guaranty law on the state bankers, no state in the Union probably has better regulated state banks. (1921, 192)

Insurance makes things better because "it sets in operation powerful social forces" of examination and monitoring. Before deposit insurance, the only people with the real incentive to monitor banks were depositors, but they couldn't do so, since bank debt by design is information-insensitive. Deposit insurance created an incentive for the party that guaranteed it, the government, to monitor banks. This is what in large part enabled the sustained prevention of crises during the Quiet Period.

But the problem of moral hazard arises in several ways, when there is an implicit promise of insurance, as discussed above, and when there is the expectation that the government will act. In the latter case, there is another issue to be discussed: the Livingston doctrine. Some types of insurance are implicit—for example, allowing suspension of convertibility—but they will cover institutions only in times of crisis. And since crises are unpredictable, there would not likely be any extra risk taking, because each individual bank cannot predict when a crisis will occur, nor can it coordinate with other banks to take risk. So a single bank will simply put itself at risk of failing. But a completely different situation arises when there is a policy that would bail out a single firm. In that case, there is no need for banks to coordinate their risk taking with other banks.

The Livingston doctrine tells us that bailouts should occur only when many institutions are in crisis. But this puts bank regulators on the horns of a terrible dilemma. What if the failure of a single bank will cause a systemic crisis? If regulators bail out the bank, then their actions may prevent a crisis. But in that case the crisis is not observed, and their actions might be taken as a policy of bailing out single institutions, reinforcing moral hazard. If they wait until there is a full-blown crisis to save many banks, so that there is no misunderstanding of their actions, the costs are potentially very high.

This dilemma is the too-big-to-fail problem.

TOO-BIG-TO-FAIL DURING THE PANICS OF 1884 AND 1890

During the National Banking Era potential bailouts came not from the government but from other banks, through clearinghouses. So the issue of too-big-to-fail can exist even without the promise of government intervention. In the Panics of 1884 and 1890, member banks of the New York clearinghouse assumed collective responsibility and decided on bailouts—and the panics were basically limited to New York City and didn't last long. This is because the New York Clearing House Association bailed out individual banks by issuing clearinghouse loan certificates. These events are particularly important to note because the revealed preference of the association of banks was a policy of too-big-to-fail during crises.

The Panic of 1884 did not turn out to be a systemic event; it was largely confined to New York City. The likely reasons that it was not a systemic event are instructive. The New York City Clearing House Association acted decisively and forcefully. The panic began with the failure of the Marine National

Bank, a smaller bank with only $4.5 million of deposits at the time it closed. This was shortly followed by the collapse of the brokerage firm of Grant and Ward.[1] Then a run ensued on the Second National Bank after evidence of fraud came to light and the bank president fled to Canada. The Metropolitan National Bank, rumored to be engaged in fraudulent activity, also faced runs, which caused it to close. Subsequently, six brokerage houses failed. The *New York Times* reported, May 3, 1889:

> When the Marine and Metropolitan Banks went down, everybody feared a season of disasters that would end no one dared think when, and would include no one dared think whom. The Metropolitan seemed destined to carry down with it scores of other concerns, and the great need was for some way to float its liabilities on the general market. Mr. [George S.] Coe devised the way. It was a combination of all the banks in the city that undertook what no one, or no ten of them, could have accomplished, and the impending ruin was averted.

The closing of the Metropolitan Bank due to runs was not an event that the clearinghouse took lightly, because the Metropolitan had extensive relations with other banks. The comptroller of the currency, Henry W. Cannon, wrote in the comptroller's annual report of 1884 that

> in this emergency the members of the New York Clearing House Association, realizing that an immediate demand for deposits would be made by their country correspondents, called a meeting at the clearing house on the afternoon of May 14, and the following plan for settling balances at the clearing house was unanimously adopted:
>
> "*Resolved*, That, in view of the present crisis, the banks in this association, for the purpose of sustaining each other and the business community, resolve that a committee of five be appointed by the chair to receive from banks members of the association bills receivable and other securities to be approved by said committee, who shall be authorized to issue therefore to such depositing banks certificates of deposit bearing interest at 6 per cent per annum not in excess of 75 per cent of the securities or bills receivable so deposited, except in case of United States bonds, and said certificates shall be received in settlement of balances at the clearing house."

After consultation with the officers and directors of the Metropolitan National Bank a committee of examination was appointed to visit the bank and ascertain if some plan would be arranged to permit it to open again for business. (33)

The investigation of the Metropolitan found a bank that was solvent but could not withstand the runs. Robert Barnett (1884) reports:

> The Investigating Committee at once commenced the examination of its affairs, and at midnight reported that there was no deficit either by the officers of the bank or by bad management. Its difficulties were due to the sudden withdrawal of deposits, and an advance of certificates to the extent of GBP 600,000 [Barnett was writing in a British journal] was made by the Committee, whereby the bank was enabled to resume business; which it did at noon on the following day, having been closed for just twenty-four hours.
>
> The action of the Clearing House Association, together with the report on the affairs of the Metropolitan Bank and its expected immediate re-opening, caused so great a feeling of relief at the opening of business on Thursday, the 15th, that it was hoped that all cause for alarm was over. (485)

An important lesson learned from this event was that clearinghouse action during a crisis would only be effective if the association prepared during non-crisis times. At a meeting on June 4, 1884, the New York Clearing House Association adopted the following resolution:

> That the experience of the associated banks in the New York Clearing House during the recent panic having shown that every member of the Association, in a time of general and serious financial disturbance, is involuntarily compelled to make common cause with every other member in the risks attending any practical expedient for general relief, or of any effective combination for the public good; it is therefore proper and necessary to enquire whether the method of business, as conducted by the several members of this Association, are uniform and correct in their operation with the public, and equitable to all the banks which are thus bound together in the Clearing House Association.

The crisis of 1890 was also limited to New York City and was of short duration. It started with the failure of a brokerage firm on November 11, 1890. The New York Clearing House held an emergency meeting that same day to provide assistance to two endangered banks, the Bank of North America and the Mechanics' and Traders' Bank, by issuing loan certificates. In the end, J. P. Morgan intervened and organized nine large banks to each contribute $100,000 for aid. This new role for J. P. Morgan would become more complicated.

THE PANIC OF 1907 AND THE FAILURE TO BAILOUT KNICKERBOCKER TRUST

In 1907 another panic occurred in New York City, with runs on the Mercantile National Bank, the New Amsterdam Bank, and the National Bank of North America. Officers of these three banks were connected with an attempt by some speculators to corner the copper market. The clearinghouse sent examiners to the three banks to determine their solvency. The Clearing House Committee, upon receipt of the examination of the Mercantile National Bank, voted to make available whatever cash the bank needed. The other two banks were also declared solvent, and they too received loans from syndicates of clearinghouse members, though these banks were not issued clearinghouse loan certificates.

Another phase of the 1907 crisis began with runs on two of the city's largest trust companies, the Trust Company of America and the Knickerbocker Trust. Trusts were a new type of financial intermediary—essentially investment banks. Importantly, trusts were not members of the New York Clearing House Association. The Knickerbocker approached the New York Clearing House for a loan but was turned down. The Knickerbocker then turned to J. P. Morgan for help, who then appointed a committee to examine the trust. It is not clear whether the examination was really undertaken or completed, but Morgan decided not to help and the trust collapsed. The panic worsened. Eventually, the Clearing House issued loan certificates and J. P. Morgan organized the rescue of the trust companies. The Panic of 1907 was one of the most severe because the trusts were not integrated into the clearinghouse mechanism. The clearinghouse was late in issuing loan certificates, and the failure of J. P. Morgan to aid the Knickerbocker Trust was quite likely a mistake.

Even before the government offered the promise of bailing out large individual institutions, banks were already trying to grasp the problem of too-big-to-fail. Almost a century later, however, after the Quiet Period, in which the government did promise action and successfully prevented crises, banking changed, and too-big-to-fail returned.

TOO-BIG-TO-FAIL AND CONTINENTAL OF ILLINOIS

In 1984 troubles arose with Continental Illinois Bank and Trust Company, the seventh largest bank in the United States at the time. It was bailed out. The Federal Deposit Insurance Corporation later explained the situation:

> The Continental open bank assistance transaction is the most significant bank failure resolution in the history of the Federal Deposit Insurance Corporation (FDIC). Continental Illinois National Bank and Trust Company (Continental), Chicago, Illinois, received interim financial assistance from the FDIC on May 17, 1984, and received permanent financial assistance on September 26 of the same year. Continental is the single largest bank ever to require financial assistance from the FDIC in the history of the United States; but it was also noteworthy for several other reasons. First, the FDIC made a public statement before a final resolution, guaranteeing that all depositors and other general creditors would suffer no loss. Second, the FDIC took a significant ownership position in the bank holding company, effectively making Continental a government-owned bank. Third, Continental was the first assisted bank in which the assets acquired by the FDIC were serviced by the bank itself under a separate servicing agreement. Finally, the Continental open bank assistance transaction affirmed for many the notion that certain banks were simply "too big to fail." (1997, 545)

The first issue with the bailout was whether it was the case that there would be a systemic crisis if the bank was not bailed out. This was viewed as being related to a second issue, which was that the bailout was extended to *all creditors*, as explained in the Federal Deposit Insurance Corporation news release of May 17, 1984:

In view of all the circumstances surrounding Continental Illinois Bank, the FDIC provides assurance that in all arrangements that may be necessary to achieve a permanent solution, *all depositors and other general creditors of the bank will be fully protected* and service to the bank's customers will not be interrupted.[2]

Both FDIC chairman (from 1981 to 1985) William Isaac and Federal Reserve Board chairman Paul Volcker argued that the failure of Continental would have caused other banks to face runs. The events unfolded during a period of heightened concern about whether Argentina, Brazil, Colombia, and Mexico could repay their debts. There were also rumors that Bolivia would suspend payments on its debt. The crisis began when Mexico informed the Federal Reserve chairman, the secretary of the Treasury, and the International Monetary Fund on August 12, 1982, that Mexico would be unable to meet its debt service obligation. There were large exposures for U.S. banks. Manufacturers Hanover, another large bank, in particular faced rumors about its Latin American exposure. The argument that in this setting the failure of Continental was especially dangerous had merit.

Because the argument had merit, in May 1984 the federal government contributed about $1 billion to prop up Continental. Continental was a money center bank that held large deposits of hundreds of smaller banks throughout the Midwest. It also was highly dependent on wholesale funding. In early May Continental faced a run by large, uninsured depositors. Irvine Sprague was the chairman of the Federal Deposit Insurance Corporation (FDIC) from 1979 to 1981, and had been on the FDIC board from 1969 to 1972. Sprague later explained that

the problem was that there was no way to project how many other institutions would fail or how weakened the nation's entire banking system might become. Best estimates of our staff, with the sparse numbers we had at hand, were that more than two thousand correspondent banks were depositors in Continental and some number—we talked of fifty to two hundred—might be threatened or brought down by a Continental collapse. (I. Sprague 1986, 155)

The comptroller of the currency intervened to rescue Continental, a rescue that saved bank depositors and bond holders of the holding company as well as the bank. The comptroller of the currency, Todd Conover, explained in subsequent Congressional testimony that

> had Continental failed and been treated in a way which depositors and creditors were not made whole, we could very well have seen a national, if not international, financial crisis, the dimensions of which were difficult to imagine. None of us wanted to find out.[3]

Continental was a bailout of a large bank, the largest bank failure in U.S. history at that time, although there had been a few other large failures. An important difference between Continental and other failures was the speed of the collapse, and this was due to how Continental funded itself. Comptroller Conover testified:

> Although Continental was weakened by asset deterioration, its losses never exceeded capital, and thus it never reached book insolvency. Rather, its near-collapse was triggered by funding problems. Beginning in the second half of 1982, the bank was forced to rely increasingly on foreign funding, as federal funds and certificates of deposit rapidly eroded. For almost two years, the overseas funding provided Continental with relatively stable, much needed liquidity. It also made the bank vulnerable to the liquidity problems that occurred in May 1984 when uncertainty about Continental's condition caused the overseas markets to close completely.
>   Clearly Continental's reliance on uninsured, short-term funds meant that it was particularly vulnerable to a loss of confidence.[4]

Continental financed itself in what was at that time a very unusual way. It relied on wholesale and largely foreign funding. One bank examiner estimated that Continental was between 60% and 70% dependent on purchased funds.[5] Partly, this was due to Illinois being a unit banking state, which meant banks could not have branches, but its funding was unusual. Like the dealer banks in the 2007–8 crisis, it relied on large, uninsured, short-term deposits. Consequently, it was vulnerable to a run. When information about Continental's deteriorating balance sheet came out, the run began:

> In May of this year, the market reacted adversely to rumors of further problems at Continental, and large depositors began withdrawing

funds. The bank was unable to stem the run, and federal intervention was required to prevent the bank's collapse.[6]

This change to reliance on short-term wholesale funding was fundamental, and in hindsight it was an important clue for understanding how the financial system was evolving. The Continental failure was due to a wholesale banking run, like the runs in 2007–8. It was the first dramatic evidence of the changes. The traditional, and comfortable, model of banking changed dramatically starting in the 1980s. It was the start of the end of the Quiet Period.

There had been large bank failures prior to Continental, but Continental received special attention—something was different. Congressman Stewart McKinney (of Connecticut; 1931–87) noted, "We have a new kind of bank. It is called too big to fail. TBTF, and it is a wonderful bank."[7]

Was the Continental decision to rescue all the creditors of Continental correct? Regulators claimed to be preventing a financial crisis. There was no crisis when they acted, but this is perhaps because they acted. The Livingston doctrine dictates that a bank can be bailed out if there is a crisis. In the case of Continental Illinois there was not yet a crisis—the logic of the bailout was to prevent one. But the Continental bailout decision *appeared* to mean that individual banks would be bailed out even when there was no crisis, a violation of the Livingston doctrine. One academic study argues that there is evidence that the bailout weakened market discipline. But what were the choices? The regulators could have let Continental fail and then acted if a crisis unfolded. That could have been very costly. Or they could have limited the insurance coverage to insured deposits, leaving the uninsured wholesale depositors to suffer losses. But that may still have resulted in a crisis because of the way that Continental was funded.

Continental Illinois raised the problem of the counterfactual. If the threat of a crisis could not be agreed upon—and that is what would have happened—then this creates an inadvertent policy issue: too-big-to-fail. It is not possible to go back in time and see what would have happened had Continental been allowed to fail, to then determine if it was right to bail it out. But the best policy is one that designs a banking system in which regulators do not face such a dilemma. But when they do, the counterfactual has to be made convincing. This is the job of economists.

LEHMAN BROTHERS

Contrary to what happened to Continental, the Knickerbocker mistake of 1907, of not bailing out a large bank during a crisis, was repeated during the crisis of 2007–8 when Lehman Brothers was allowed to fail. Lehman filed for bankruptcy on September 15, 2008. The next day the Reserve Primary Fund, a U.S. money market fund with over $50 billion in assets, broke the buck, and the government stepped in to rescue AIG. Fed Chairman Ben Bernanke told the Financial Crisis Inquiry Commission that government officials understood a Lehman bankruptcy would be catastrophic:

> We never had any doubt about that. It was going to have huge impacts on funding markets. It would create a huge loss of confidence in other financial firms. It would create pressure on Merrill and Morgan Stanley, if not Goldman, which it eventually did. It would probably bring the short-term money markets into crisis, which we didn't fully anticipate; but, of course, in the end it did bring the commercial paper market and the money market mutual funds under pressure. So there was never any doubt in our minds that it would be a calamity, catastrophe, and that, you know, we should do everything we could to save it. (Financial Crisis Inquiry Commission 2011, 339)

The failure of Lehman Brothers paralyzed the interbank market, where short-term borrowing and lending froze. Market participants did not know how large other financial intermediaries' exposures to Lehman Brothers were and refused to trade. Henry Paulson, the treasury secretary at the time, described the result of the Lehman failure:

> We had a system in crisis. Credit markets froze and banks substantially reduced interbank lending. Confidence was seriously compromised throughout our financial system. Our system was on the verge of collapse, a collapse that would have significantly worsened and prolonged the economic downturn that was already underway. (Paulson 2008)

Figure 10.1 shows a measure of counterparty risk in the interbank market and a measure of the risk in the subprime mortgage market. Counterparty

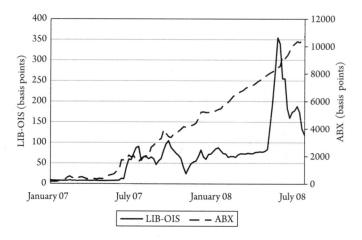

Figure 10.1 Counterparty Risk (LIB-OIS) versus Fundamentals (ABX)
Source: Gorton and Metrick, forthcoming.

risk is measured by the difference between three-month LIBOR, the rate at which banks borrow and lend to each other in the London dollar market. Subprime risk is measured as the spread on an index of BBB subprime-linked securities (ABX). Subprime risk continues to deteriorate during the whole period shown; the spread increases and increases. But, in the interbank market, the Lehman failure is shown as the large spike.

The failure of Lehman Brothers stunned the market because participants apparently thought that no large institution would be allowed to fail. Why was Lehman allowed to fail? Bernanke maintained that Lehman did not have the collateral to justify a loan from the Fed of sufficient size to save them. Perhaps so; during a crisis it is very hard, even impossible, to determine the value of assets. But the looming catastrophe was clear, and by the Livingston standard, Lehman should not have been liquidated. It seems widely agreed that this was a mistake. Of course it is easy to say that it was a mistake after the fact—we observed the crisis. But one cannot help but think that various political realities played a role.

Prior to Lehman's failure many economists and regulators said during the crisis that a big bank must be allowed to fail. No one admits this now. The notion of moral hazard was so ingrained, because of Continental, that the idea of punishing a bank was taken as paramount. Paul Volcker had articulated this logic decades earlier:

The 1980s exposed various excesses which I think, to some degree, were becoming apparent in the 1970s. I can remember very clearly sitting in my office then, as President of the Federal Reserve Bank of New York, thinking what this country needs is a first-class bank failure to teach us all a lesson. But please God, not in my District. When I went to Washington, I had the same feeling. We need a clear lesson from market discipline, but please dear God, not in my country.[8]

One can only imagine the outcry if no bank had been allowed to fail. The counterfactual would never have been convincing. And if Lehman had been bailed out, the political firestorm might have resulted in a much worse conflagration, maybe the inadvertent insolvency of many more institutions. This political dilemma resulted in punishing the bankers as an example.

The principal issue concerns the problem of counterfactuals and the effects of counterfactuals on expectations. Regulators could never show convincingly that there would have been a financial crisis had they not rescued Continental. Nor can the Federal Reserve ever show that the crisis would have been worse in 2007–8 had they not acted. And it is clear that rescuing big banks during crises is not a policy that is caused by the government, as the examples from the pre–Federal Reserve period show.

The bottom line is that the *Livingston* case and subsequent history suggests that banks should be liquidated if they cannot honor their debt in noncrisis periods, but not during a crisis. The failures to rescue the Knickerbocker Trust or Lehman Brothers may have been mistakes, just as the bailout of Continental Illinois perhaps was. But the alternative to letting Lehman Brothers go bankrupt may have been worse because of the way banking changed from around the time of Continental Illinois.

As charter value disappeared, and the original design of bank regulation became less effective, moral hazard and too-big-to-fail became important issues, particularly after Continental Illinois failed and was bailed out. This showed that there is an inevitable dilemma for bank regulators if the system of bank regulation cannot credibly prevent crises.

An important implication of the Livingston doctrine is that banks cannot coordinate to engage in moral hazard if they are only bailed out when there is a crisis. They cannot coordinate risk-taking decisions and there are no moral hazard or too-big-to-fail problems. But Continental Illinois showed that determining when there is a crisis is difficult. How do we know that there would have been a crisis? How do we know when we are in a crisis? The earlier period made this clear: there was a panic.

Moral hazard and too-big-to-fail are not causes of the underlying problem—financial crises. If bank regulation can be designed to avoid crises, these dilemmas for regulators can be avoided, at least for while. The problem does not exist if a Quiet Period can be recreated.

XI. BANK CAPITAL

Against such panics, Banks have no security, *on any system*; from their very nature they are subject to them, as at no time can there be a Bank, or in a country, so much specie or bullion as the monied individuals of such a country have a right to demand. Should every man withdraw his balance from his banker on the same day, many times the quantity of bank notes in circulation would be insufficient to answer such a demand.

—David Ricardo

Throughout American history the banking system has been designed, by Congress or state legislatures, to try to achieve stability, to prevent crises. The Quiet Period suggests it is possible to do this successfully. There are enticements, like charter value, that encourage banks to not take too much risk. There are also regulations, like reserve requirements—how much cash a bank has to have on hand; and capital requirements, limitations on how much the bank can borrow. And there are bank examinations. Through a combination of these, stability might be achievable. But it is a delicate balance of pay-offs and punishments—if there is no profit in being a bank, bank capital will exit the industry.

Conceptually, there are two issues, as George Barnett explained in 1911:

The banking question in the United States includes at least two prob-lems. The more serious of these is the prevention of panics, such as those which occurred in 1893 and 1907. The less urgent, but important, problem is the minimizing of losses through bank failures. The two problems are not entirely distinct since panics, directly and indirectly, have been responsible for many of our bank failures, but the two may be considered as separate since most bank failures are due, not to the breaking down of the general credit structure, or the resultant depreciation in values, but entirely to causes peculiar to the particular institutions involved. (270)

From 1934, when deposit insurance was adopted, until the 1980s, bank regulators focused on bank examinations rather than capital requirements. That was a period of high charter value, when banks internalized risk management. There was little financial innovation. Prior to the Federal Reserve System, clearinghouses focused on reserve requirements and restrictions on the payment of interest on deposits. Capital requirements, though present, were not the focus. The reasons for this are clear. Banking panics are about cash, so having enough cash on hand, if possible, means holding reserves and not lending them out for interest. Bankers and bank regulators understood that crises are about cash. Tynan Smith and Raymond Hengren of the FDIC, for example, write:

> Capital is not the sole answer ... to the problem of keeping a bank's doors open. Regardless of the size of a bank's capital, it will continue to function as a going concern only so long as it has on hand or can obtain cash to meet the claims of depositors. ... Whenever banks are faced with heavy withdrawals of deposits, either because of general economic crises or local or regional situations, the essential problem is one of liquidity rather than of capital. ... The equity ratio has relatively little bearing on the ability of a bank to obtain cash when it is needed. (1947, 557)

A systemic financial crisis is an event in which the banking system is insolvent, which means debt contracts cannot be honored with cash because assets cannot be sold. In that event no amount of capital short of 100%—so there is no bank debt—can prevent a crisis. The recent financial crisis reinforced this point. For example, in discussing Lehman's impending failure, one New York Fed official wrote to his colleagues: "Balance-sheet capital isn't too relevant if you're suffering a massive run" (Financial Crisis Inquiry Commission 2011, 324). If there is a run on the banking system, there is no buyer large enough to buy enough bank assets without prices plunging. High capital ratios cannot prevent runs.

That crises are about cash and not capital should be clear. David Ricardo also made this point:

> It remains to be considered, whether the ability of the Bank to pay their notes in specie would be increased by an increase of their capital. The ability of the Bank, to pay their notes in specie, must depend upon the proportion of specie which they may keep, to meet the probable demand for payment of their notes; and in this respect their power cannot be increased, for they may now, *if they please*, have a stock of specie, not only equal to all their notes in circulation, but to the whole of the public and private deposits, and under no possible circumstances can more be demanded of them. But the profits of the Bank essentially depend on the smallness of the stock of cash and bullion; and the whole dexterity of the business consists in maintaining the largest possible circulation, with the least possible amount of their funds in the shape of cash and bullion. (1876, 431–32)

Nevertheless, the confusion about the meaning of a systemic crisis and the role of bank capital continues. In August 2011 at the Federal Reserve Bank of Kansas City's Jackson Hole Symposium, a leading finance official said that European banks were in need of an "urgent recapitalization." To this, the *Financial Times* reported that these comments "missed the point of banks' current difficulties. 'The key issue is funding,' said one experienced central banker. 'Banks in some countries have had trouble securing liquidity in recent weeks and that pressure is going to mount. To talk about capital is a confused message'" (August 28, 2011). Yet there has been a narrow focus on capital ratios at banks since the early 1980s. Deposit insurance and the Quiet Period made it seem that bank failures are caused by idiosyncratic events, like fraud, or odd shocks. In the case of a single bank, capital can absorb losses, minimizing the use of insurance funds. When charter values declined starting in the 1980s, banks began to fail. But the failures were not a systemic event; they reflected the deterioration of commercial banks' business models. In George Barnett's classification above, this was the "less urgent, but important" problem of minimizing losses.

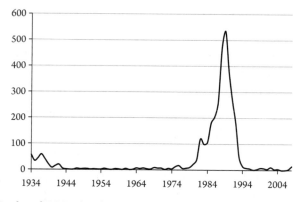

Figure 11.1 Number of U.S. Bank Failures, 1934–2008
Source: Federal Deposit Insurance Corporation.

Figure 11.1 shows the Quiet Period and the period of the 1980s when there was an increase in bank failures as charter values declined.

The failures in the 1980s, reflecting a decline in charter values, were not viewed as a harbinger of a systemic crisis—systemic crises in the United States were supposedly impossible. The issue at hand was making sure the deposit insurance fund did not run out of money, as the Federal Savings and Loan Insurance Corporation did. The FSLIC became insolvent in the 1980s due to the thrift crisis in which about 750 savings and loans failed. The insurance fund itself had to be bailed out. Bank capital requirements were part of protecting insurance funds from insolvency.

Nevertheless, capital requirements are important and affect the likelihood of a bank becoming insolvent. But they are not the solution to a systemic event. Designing a bank regulatory system that is not susceptible to bank runs should be the first priority. Only as a part of this comprehensive design should capital requirements have a role.

INTEREST ON DEPOSITS AND CAPITAL REQUIREMENTS

Before the advent of the Federal Reserve, the banks themselves, through clearinghouses, focused on reserves and on interest rates on deposits, especially on interbank deposits. The perceived problem was called "reserve pyramiding." Banks wanted to earn interest on their reserves, and so they would lend their reserves to other banks. This chain went from rural banks to larger banks and then to New York City banks. The pyramid would end up with the money being lent out so that it would earn enough to cover the interest in reserves that was promised. But if it was ultimately lent out, it could not serve as reserves. In fact, they were called "fictitious reserves." Such fictitious reserves put the whole system at greater risk because the reserves could not be called in fast enough—they weren't really reserves. George S. Coe, in his famous proposal of June 4, 1884, to the New York Clearing House Association, argued that the interest rates on deposits should be zero and that the clearinghouse should adopt this rule:

> From the very start the vicious practice of paying interest for the custody of the people's cash reserves pursues such funds like an enemy from place to place and impairs their integrity at every point. And when those deposits have at last concentrated in New York banks, the same evil overtakes them there, all tending to the reduction of tangible cash assets to the lowest point, and to the weakness and impoverishment of the whole country. Arrest this practice here, at the termination of the line, and the reform will, of necessity, run back through every link of the chain in other cities, adding strength to the whole incalculable benefit of the nation. Every institution that accepts the reserves of the community, agreeing to return them upon instant demand, gives a full equivalent in their faithful care. It is in duty bound to retain so large proportion of such deposits, in actual cash, that no other compensation can be safely allowed. (48)

Coe's proposal was not adopted at that time. But later, the Banking Act of 1933 included a prohibition of interest payments on all demand deposits. By the 1930s, the logic for this had changed since George S. Coe's time. Since deposits were to be insured, the fragility of the system was not the issue.

The Banking Act of 1933 required that regulators consider the "adequacy of the capital structure," but no attempt was made to enforce explicit capital requirements until 1982. Instead, there were subjective capital standards, based on the results of examinations of individual banking organizations. Regulators would compare a bank's capital-to-asset ratios to other banks with common characteristics, such as asset size, and try to ensure that banks with capital ratios lower than their peer group's average raise their capital ratios. The system used to examine and monitor banks was the "CAMEL" ratings system, which stands for the five components of a bank's condition, as assessed by the bank examiners: capital adequacy, asset quality, management, earnings, and liquidity. A sixth component, a bank's sensitivity to market risk was added in 1997, so the acronym was changed to CAMELS. In this system, capital was only one component.

As banks failed in the 1980s, the concern was about the risk exposure of the deposit insurance system. As a result, the method of determining required capital by comparing a bank's capital to that of a peer group of banks was replaced by specific minimum requirements. The declining charter value led to increases in bank risk. The new capital requirements forced banks with low capital ratios to increase them, which meant that banks could not use as much borrowed money. All banks and bank holding companies were required to hold primary capital equal to at least 5.5% of assets by June 1985.

Risk-based capital requirements, based on the different ways banks lent their capital, became effective in 1990, and the passage of the Federal Deposit Insurance Corporation Improvement Act in 1991 explicitly required regulators to force bank compliance. Similar trends held internationally. In 1988 bank regulators of the G10 countries plus Switzerland and Luxembourg coordinated their policies, focusing on risk-based capital requirements. This was the "Basel Accord," named after the city in Switzerland that is home to the Bank for International Settlements, a meeting place for central bankers created after World War I, which coordinated the development and signing of the Basel Accord.

The Basel Committee of Banking Supervision was established in 1974.[1] Each member country is represented by its central bank and the authority responsible for domestic banking supervision (if this is not the central bank). The Basel Committee has no formal supervisory authority. It coordinates the formation of supervisory standards and recommends their adoption. The original mandate of the Committee was to face the regulatory challenge posed by the increasing internationalization of banking in the 1970s. The collapse of the German Herstatt Bank and the New York–based Franklin National Bank in 1974 showed that bank failures were no longer confined to one country, and that coordinated international action was needed to prevent future bank failures from spilling over borders. The Committee's first proposal, the 1975 Basel Concordat, established rules determining the responsibilities of home and host country regulators vis-à-vis cross-border banks.

The Basel Committee introduced the Basel III capital requirements in the fall of 2010. The new rules are considerably more sophisticated in how they measure capital and in how they are linked to measures of risk. Also, for the first time there are requirements about holding liquid instruments. The new Basel III rules require banks to hold 7% "core" capital against risk-weighted assets, and for the largest banks there is an additional requirement of up to 2.5%. Some still thought this wasn't good enough. As the general manager of the Bank for International Settlements put it (Caruana 2010, 2): "*Better* capital is not enough. As the financial crisis painfully revealed, we need *more* capital in the banking sector." This was the main response to the recent financial crisis. Yet it still reflects the error of not understanding that systemic crises are about obtaining cash.

There is almost no evidence that links capital to bank failures. Every generation seems to rediscover this. The recent crisis was not centered on commercial banks but on dealer banks. The fact that an entire shadow banking system had developed, completely undetected by bank regulators, would suggest that the greater problem is one of measurement of economic activity rather than just capital. The commercial banks that failed in the recent crisis held on average more capital than Basel III required.

THE PURPOSE OF BANK CAPITAL

The output of banks is debt. What are the inputs to the creation of bank debt? Bank capital, combined with the bank's choice of assets and the regulatory environment, determine the ability of banks to create secretless debt that trades at par. Bank capital is one input, but the others are also important.

Over the last two hundred years there has been significant technological progress in banking. There have been important legal changes regarding negotiable instruments, bankruptcy, and foreclosure; advances in accounting; improvements in information technology, including the railroad and the telegraph, as well as computers; improvements in check clearing; advances in making credit decisions; increasing specialization and division of labor in the functions of bank personnel; improvements in portfolio management and liquidity management; better hedging instruments like interest swaps and credit default swaps; and improved methods for dealing with crises, like clearinghouse loan certificates and the Fed's discount window. All of these changes increased the efficiency of how banks use their capital. As banking developed over the centuries, the proportion of bank capital needed as an input to create usable debt declined.

In many areas the changes were very significant. I will give a few very brief examples. The first involves changes in bankruptcy law and the accompanying litigation. Banks make loans, which are debt contracts. When there are defaults, unpaid debts are forcibly collected. Governments, and courts in particular, have been called upon to essentially regulate the debt collection process, following state or federal bankruptcy codes. One way to measure the progress of the evolution of the personal and firm bankruptcy process is to examine the extent to which state supreme courts (SSCs) ruled on debt-related cases. Figure 11.2 provides a sense of the progress that has been made in streamlining the process of dealing with defaults.

The figure is suggestive. It shows the decline in the number of state supreme court opinions that were related to debtor protection or creditor rights. This decline was proportional and in absolute terms. This has been attributed to improved contract design, the development of alternatives to litigation, and the Quiet Period, which resulted in fewer disputes. This meant that banks needed less capital to operate efficiently.

A second example of an important change is the development of credit reporting agencies, firms that provided reports, and eventually ratings, on

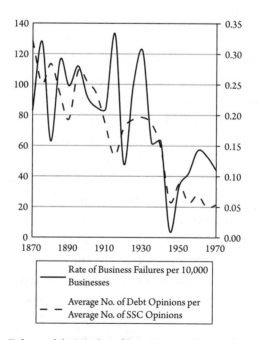

Figure 11.2 Business Failure and the Number of State Supreme Court Debt Case Opinions
Source: Kagan (1984).

merchants, and eventually individuals. The earliest "mercantile agency," as it was called, was established by Lewis Tappan in 1841. Tappan's Agency, and competitors such as the Bradstreet Mercantile Agency, founded in 1849, sold reports to subscribers. It took some time, and dealing with lawsuits, to convince subscribers of the accuracy of their reports. Eventually, the agencies relied on direct interviews with businessmen. Madison (1974) describes an example of technological change in credit reporting:

> The Dun Agency was one of the earliest enterprises to recognize the potential of the typewriter. Although the writing machine was little more than a curiosity item, Dun executives thoroughly investigated Remington's new model in 1874 and placed an order for 100 machines. At about the same time, practical carbon paper became available in large quantities. The process of replacing clerks copying in longhand and reading reports to subscribers was soon underway as the Agency quickly introduced typewriters and carbon paper in the New York offices and the branches. In the fall of 1875 the firm sent to all branch managers a manual containing twenty-one pages of instructions for use of the typewriter.

Compared with the Dun Agency's adoption of the typewriter in 1874, one need only imagine what is needed to securitize a portfolio of, say, 20,000 home mortgages to understand the distance technologically traveled since then. To securitize mortgages, a large amount of information is needed, like credit scores, income information, loan-to-income ratios, details of each mortgage, and so on. Securitization would be impossible without computers.

Other examples include the development of accounting and bookkeeping, and the increasing division of labor within the banking firm—the professionalization of banking. In 1899 the multivolume *Treatise on Bookkeeping and Stenography* was published. It was around that time that books on credit analysis first appeared. The "credit man" and the "credit office" came into being. The "Credit Men's Association" was established in 1893:

> The purpose of the National Association was well stated in Article II of the Constitution: "The object of the organization shall be the organization of individual men and associations of credit men to make more

uniform the basis upon which credit rests; to demand a change of laws unfavorable to honest debtors and the enactment of laws beneficial to commerce in the several states; to improve methods of diffusing information of gathering data with respect to credits; to improve business customs; to provide a fund for the protection of members against injustice and fraud." (Hagerty 1913, 226)

By 1911 the Proceedings of the Sixteenth Annual Convention of the National Association of Credit Men ran over six hundred pages. In 1920, the retail charge account first appeared, later leading to the invention of the credit card. Modern underwriting methods continually improved.

Improvements in electronic payments and information technology, starting in the early 1970s, also caused a revolution in banking, creating telephone banking services, ATMs, point-of-sale terminals, the national automated clearinghouse association, and so on. All of this came from the computer. George S. Eccles (1902–82) was a banker who lived through this:

> The electronic computer spawned new banking services—often at substantial costs to banks, and with no certainty of accrued benefits greater than the costs. It became a battering ram against the ramparts of legal restraints on the territorial expansion of banking enterprises. It stimulated the rise of new kinds of nondeposit funds, and helped expand the global reach of banking. It was among the factors that forced a redefinition of "money." It posed new problems of security for financial transactions, and engendered new controversies over the rights of privacy. It created subsets of new professions within the profession of banking. Its very existence inspired demands for more information from banks by private financial analysts, more demands by governmental regulatory agencies for more reports, along with more regulations bearing on the accuracy and disclosure of transactions between banks and their customer. (Eccles 1982, 126)

All of these changes meant a decreased need for bank capital as an input into the creation of bank debt. Figure 11.3 shows the trend in the average U.S. bank capital ratio over 176 years.

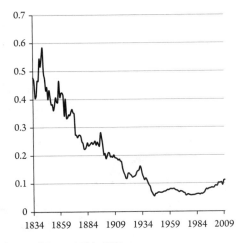

Figure 11.3 U.S. Bank Capital Ratio, 1834–2010
Sources: from 1834 to 1933: Susan B. Carter, Scott Sigmund Gartner, Michael R. Haines, and Alan
L. Olmstead, eds., *Historical Statistics of the United States, Earliest Times to the Present* (Cambridge,
UK: Cambridge University Press, 2006), 3:653 and 3:654; from 1934 to 2010: FDIC Historical
Statistics on Banking website: http://www2.fdic.gov/hsob/hsobRpt.asp.

The figure captures only one input, bank capital, but it is dramatic. It seems
that over the last 176 years banks have become more efficient at using bank
capital to manufacture debt. This is a period during which real income per
person in the United States increased by a factor of twelve (from 1870 to
2010), despite frequent crises.

This long-run decline in capital ratios is a worldwide phenomenon,
as shown in figure 11.4. Though the figure is a bit hard to read, it is clear
that the trend is downward in all countries, though it only goes to 1939.
This is a worldwide improvement in the efficiency of bank-debt
creation.

And interestingly, figure 11.5 shows that capital input was actually higher
in countries that did not have capital requirements.

The improvements in the creation of bank debt do not correspond to a
simple increase in the size of the banking system. The size of the banking
system is related to the creation of value in the economy—the gross national
product. There is no real change in the ratio of bank assets or loans to the
gross national product, or to economist Joseph Davis's measure of industrial
output for the earlier period.

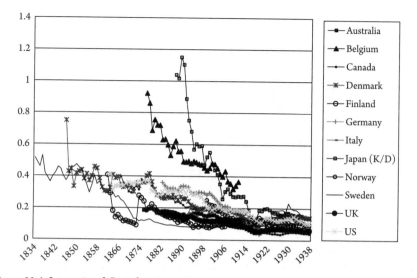

Figure 11.4 International Capital-to-Assets Ratios, 1834–1939
Source: Grossman (2007).

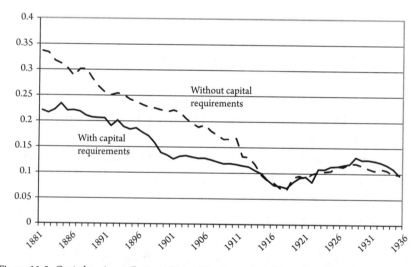

Figure 11.5 Capital-to-Assets Ratios, 1881–1939: Countries With and Without Capital Requirements
Source: Grossman (2007).

Bank capital is an important input into the manufacture of bank debt. But with improvements in the methodology for making credit decisions, the management of the underwriting and risk management processes, information technology, and the design of bank regulation, banks have steadily reduced the amount of capital needed. This is technological progress in the production of bank debt for trading purposes.

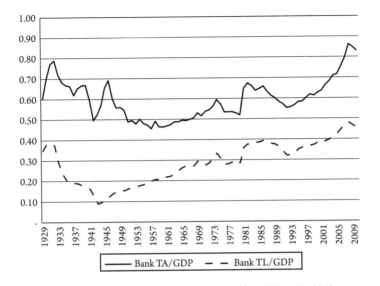

Figure 11.6 U.S. Banks' Total Assets and Loans, Normalized by GDP, 1929–2010
Source: Susan B. Carter, Scott Sigmund Gartner, Michael R. Haines, and Alan L. Olmstead, eds.,
Historical Statistics of the United States, Earliest Times to the Present (Cambridge, UK: Cambridge University Press, 2006), Cj252, Cj253; U.S. Bureau of Economic Analysis.

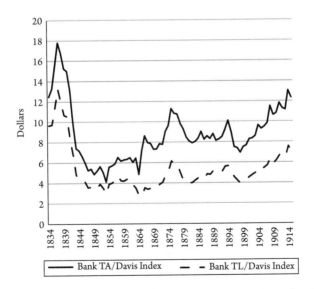

Figure 11.7 U.S. Banks' Total Assets and Loans, Normalized by Davis's Industrial Production Index, 1834–1915
Source: Susan B. Carter, Scott Sigmund Gartner, Michael R. Haines, and Alan L. Olmstead, eds.,
Historical Statistics of the United States, Earliest Times to the Present (Cambridge: UK, Cambridge University Press, 2006), Cj252, Cj253; Davis (2004).

Bank capital was not the focus of bank regulation until recently. In the 1980s regulators began focusing on bank capital as a buffer against idiosyncratic bank failures and associated losses that could have bankrupted the deposit insurance fund. But it has been recognized that historically systemic bank crises are about cash. They can be prevented or mitigated by the design of regulatory infrastructure, whether it is public or private. They cannot be prevented by bank capital.

XII. FAT CATS, CRISIS COSTS, AND THE PARADOX OF FINANCIAL CRISES

"The classic lesson of financial crises is governments wait to act,"
[U.S. Treasury Secretary Timothy] Geithner told NBC's "Meet the
Press." "They wait too late. And that means more damage to
the economy, higher deficits in the future and greater cost to the
taxpayer. And we're not prepared to take that approach."

— John Schoen, MSNBC.com, March 29, 2009

When governments and central banks wait to respond to a financial
crisis, the costs mount. Why wait? Perhaps waiting, with mounting
costs, creates the sense of urgency needed to galvanize them to respond. Perhaps we misunderstand crises.

In fact, there are two problems that cause governments to wait to act. First,
governments often do not know there is a crisis until it is full blown.
Before central banks and governments were expected to intervene in crises,

households would trigger a crisis by bank runs. The crisis was obvious to all. Now, when central banks and governments intervene, crises grow before they become apparent. When Congress amended the Trading with the Enemy Act in March 1933, they stipulated that in addition to a "time of war," the act would come into play "during any other period of national emergency declared by the President." In other words, it is up to the president to declare a crisis.

The second reason for a delayed response is another simple fact: saving the banking system means saving the bankers. Inevitably, politics affects the crisis response. Since bailouts are payments to bankers at the expense of taxpayers, they are unpopular. "I did not run for office to be helping out a bunch of, you know, fat-cat bankers on Wall Street," President Obama said on *60 Minutes*. I look to this as a reason for the delayed response.

THE PARADOX OF FINANCIAL CRISES

The Livingston doctrine says that in times of crisis banks should be bailed out. We do not want to liquidate the banking system, because that will destroy the economy. But a bailout is a regressive tax—it takes money from the people and saves the banks *and the bankers.* This paradox is what I think U.S. Treasury Secretary Timothy Geithner was getting at when he said, "The central paradox of financial crises is that what feels just and fair is the opposite of what's required for a just and fair outcome" (*New York Times*, November 5, 2011). To save Main Street, Wall Street must be saved.

This paradox is central to the Wall Street versus Main Street populist paradigm. In any market economy, the real economy and the financial sector are intimately connected. Main Street and Wall Street are Siamese twins—each would die without the other.

The financial system is the central nervous system of a market economy; without a financial system there is no economy. And, historically, no banking system has ever been intentionally liquidated. In the modern era of central banks, there have been large costs in avoiding the liquidation of banking systems. But since saving the banks means that bankers are also saved, there has always been political tension that has surrounded every financial crisis. This makes reform difficult too.

This tension has played out in every single crisis, and has always led to two narratives, one of a crisis caused by greedy, wicked, fat-cat bankers, driven by

Figure 12.1 The Siamese twins of Main Street and Wall Street. Drawing by Harry Bliss.

misaligned incentives, and another of a financial crisis related to a structural feature of market economies—the use of vulnerable bank debt. One says bailouts are handouts to bankers, and the other that bailouts are needed to save the banking system.

The idea of evil bankers is as old as capitalism. Here's a description from the populist viewpoint, from the official journal of the Farmers' State Alliance in 1896:

> The banking business is an evil. Bankers are leeches on the business body. When bankers prosper the people mourn. Banking destroys more wealth than any other business.... The banking interest is a money combine that corrupts legislatures, Congress and the Administration, as is

now the case, and leads to national disgrace and disaster. The country is now in the clutches of the bank combines and it may require a revolution to extricate it. Down with the banks![1]

Not so different from White House economic adviser Austan Goolsbee talking about senior executives of AIG during the recent crisis: "It's almost like these guys should have gotten the Nobel Prize for evil."[2]

Every crisis is a public comeuppance for bankers, and the cycle begins again, as explained by the *Nation*, after the Panic of 1873:

> It is...highly gratifying to those who consider yachting a senseless amusement to reflect that the panic will probably diminish the number of yachts.... "We shall now," they say, "have fewer fast horses, and less champagne, and less gaudy furniture, and more honest work and plain, wholesome food."
>
> The curious thing about this expectation is that it has survived innumerable disappointments without apparently losing any of its vigor. It was strong after 1837, and strong after 1857, and stronger than ever after 1861. (October 9, 1873, 239)

But aside from the "bankers are evil" narrative, there is also the other point of view:

> There have been five severe commercial panics in this country; four of them important and far reaching; the fifth, severe at the time but of short duration. The really first class panics occurred in 1837, 1857, 1873, and 1893; the lesser one, in 1884. The question which everybody would like to know the answer to, at the present time, is, which kind of panic and depression are we having now—the long kind or the short kind?
>
> To begin with, let us separate ethics and economics, and keep them vigorously apart. Wickedness did not cause the 1907 panic; it never caused any panic. (*Railroad Gazette*, December 27, 1907, 769)

The idea that there is a structural problem with the debt of the banking system does not matter to those seeking to assign individual blame. After a crisis, we cannot take revenge on the system, or at least we haven't historically. The idea that capitalism is a system means that millions of people make decisions, based on prices and their budgets, and they innovate, causing change. Banking is different only in that there is a specific regulatory environment. Deposit insurance was adopted, the Quiet Period ensued, things changed, and an old problem reemerged. Crises are a structural problem.

This is not a satisfying explanation for many. How could the financial crisis of 2007–8 have happened without anyone being responsible or going to jail? On the face of it, the idea that a small number of people engaged in criminal activity and caused a systemic financial crisis, over and over again in the history of market economies, is ridiculous. Millions, billions, of people make decisions and over time the system morphs. Indeed, the real question raised is who can be held responsible for capitalism. It was this tension between saving the banking system and saving the bankers that led to Lehman. There are large costs in getting it wrong.

Yet the paradox dooms reform, and if left unchecked some economies essentially commit inadvertent suicide. Indonesia during the Asian Crisis is perhaps an example of this. The crisis in Indonesia, starting in August 1997, had evolved by May 1998 into a currency, financial, natural, economic, and political crisis. Ethnic and religious conflicts erupted between indigenous Indonesians and Chinese Indonesians, and between Muslims and Christians. In May 1998 President Suharto "retired" after four students were killed during a demonstration, followed by riots in which over one thousand people died.

It did not get as bad in the United States, though I, for one, cannot forget the death threats, or Senator Charles Grassley's suggestion that AIG executives resign or commit suicide. Think back to the Congressional hearings related to the crisis—these were not models of dispassionate consideration. The experience of the crisis was reminiscent of Sinclair Lewis's novel *It Can't Happen Here*. It reminds us, or at least me, of the fragility of the rule of law. But even without such a dramatic turn of events as in Lewis's book, we were unable to have a national discussion about the financial crisis because of the financial-crisis paradox. And the policy decisions about the crisis will have a long-run impact.

THE COSTS OF CRISES

Financial crises are very costly.

And they're much more expensive to resolve now than in the period before central banking and government interventions. For example, the Asian crisis cost Thailand 97.7% of its output as a percentage of GDP, and its fiscal cost was 43.8% of GDP. The output cost for Indonesia was 67.9%, and the fiscal cost was 56.8%. Uruguay in 1981 lost 87.5% output and 31.2% fiscally. There are instances of crises where the entire banking system became insolvent. Many of the modern-day crises involve political unrest, riots, increases in poverty, and high unemployment. Unemployment is unhealthy—the human toll is enormous. The costs are usually much smaller for crises in developed economies, although the definition of a crisis is the same. In Japan, for example, the output loss was 17.6% of GDP and the gross fiscal cost was 14%—still very high.

It is difficult to compare costs of crises in the modern era to, say, the costs during the National Banking Era. The costs during the National Banking Era were measured by the realized loss per dollar of demand deposits and the percentage of national banks that failed. The measures of costs in the modern era are not as precise. Another possible difference is that finance and banking are more central to the economy and more global now than in the nineteenth century. Nevertheless, in the earlier period there were no instances where whole banking systems were insolvent after the crisis. This is not an argument for going back in time, but a point that needs to be understood.

Increased crisis costs seems to be an important difference between the bank runs before and after central banking. The timing of the panics in the pre-Fed era was not delayed by expectations of action by the government and the central bank. In the pre-Fed era, clearinghouses appear to have been able through suspension of convertibility and loan certificates to mitigate the effects of financial crises. The losses on deposits and the number of bank failures were very small, although we do not know if suspension of convertibility exacerbated recessions. We do know that in the earlier era whole banking systems did not end up insolvent.

Expectations of government and central-bank actions in the modern era mean that there are no bank runs unless those expectations are not met, if the response is delayed. In the modern era, crises are events in which the net worth of the banking system has been almost or entirely wiped out. Using this definition of a crisis—that the net worth of the banking system is eliminated—researchers Gerard Caprio and Daniela Klingebiel found eighty-six episodes of systemic banking system collapse in sixty-nine countries from the late 1970s through 1995. And the losses seem quite high, 10–20% of GDP in many cases and sometimes as high as 40–55% (Caprio and Klingebiel 1996, 1997). This never occurred in the earlier period, before governments intervened. Compared to the earlier period in the United States, governments in the crises of the modern era tend to intervene late and inefficiently.

Part of the problem is that there is no mechanism for determining when there actually is a crisis. An advantage of a banking panic is that depositors assess the new information and decide whether to run to their banks or not. If they run, then there is a crisis. But with deposit insurance there is no such device. Intervention is either early, as with Continental Illinois, or, more typically, late. Often, it seems that the losses from a crisis have to reach a very high level for a consensus to act to emerge. Central banks may be able to act earlier if they are independent and can withstand political pressure. But even then the policies may not be effective. In many cases, for example, large amounts of money are used to try to address a crisis, only to fuel further problems, aggravating instability through a currency crisis or complicating monetary policy.

It is not easy to determine the costs of a crisis. First, a crisis must be defined. Caprio and Klingebiel define a crisis as a situation in which the entire capital of the banking system is exhausted or where there is significant evidence of problems in the banking system, such as bank runs, forced bank closures, forced mergers, or government takeovers of banks (1996). Most subsequent studies have followed this definition.

Generally speaking, there are four types of potential costs of a financial crisis: (1) deadweight losses from fiscal transfers, (2) output losses and increases in unemployment when aggregate real output goes down relative to trend, (3) misallocations of resources due to the crisis and the government's actions to try to ameliorate the crisis, and (4) the costs to social well-being, such as stress or depression due to unemployment, loss of income and wealth, and even suicides.

All these measures of costs have problems. A bank bailout is a transfer from taxpayers to bankers. This is not necessarily a cost but a redistribution of income from taxpayers to bankers. But there may be deadweight losses, as this money may have been spent more efficiently otherwise. A deadweight loss is a waste. While these losses are hard to determine, they are significant. But since these are hard to measure, the fiscal costs are usually cited as a measure, which is only reasonable if the deadweight costs are proportional to, or increasing in, these transfers.

Regarding lost output, there is the problem of separating the output lost because of a crisis from the output lost because of a recession, which the financial crisis may just reflect or may contribute to. One way to try to distinguish output losses due to a crisis from those due to other factors is by trying to match a crisis country with a similar, neighboring country that had an economic downturn but no banking crisis. This requires finding such pairs. Crises are often clustered by region, as with the banking crises in Latin America in the early 1980s, 1990, and the mid-1990s; the Nordic banking crisis in the late 1980s and early 1990s; and the East Asian crisis in 1997–98. While imperfect, the evidence suggests that, on average, banking crises increase the cumulative output gaps by 13% of GDP.

The third cost, a misallocation of resources, though it may be significant, has so far proven impossible to estimate.

Social costs are also hard to measure, but there have been efforts. For example, one study found that in Indonesia "the poverty rate increased from the lowest point of around 15 percent at the onset of the crisis in the mid of 1997 to the highest point of around 33 percent nearing the end of 1998. This maximum increase in poverty rate during the crisis of 18 percentage points implies that around 36 million additional people were pushed into absolute poverty due to the crisis" (Suryahadi, Sumarto, and Pritchett 2003, i). For the United States, economists Janet Currie and Erdal Tekin, in a paper entitled "Is the Foreclosure Crisis Making Us Sick?," wrote that the answer is yes:

> We find that an increase in the number of foreclosures is associated with increases in medical visits for mental health (anxiety and suicide attempts); preventable conditions (such as hypertension); and with increases in a broad array of physical complaints that are plausibly stress related. The effects are much larger for blacks than for whites, consistent with the perception that African-Americans have been particularly hard hit. (2011)

Also, crises affect people's attitudes, their outlook on life, and their sense of well-being; they become pessimistic. Based on surveys, researchers find that as unemployment rises and home foreclosures increase, people become more pessimistic about the future. They report decreases in their sense of well-being and increases in stress. But such measures and surveys are not available in most countries in a comparable form.

Because of the difficulties of measuring the costs of crises, research has tended to focus on the fiscal costs and output losses. In figures 12.2a and 12.2b, the fiscal cost is the net fiscal cost as a percentage of GDP for five years (the year

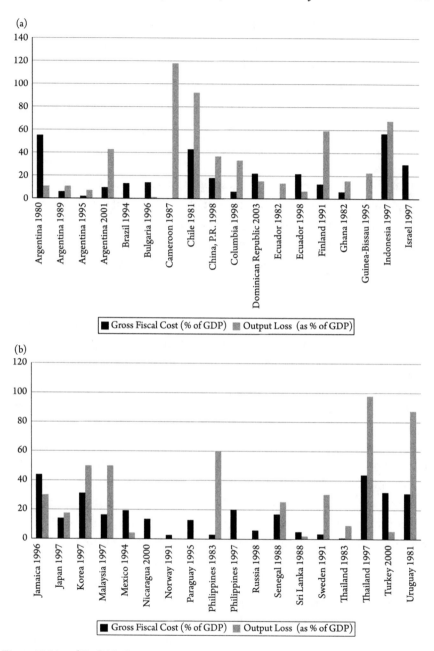

Figure 12.2A and B Crisis Costs
Source: Laeven and Valencia (2008).

the crisis started and the next four years). The output loss is based on extrapolating a trend for real GDP and then comparing the differences between the trend GDP and the actual GDP for the crisis year and the next three years. These figures suggest large costs of financial crises.

"GOODWILL" AND ZOMBIES: THE EXAMPLE OF THE U.S. SAVINGS AND LOAN CRISIS

Why are the costs of resolving modern financial crises so high?

Many modern crises are much different than historical banking panics, because there may be little oversight of banks, and the banking system may deteriorate for some time before the crisis becomes apparent to authorities. Often in a modern crisis a banking system that is already weak or fragile is hit by a shock that decimates it. The shock can be a sudden, large deterioration of the exchange rate or an increase in interest rates.

An instructive example is the U.S. savings and loan industry. This crisis was not a systemic crisis, since it was confined to one sector, but it was costly to clean up. The S and L industry had its origins in the Great Depression. It was composed of financial intermediaries, called thrifts, which made long-term, fixed-rate mortgages and financed them with demand deposits. When interest rates rose in the late 1970s and early 1980s, these thrifts found that the rates they had to pay to attract deposits were higher than the rates on the mortgages they had already contracted. They were borrowing at 6% and earning 3% on the mortgages, for example, earning a negative spread. Hundreds of thrifts were insolvent as a result. Deregulation was one of the responses, which allowed thrifts to engage in new investments, and capital requirements were lowered. The resulting failures bankrupted the thrift insurance fund, the FSLIC.

But there was still a problem. Insolvent thrifts were allowed to remain open, mostly because of the depleted resources of the Federal Savings and Loan Insurance Corporation, and their assets weren't sold to new investors. The Federal Home Loan Bank Board chairman Richard Pratt put it this way in testimony before Congress: "The Bank Board...did not have sufficient resources to close all insolvent institutions, [but] at the same time, it had to consolidate the industry, move weaker institutions into stronger hands, and do everything possible to minimize losses during the transition period. Goodwill was an indispensable tool in performing this task."[3] "Goodwill" refers to the practice of forbearance, allowing insolvent thrifts to remain open even though they had negative net worth. Forbearance was described by Ed Kane as turning insolvent thrifts into "zombies"—effectively dead but still operating.[4] Eventually, the Resolution Trust Corporation was established to liquidate the assets of insolvent thrifts. The bailout of the thrift industry ultimately cost $180 billion, which was 3.2% of GDP.

The S and L crisis is instructive as to where losses come from in crises. One typical problem in modern crises generally are the losses in bank value due to a delay in resolving—closing or selling—a potentially insolvent bank. What happens when an insolvent bank is not closed? The S and L, while insolvent, continues to operate and enjoy the benefit of deposits that are insured.

In this case, the management of the S and L can essentially loot the firm. In a famous paper George Akerlof (2001 Nobel Prize winner) and Paul Romer explained that in these zombie settings "firms have an incentive to go for broke at society's expense (to loot) instead of go for broke (to gamble for success). Bankruptcy for profit will occur if poor accounting, lax regulation, or low penalties for abuse give owners an incentive to pay themselves more than their firms are worth and then default on their debt obligations" (1993, 2). The examples they study are Chile and the S and L crisis. In their conclusion they highlight some of the reasons that looting can lead to high costs:

> Why did the government leave itself exposed to abuse? Part of the answer, of course, is that actions taken by the government are the result of the political process. When regulators hid the extent of the true problem with artificial accounting devices, when congressmen pressured regulators to go easy on favored constituents and political donors, when the largest brokerage firms lobbied to protect their ability to funnel brokered deposits to any thrift in the country, when lobbyists for the savings and loan industry adopted the strategy of postponing action until industry difficulties were so large that general tax revenue would have to be used to address problems instead of revenue raised from taxes on successful firms in the industry— when these and many other actions were taken, people responded rationally to the incentives they faced within the political process. (59)

Looting is not moral hazard as the term was used before. Moral hazard refers to actions by solvent firms. Looting is a brazen act of theft. It requires a particular political environment.

ACTING LATE: POLITICAL PROBLEMS IN REACTING TO CRISES

The political dangers of bailouts help cause governments to act late. In emerging markets, for example, failing banks are less likely to be taken over by the government before elections. But it is not only emerging markets. There are certainly cases in developed economies where it seems clear that the government was late in intervening. Either there is confusion about the crisis or there is a policy of forbearance that is adopted explicitly or implicitly due to political constraints. To take one example, there was no bank run in Japan in the 1990s. Instead, the government engaged in forbearance, resulting in prolonged losses and stagnation. The U.S. savings and loan crisis also did not see bank runs but did involve a long period of costly forbearance. Forbearance typically results in even greater losses. The actions of the government can prevent bank runs but seems to increase the costs of crisis resolution if there is a crisis. In the latter case, government itself is then a problem.

The U.S. government intervened late in the crisis of 2007–8. It was clear that there was an impending problem with subprime mortgages by late 2005. Certainly something was apparent by early 2007, when more and more problems arose with the failure of several subprime mortgage originators and the decline in the ABX index, an index linked to securitized subprime mortgages. In August 2007 withdrawals in the repo market began to rise, and there was a run on Structured Investment Vehicles (an independent managed fund that buys asset-backed securities and finances itself with commercial paper), leading to fear among money market mutual funds. The fall of 2007 was a crisis. I submitted an op-ed piece to newspapers in January 2008 that read in part:

> The problem is that millions of subprime mortgage holders cannot afford their mortgage payments when their mortgage interest rate resets, after two or three years from initiation. But they cannot find financing to get new mortgages that they can afford. Meanwhile, for financial institutions and investors, the lack of information about which securitized mortgage bonds are really in trouble has caused credit markets to seize up. With no credit, there is no investment, and there is a recession.
>
> There's another problem. Unlike historical banking panics, the current one involves the "shadow banking system," the system of risk transfer mechanisms that has moved credit risk around the globe. The

institutions in place to deal with banking panics date back to the Great Depression. They are not particularly relevant for the current crisis.

I advocated that Freddie Mac and Fannie Mae refinance all subprime mortgages at their initial teaser rate. This was eight months before Lehman failed. I am convinced that had this been done the crisis could have been largely avoided. From the rejection of this op-ed piece I realized that the panic was not visible to most people, the press, politicians, and the regulators. The crisis was not observed and not understood. Regulators, academics, and the media did not understand that there was a crisis. In fact, there had been a bank run, but it was a run on repo, which involved banks that were not regulated commercial banks. So the run was not observed. There needed to be large visible losses to galvanize the government to action. We had to wait until large firms were visibly in trouble. Because economists misunderstood the crisis, there was no clarity about the events. And the political constraints—many of which were created by the response—delayed action.

The only good news overall is that democracies seem to do better with crises than nondemocracies. Philip Keefer, a World Bank economist, in a study of thirty-five countries over the years 1970–2000, found that "although democracies are no less likely to experience banking crises, in the event of a crisis, competitively elected governments intervene more rapidly in insolvent banks and make transfers to them that are between 10 and 20 percent of gross domestic product less than those made by nondemocratic governments" (2007, 607).

BENEFITS OF CRISES?

We could design a financial system that avoids crises, for a period of time at least, but the design faces the problem of risking a crisis on the one hand or being financially repressive on the other. We could constrain banking in the extreme or allow financial innovation, which may be risky. This trade-off seems to be realistic. Economists Romain Rancière, Aaron Tornell, and Frank Westermann (2008) found that countries that have experienced occasional financial crises have tended to grow faster than countries that have not experienced crises. Their sample includes both developed and emerging economies.

If a policymaker, whose goal is to maximize GDP growth, could choose whether to have periodic crises or not, the policymaker might choose to have crises rather than to have low growth. It depends how society feels about economic volatility. The policy issues here seem related to an issue raised by Robert Lucas in his 2011 Milliman Lecture at the University of Washington, "The U.S. Recession of 2007–201?": "Is it possible that by imitating European policies on labor markets, welfare, and taxes [the] U.S. has chosen a new, lower GDP trend?" Lucas was talking about the policy responses to the financial crisis of 2007–8. The issue is whether the policies adopted in the financial sector, according to the Dodd-Frank legislation, will have the same effects of reducing growth.

The point about the design trade-off can be seen in Thailand and India. GDP per capita grew by 162% over the period 1980–2002 in Thailand, despite the Asian Crisis, while India's GDP per capita grew only 114% over the same period, with no crises.

Figure 12.3 shows the credit boom and subsequent crash, coinciding with the Asian Crisis.

The credit boom led up to the crisis in Thailand. Figure 12.4 shows real GDP per capita in the two countries. Despite the effects of the crisis in Thailand, real GDP growth is everywhere above that of India.

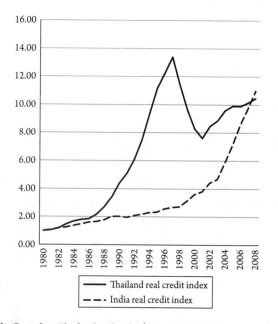

Figure 12.3 Credit Growth in Thailand and India (values for 1980 have been normalized to one)
Source: Rancière, Tornell, and Westermann (2008).

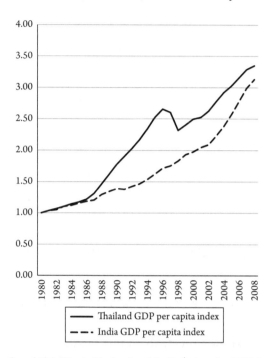

Figure 12.4 Growth and Volatility in Thailand and India (values for 1980 have been normalized to one)
Source: Rancière, Tornell and Westermann (2008).

The figure is suggestive of the trade-off. What is the benefit that may be accruing to Thailand in this example? There are several possibilities. One possibility has to do with the positive benefits of a credit boom. In a credit boom, if more and more firms are getting loans and are making efficient investments, then output is going up. A credit boom means that banks are lending. If banks are not constrained in their lending, then they can lend to firms based on their assets, even if those assets are not thoroughly investigated. In that case, firms without good collateral might be able to borrow, increasing the output of the economy. Output is going up, but so is fragility, as more and more firms are borrowing without the bank investigating the quality of the backing for the loans. A small shock can then cause the firms to be investigated, and loans are cut off to those without sufficient collateral.

If growth is constrained by an inability to borrow, then banks might be encouraged to lend anyway if there is explicit or implicit insurance. Greater leverage for the economy as a whole allows greater investment, but at the price of greater fragility. The government can smooth the risk through time,

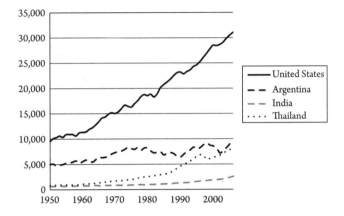

Figure 12.5 Per Capita GDP (1990 International Geary-Khamis dollars)[5]
Source: Angus Maddison, Historical Statistics of the World Economy: 1–2006 AD.

but will tax future generations if there is a bailout. However, the net effect can still be positive.

We simply don't know enough about these issues yet to say what the best policies are. A key point is that the policies we are talking about, which lead to the two cases of India or Thailand, are not likely to consist of simply one piece of legislation or one regulatory regime but the accumulation of policies over some period of time. In the preface I mentioned Argentina as a likely example of what happens when there is a series of bad policies. Figure 12.5 shows per capita GDP for the United States, Thailand, India, and Argentina. These growth paths reflect many policy decisions made over time, as well as other factors, such as good and bad luck.

Compared with the United States and Argentina, the difference between India and Thailand is not so dramatic. The real policy errors can be seen in the case of Argentina. But every policy decision and act of Congress contributes to the buildup of a growth path that over a long time will resemble one of those in the figure.

Crisis costs seem very large in the era of central banks and government intervention. This is likely due to delayed, and sometimes misguided, responses to a crisis. The government authorities seem not to know when the crisis has started, and often there is no bank run to signal the onset of the crisis, because market participants expect the authorities to act. This does not mean we should try to regain the past. Rather, it shows that banking systems should be designed to avoid crises, and if they cannot be avoided then central banks should be capable of detecting crises and acting without political interference.

The ability to act without political interference is rare, because crisis responses are inevitably political, as saving the banking system means saving bankers. Politics quickly creates an anti-intellectual environment causing flawed reforms to be implemented. But even intelligently designed reform faces a dilemma. While it would be best to design a system of bank regulation that avoids crises, this also runs the risk of financial repression. There may be large costs to avoiding crises altogether.

XIII. THE PANIC OF 2007–8

[Former Connecticut senator Christopher] Dodd described the worst part of the crisis in September of 2008, the "night of a most extraordinary meeting, with Treasury Secretary Henry Paulson, Federal Reserve Chairman Ben Bernanke, and leaders of both parties in then-House Speaker Nancy Pelosi's meeting room. Bernanke said: 'Unless you act in the next few days the financial system in the U.S. and the rest of the world will melt down.' The air left the room" he said. "There were ageless moments of quiet."

—Kathleen McBride

The global financial crisis that began in the United States in the summer of 2007 was triggered by a bank run, just like those of 1837, 1857, 1873, 1893, 1907, and 1933. That's why I have spent so much time on the history of these crises.

This crisis was the worst since the Great Depression, and it has had devastating effects that continue today. The crisis began with a financial panic, a run on short-term money market instruments. It was a systemic event. Fed governor Ben Bernanke reported that of the thirteen "most important financial institutions in the United States, twelve were at risk of failure within a period of a week or two" (Financial Crisis Inquiry Commission 2011, 354). Asset prices plummeted, credit markets froze, production and investment sharply declined, and millions lost their jobs. It appeared for a time that we were on the verge of a depression, but central banks engaged in extraordinary efforts to stabilize the economy. These events were momentous. What began with a bank run led to a deep recession in the United States and many countries around the world.

The Panic of 2007–8 should clarify our understanding of crises. First, it was a systemic financial crisis, so the idea that this could not happen in the United States is not true. Second, the crisis was triggered by a run, on repo and on asset-backed commercial paper. It was a banking panic that started on August 9, 2007. The crisis (if not the response) resembled the bank runs of the pre–Federal Reserve era. Repo and commercial paper are money, forms of bank debt that grew to significant amounts and were vulnerable to being run on. They were largely provided outside the regulated commercial banking sector.

The deterioration of house prices and defaults in the subprime mortgage market were not enough to cause a systemic crisis by themselves. But, like the earlier era, when news of a shock arrived, bank creditors went to monitor the banks: Did they have the money? The run was a demand for cash, and repo agreements and commercial paper were not renewed. This time there was no suspension of convertibility and no bank holidays. To meet cash demands financial intermediaries had to sell assets, causing the prices of all assets to go down. This was difficult because the assets were bonds that were designed to be secretless and information-insensitive. When they became information-sensitive, they became hard to sell to raise sufficient cash, so the Federal Reserve stepped in to buy assets. The crisis was magnified when Lehman Brothers was not bailed out. In the end a number of major financial firms disappeared: Bear Stearns, Merrill Lynch, Wachovia, Lehman Brothers, Washington Mutual, and Countrywide. Securitization shrank dramatically and went dormant. The economy became moribund. The malaise continues and the future does not look bright.

Table 13.1 shows that the recession of 2007–9 was more severe than the average U.S. postwar recession. Investment and employment declined by much more in the United States than in other countries. Note the declines in investment, employment, and output.

We can also examine individual cycles, including the Great Depression, for comparison as seen in table 13.2.

The latest recession ranks as one of the worst in recent U.S. history, but it was not as severe as the Great Depression or the recession of 1937–38. We

Table 13.1 The 2007–8 Recession in Perspective: Changes in per Capita Variables for Each Peak-to-Trough Episode (%)

	Output	Consumption	Investment	Employment	Hours
U.S., Postwar Recessions vs. 2007–8 Recession					
Average Postwar Recessions	-4.4	-2.1	-17.8	-3.8	-3.2
2007–8 Recession (2007 Q4–2009 Q3)	-7.2	-5.4	-33.5	-6.7	-8.7
2007–8 Recession, U.S. vs. Other High Income Countries					
United States	-7.2	-5.4	-33.5	-6.7	-8.7
Canada	-8.6	-4.6	-14.1	-3.3	-
France	-6.6	-3.4	.12.6	-1.1	-
German	-7.2	-2.9	-10.2	0.1	-
Italy	-9.8	-6.6	-19.6	-3.0	-
Japan	-8.9	-3.6	-19.0	-1.6	-
United Kingdom	-9.8	-7.7	-22.9	-2.9	-
Average Other High-Income Countries	-8.5	-4.8	-16.4	-2.0	-

Source: Ohanian (2010)

Table 13.2 The 2007–8 Recession and the Great Depression

Recession	Duration (months)	Decline in Real GDP: Peak to Trough (%)	Unemployment: Maximum reached during Recession (%)	CPI: Change from Peak to Trough (%)
1929–33	43	–36.21	25.36	–27.17
1937–38	13	–10.04	20.00	–2.08
1945–45	8	–14.48	3.40	1.69
1948–49	11	–1.58	7.90	–2.07
1953–54	10	–2.53	5.90	0.37
1957–58	8	–3.14	7.40	2.12
1960–61	10	–0.53	6.90	1.02
1969–70	11	–0.16	5.90	5.04
1973–75	16	–3.19	8.60	14.81
1980	6	–2.23	7.80	6.30
1981–82	16	–2.64	10.80	6.99
1990–91	8	–1.36	6.80	3.53
2001	8	0.73	5.50	0.68
2007–9	18	–5.10	9.50	2.76

Source: Wheelock (2010), updated from the Bureau of Economic Analysis (2011).

did not have another Great Depression likely because of the extraordinary actions taken by the Federal Reserve.

To stem the crisis, the Federal Reserve lent a total of $1.1 trillion to financial firms. Four banks—Citigroup, Bank of Scotland, and Barclays Group—borrowed $233 billion, as shown in the table 13.3. These Federal Reserve programs were in addition to the U.S. government's Troubled Asset Relief Program (TARP), which allowed the U.S. Treasury to insure or buy up to $700 billion of troubled assets. Further, there was the American Recovery and Reinvestment Act of 2009 of about $800 billion. The amounts involved in fighting the crisis, attempting to stem its deleterious effects and prevent a total meltdown, are staggering.

It will be some time before we are in a position to evaluate the effects of these sums. We can't see the counterfactual of what would have happened had we not summoned these vast resources. But we can make progress in understanding what happened. Indeed, we must make progress—we cannot wait for decades to try to redesign bank regulation.

EXPLAINING WHAT HAPPENED

The subprime shock was not large enough to account for the crisis. At the time of the crisis there was about $1.2 trillion of subprime mortgages outstanding. Even if every single one of these mortgages defaulted with no recovery at all, it would not by itself explain the magnitude of the crisis. Furthermore, the losses on subprime mortgages have not been so large. Sunyoung Park examined trustee reports on February 2010 for 88.6% of the notional amount of subprime bonds issued between 2004 and 2007. She calculated the realized principal losses on the $1.9 trillion of AAA/Aaa-rated subprime bonds issued between 2004 and 2007 to be 17 basis points as of February 2011 (Park 2012).[1] These are the realized losses up to that date. It will probably be twenty years before the final number can be tallied, and that depends on many factors.

The point that the expected losses do not seem high was made by the Financial Crisis Inquiry Commission report by looking at the ratings on subprime mortgages. The FCIC noted that "overall, for 2005 to 2007 vintage tranches of mortgage-backed securities originally rated triple-A, despite the mass downgrades, only about 10% of Alt-A and 4% of subprime securities had been 'materially impaired'—meaning that losses were imminent or had

Table 13.3 Institutions with the Largest Borrowing in the Federal Reserve Emergency Programs, December 2007 through July 2010, $ billions

Borrowing Company	TAF	PDCF	TSLF	CPFF	Subtotal	AMLF	TALF	Total Loans	Percent of Total
Bank of America	$48	$6	$8	$6	$67	$0	—	$67	6%
Citigroup	15	8	27	8	58	—	—	58	5
Royal Bank of Scotland (UK)	25	—	23	10	58	—	—	58	5
Barclays Group (UK)	24	2	15	10	50	—	—	50	4
UBS (Switzerland)	7	—	9	18	35	—	—	35	3
Deutsche Bank (German)	9	—	22	—	30	—	—	30	2
Wells Fargo	25	—	—	—	25	—	—	25	2
Dexia (Belgium)	10	—	—	13	23	—	—	23	2
Credit Suisse (Switzerland)	—	—	21	—	21	—	—	21	2
Bank of Scotland (UK)	20	—	—	—	20	—	—	20	2
Commerzbank (Germany)	16	—	—	4	20	—	—	20	2
Goldman Sachs	—	—	17	—	20	—	—	20	2

(continued)

Table 13.3 Continued

Borrowing Company	TAF	PDCF	TSLF	CPFF	Subtotal	AMLF	TALF	Total Loans	Percent of Total
Merrill Lynch	—	2	14	—	19	—	—	19	2
BNP Paribas (France)	11	—	3	4	19	—	—	19	2
Société Générale (France)	17	—	—	—	17	—	—	17	1
Morgan Stanley	—	8	8	1	17	—	—	45	4
Wachovia	16	—	—	—	16	—	28	16	1
JP Morgan	13	—	3	—	16	—	—	31	3
AIG	—	—	—	15	15	—	—	15	1
Norinchukin (Japan)	15	—	—	—	15	—	—	15	1
All Other Borrowers	204	4	11	94	313	13	211	$1,139	47
Total	**$474**	**$35**	**$179**	**$183**	**$870**	**$29**	**$240**	**$1,139**	**100%**

Source: U.S. Government Accountability Office (2011, 132). The acronyms are as follows: TAF: Term Auction Facility; PDCF: Primary Dealer Credit Facility; TSLF: Term Securities Lending Facility; CPFF: Commercial Paper Funding Facility; AMLF: Asset-Backed Commercial Paper Money Market Mutual Fund Liquidity; TALF: Term Asset-Backed Securities Lending Facility.

already been suffered—by the end of 2009" (Financial Crisis Inquiry Commission 2011, 228–29). If the shock wasn't so large, how did we get a crisis?

Another aspect of the crisis is that all bond prices fell, not just subprime-related bonds, and the prices of all manner of asset-backed securities fell. Furthermore, the nonsubprime bond prices track measures of interbank risk, not measures of subprime fundamentals. Why did the prices of, say, AAA/Aaa credit card asset-backed securities plummet when this asset class had nothing to do with subprime mortgages, and had not experienced losses?

Each of the four lines in table 13.3 is a "spread," the difference between the yield on a security and the yield on an otherwise equivalent riskless security. A spread represents the compensation for risk an investor receives. For example, if the spread is 1%, then that is the difference between what the bond yield is in the market and what the yield is on a U.S. Treasury bond of the same maturity. A bond yield is inversely related to a bond's price, so when spreads go up, the bond price falls correspondingly. Spreads up means bond prices are falling.

One of the lines shown in figure 13.1 is the difference between LIBOR, the rate at which financial firms borrow and lend to each other, and the overnight index swap (OIS), a popular measure of the yield on a riskless instrument. The spread LIBOR rate minus the OIS rate measures the risk in the interbank market. You can see that this line starts to rise dramatically in August 2007 and then really skyrockets when Lehman fails.

The other three lines are the spreads on three categories of AAA/Aaa asset-backed securities. The three categories of loans that have been securitized into bonds are student loans, credit card loans, and auto loans. These loans have nothing to do with subprime mortgages, and they have never had losses. You can see that the spreads for these three types of bonds are moving very closely with the measure of risk in this new type of "banking" system.

For simplicity, the figure does not include subprime spreads, which rose continuously starting in January 2007. In other words, subprime spreads did not move with the measure of counterparty risk, which is what would have happened if that was the whole story.

From the point of view of historyless economics, each crisis is special and has its own explanation, such as a special emphasis on the subprime mortgages. But remember William N. Parker's words, worth quoting again, about economists who have no knowledge of economic history: "Such an economist becomes a shallower, narrower analyst with feeble capabilities for

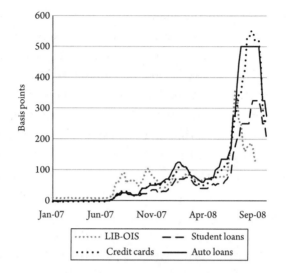

Figure 13.1 Spreads on AAA/Aaa Asset-Backed Securities and Bank Counterparty Risk
Source: Gorton and Metrick, forthcoming.

adapting the theory and statistics he has mastered to new and strange social environments. All problems strike such a one as new" (1986, 9).

The banking system evolved over the last twenty-five years in a number of fundamental ways. The regulated commercial banking sector began securitizing loans, which were used in large part by a new banking system. Known as "shadow banking," it provided a deposit-like banking system for nonfinancial firms and institutional investors, not for households and small businesses that could go to commercial banks. Nonfinancial firms and institutional investors deposit money short-term, earn interest, and are assured of the safety of their deposit by taking collateral in the form of bonds. Securitization meets the need for collateral, which often took the form of asset-backed securities. Prior to the crisis, there was a shortage of collateral, which was needed for purposes of mitigating counterparty risk in derivatives, for clearing and settlement systems, and for repo.

The banking system based on repo became very large prior to the crisis. Although there are no official data measuring the overall size of this market, various estimates suggest that it was around $10 trillion, the same size as total assets in the U.S. commercial banking sector, but we don't know for sure. The European repo market, universally viewed as being much smaller than that in the United States, was EUR 4.87 trillion ($3.5 trillion) in June 2009, having peaked at EUR 6.78 trillion ($5.1 trillion) in June 2007, a fall of 31%, according to the International Capital Markets Association European Repo Market Survey, a fairly comprehensive survey. Asset-backed commercial paper (ABCP) was also large, but nowhere near as large as repo. ABCP in the United States peaked at about $1.2 trillion in July 2007.

Not only was repo a very large market, but the "banks" which specialized in this kind of banking had become large as well. These repo banks were broker-dealer banks, the old investment banks, the largest of the commercial banks, and many foreign banks. Officially, the U.S. banks that were large players in repo were broker-dealers, "dealer banks" for short, not regulated depository institutions.[2] These are the firms that are often in the press, Goldman Sachs, Citi, Morgan Stanley, and so on.

The ratio of the total assets of the dealer banks to the total assets of the commercial banks grew from 6.3% to about 30% from 1990 until 2006, just before the crisis, an increase of 376%. The Securities and Exchange Commission filings of Goldman Sachs, Merrill Lynch, Morgan Stanley, Lehman Brothers, and Bear Stearns show that these five former investment banks together had financial assets worth $1.4 trillion, 48% of which was pledged as collateral at the end of 2006.

On August 9, 2007, after months of problems in the subprime mortgage market and increasing uncertainty about assets backed by subprime mortgages, a bank run began through an increase in repo "haircuts." A haircut is a demand by a depositor for collateral valued higher than the value of the deposit. Usually, if an institutional investor deposits $100 million overnight in a repo, the collateral would be bonds with a market value of $100 million. The bank would pay a 3% repo rate and receive 6% on the bond collateral, even though the institutional investor has taken possession of the bonds. In this case, the repo deposit is financing 100% of the bond. But if the next day the institutional investor is nervous, he could deposit only $90 million overnight, and demand $100 million collateral. This is like the institutional investor withdrawing $10 million from the bank. It is a 10% haircut. Now the bank has to come up with $10 million dollars from some other source to finance the bonds it offered as collateral.

If there is no new funding forthcoming, the borrowing bank must sell assets, or deleverage. When many firms are forced to do this—all selling assets—there are fire-sale prices. This is what happened in real life. By September 2009, repo transactions by primary dealers (the banks eligible to trade with the Federal Reserve) had fallen by about 50% from the level of activity prior to Lehman's bankruptcy. The *Financial Times* reported that "overall repo activity in the US during the first six months of this year has fallen to levels not seen since 2003" (Michael Mackenzie, "Bank Runs Left Repo Sector Exposed," September 10, 2009).

Repo haircuts depend on the identities of the counterparties to the transaction and on the nature of the collateral. Haircuts were remarkably low prior to the crisis. But when they rose, they went up the most on subprime-related bonds, but they also rose significantly on all asset-backed securities (and eventually somewhat on corporate bonds). The increase in haircuts resulted from a suspicion of the appearance of secrets concerning the value of very complicated securities. Securities that had been designed to be secretless became suspicious.

Haircuts rose steadily during the crisis, with the largest increases following the bankruptcy of Lehman Brothers. To fund the increasing amount of collateral needed, repo firms were forced to sell assets, and they wanted to sell the most valuable assets that would raise the most money, like AAA/Aaa assets, which were unrelated to subprime. But all the dealer banks did the same thing and sold the same assets. This dumping of assets is what caused all bond prices to plummet during the financial crisis, not just the prices of subprime-related bonds. Hence figure 13.1 showing the spreads on AAA/Aaa asset-backed securities related to credit card receivables, auto loans, and student loans skyrocketing.

Figure 13.2 reveals the banking panic for a sample of dealer banks. It shows the average dollar amount of financial instruments owned by Goldman Sachs, Merrill Lynch, Lehman Brothers, Morgan Stanley, Bear Stearns, Citi, Bank of America, Wells Fargo, and Wachovia.[3]

The solid line is the average percentage of financial assets that were pledged as collateral to depositors. You can see that prior to the crisis, 50% of dealer banks' financial assets were pledged, and that during the crisis this drops to below 30%.[4]

The panic also affected other money markets. There were withdrawals in the commercial paper market when investors chose not to reinvest in asset-backed commercial paper or in the commercial paper of financial firms. Recall that commercial paper is short-term debt issued by firms, as well as by asset-backed commercial paper (ABCP) conduits, managed vehicles that buy asset-backed securities (bonds backed by pools of loans) using commercial paper. ABCP conduits are limited-purpose operating companies that undertake arbitrage activities by purchasing mostly highly rated medium- and

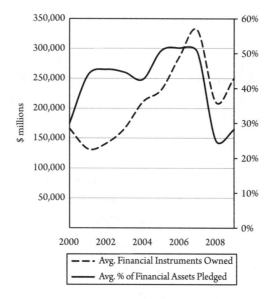

Figure 13.2 Repo Banks and the Crisis
Source: Securities and Exchange Commission 10-k filings.

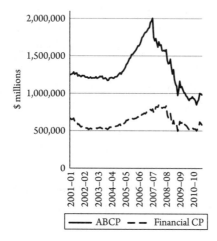

Figure 13.3 Financial and Asset-Backed Commercial Paper Outstanding (seasonally adjusted)
Source: Federal Reserve System.

long-term asset-backed securities and funding themselves with cheaper, mostly short-term, highly rated commercial paper and medium-term notes.

Once the repo banks were in trouble, there were large withdrawals from prime brokerage (dealer bank) accounts. On Monday, September 15, 2008, for example, hedge funds asked to withdraw $10 billion from Morgan

Stanley. The Financial Crisis Inquiry report describes this as turning into a $32 billion torrent of withdrawals by Wednesday.

The runs on repo, commercial paper, and prime brokerage accounts resulted in a breakdown of the central nervous system of the economy—financial firms. As lending stopped, the crisis spread to Europe and to the nonfinancial sector of the U.S. economy. Like the banking panics of the National Banking Era, this panic happened near the business cycle peak. The panic started in August 2007, and the National Bureau of Economic Research dated the peak to December 2007. The panic was not irrational, as the problems in the housing market were becoming increasingly apparent. Like the panics of the earlier era, this one exacerbated the recession, the ongoing malaise.

THE LESSONS TO BE LEARNED

The financial crisis of 2007–8 should provide some clarity in our thinking about crises because it was started by a bank run. The bank money involved was repo and ABCP—uninsured, privately produced money, not demand deposits. And those running on the banks were not households but institutional investors, other banks and nonfinancial firms. The "banks" that were the subject of the runs were not the regulated commercial banks but dealer banks. And even though the run was not seen by anyone other than those at these financial firms, it was still a bank run, similar to those of the period before the advent of the Federal Reserve system.

The recent crisis had a sort of purity to it that should allow us to understand the root cause of financial crises. Dealer banks were institutions that had never been bailed out before, and their debt was not insured. At least at the outset of the crisis, the run was not contaminated by expectations about the government's crisis responses. It is hard to understand how policies of too-big-to-fail and moral-hazard-related incentives emanating from government regulation could have affected the dealer banks. The government did not know of the existence of the shadow banking system. Further, in light of the testimony of dealer bank CEOs before the Financial Crisis Inquiry Commission, it is doubtful if even the dealer banks understood the changes to the financial system.

An important problem with understanding financial crises has been that the underlying structural problem with bank debt has been obscured by government actions and by the idiosyncrasies of each crisis. A common—if somewhat vague—view of crises is that they are caused by some combination of government policies, bad events, and greed. Each crisis is then seen as a unique event. This view implicitly sees historical crises as essentially irrelevant for study, because the government has different policies now compared to then, and "the world was different back then."

Capitalism has some inherent structural features that are common to all market economies. One common feature of market economies that I have emphasized is the vulnerability of private bank money. The important lesson is that all short-term bank debt is vulnerable to runs. Because the financial crisis involved a parallel banking system, separate from regulated commercial banks or demand deposits, this point should be clear. This lesson is not new. For example, Bonamy Price in his textbook of 1876, *Currency and Banking*, wrote that "such crises...are inherent in banking" (132). Only the lack of an understanding of history can keep us from seeing this lesson, and only the paradox of financial crises can keep us from doing something about it. Those are lessons too.

A crisis is an unpredictable event, even if the buildup of fragility—the credit boom and asset price increases—is observed. The financial crisis of 2007–8 was unexpected. It was unexpected because the evolution of the financial system over a thirty-year period was not understood. Any market economy constantly evolves, changes, transforms. Competition and the urge to innovate are central to market economies. Millions of people make decisions about whether to open a money market account or to buy a home with a subprime mortgage. Firms decide to retain more cash in more sophisticated treasury departments that invest in short-term money market instruments. Banks introduce securitization. The government fosters homeownership with subsidies via quasi-government firms. Financial firms offer new products. And so on.

Given the constant of constant change, the only question is: How is the system evolving? Even now the financial system is reconfiguring. This suggests that the idea that any one policy, such as deposit insurance, would forever solve the problem of crises is naive. Probably no one is in a position to see and understand these changes. The government is likely to be constantly behind the changes in terms of measuring the changes and in adopting new regulations. Although we can improve with better measurement of risk and proactive regulations, perhaps the best that can be done is to try to create an environment where crises are infrequent.

Another lesson follows from this, a lesson concerning the central bank. Because of the paradox of financial crises, central banks must be independent so that they can take unpopular actions to keep the banking system from being liquidated. And there cannot be inflexible rules that the central bank must follow in crises. During noncrisis times most economists think that the central bank should focus on fighting inflation based on rules rather than discretion. But in crisis times it is the opposite. Central banks must have discretion, sometimes to take unprecedented actions. There cannot be rules, because the crisis is not predictable and the unfolding of the crisis is very fast. If the timing and the sequence of events of a crisis could be predicted, so that reasonable rules could be adopted, there would not be crises, because they would be so well-understood.

This does not mean that there are no guidelines for the central bank in times of crisis. The classic rule of Walter Bagehot, articulated in his 1873 book *Lombard Street*, is that in a panic, the central bank should lend freely (that is, without limit) to solvent firms, against good collateral, and at "high rates." The idea is that by lending freely, the central bank can provide enough liquidity to satisfy the demands for cash by those running on the banks and thereby prevent costly deleveraging. But this rule is somewhat ambiguous. First, when is there a "crisis"? And furthermore, in a crisis, what is a "solvent" firm, what is "good" collateral, what is a "high rate"? These are judgment calls that the central bank must make, and make quickly. It is hard to see how the answers to these questions could be prespecified as rules. And if they could, these rules would likely not be followed in the next crisis.

The Livingston doctrine, that a bank should not be liquidated in a crisis, comes from the idea that in a crisis there is no way of knowing which firms are solvent and which are not. The problem is systemic. The entire system cannot honor demands for cash, and the counterfactual of whether a firm would be solvent were it not for the crisis cannot be answered. So it is best not to liquidate banks in a crisis. But even this rule may not be optimally followed, as with Lehman Brothers. The paradox of the financial crises may dictate that a bank be allowed to fail to keep the central bank from being eviscerated by the populist backlash. It is hard to imagine what "independence" for a central bank would mean in a way that could prevent this problem under all circumstances. So whether to let a bank fail or not is also a judgment call by the central bank.

RETHINKING BANK REGULATION

To design a bank regulatory environment that addresses the vulnerability of bank debt and fosters economic growth is possible in principle. But because of the paradox of financial crises, it might not be possible in practice.

The National Bank Acts and federal deposit insurance suggest that it is possible to create money that is not crisis-prone. But, let's face it, the beneficial consequences of these acts of legislation were probably the outcomes of luck rather than design. The National Bank Acts were passed to finance the Civil War, and created a uniform currency only as a lucky by-product. Federal deposit insurance was passed because it was demanded by the public, not because economists and regulators wanted it. And in the aftermath of the current crisis we can still see the debate dominated by antibanker sentiments—not exactly an environment where we can expect design of intelligent banking regulations.

Still, something should be done about the shadow banking system. One can take either of two points of view here. First, we could recognize that the shadow banking system is a genuine banking system, in which case we would seek to preserve it but make it much less vulnerable to a run. Second, we could try to squelch it. My Yale colleague Andrew Metrick and I put forth a proposal that expresses the first point of view.[5]

The basic idea is to address the central weakness of the shadow banking system's vulnerability, but in a positive way, so that this banking system can continue to perform its functions. We do not want to liquidate, or inadvertently destroy, this banking system. On the contrary, we want to restore confidence in it. To achieve that, the overarching goals of the proposal are to bring securitization under the regulatory umbrella and to provide a system of collateral production that can back repo without being so vulnerable to runs.

There are two key ideas. The first is the creation of a new category of regulated banks, called narrow funding banks (NFBs). These banks would be contained entities that could not engage in any activity other than purchasing asset-backed securities, government bonds, and agency bonds, according to regulations restricting the composition of their portfolios. These purchases would be financed by issuing long-term debt or medium-term debt, or by repo. All asset-backed securities would have to be sold to NFBs. NFBs would be stand-alone entities with capital requirements, and would be examined by bank examiners. They would not be allowed to take deposits but would have access to the discount window of the Federal Reserve System.

Secondly, regulate repo. While there would be no restrictions on the amount of repo that banks could engage in, there would be limits on how much repo nonbanks could engage in. Nonbank counterparties would be allowed to engage in repo with a regulated bank.

This system would place the government in an oversight role in the securitization and repo markets, and ensure that the safety of the collateral for repo would be overseen. Collateral would consist of the debt issued by NFBs, or, if the transaction was conducted with another NFB, it would be bonds from their portfolio, namely, ABS, treasuries, or agency bonds.

Re-creating confidence in the shadow banking system is essential for economic growth. This proposal takes the view of the Free Banking and National Banking Eras that the backing collateral must be produced in such a way that it is secretless and such that if there is a problem, then there is access to the discount window of the Federal Reserve System.

Recent legislation in response to the Panic of 2007–8, the Dodd-Frank bill, does not take the approach associated with the previous legislative successes. It does not address the fundamental problem that there exist new classes of bank debt that are large and not sufficiently backed. It does not identify, and ring-fence, a set of institutions that are designated as having certain privileges in exchange for following certain rules. On the contrary, the centerpiece of Dodd-Frank does the opposite. The proposed Financial Stability Oversight Council (FSOC) has discretion to identify "systemically important" nonbank financial companies. The Council has enormous power; the vast majority of the regulations are yet to be written. Moreover, the legislation appears to give regulators discretion to modify statutory standards and issue exemptions. Focusing on improving discretionary government intervention seems misguided, because it misses the underlying problem of the vulnerability of bank debt. The government is unlikely to intervene as promptly as in the nineteenth-century panics, as it is unlikely to have information promptly, and even with the information there are political constraints. Ironically, it seems that large losses have to be experienced in order to galvanize politicians to respond. It would be better to design a regulatory system under which there is no need for a discretionary response.

The financial crisis of 2007–8 is another demonstration that in market economies there is an inherent vulnerability of bank debt. There is a demand for short-term, secretless debt, but the private sector cannot produce riskless collateral. The experience of 2007–8 should clarify the meaning of bank money and of a "crisis." This is a basic structural problem and should be addressed in a positive way, a way in which the shadow banking system can fulfill its role in the economy without being crisis-prone.

The crisis was confusing because the bank run was not observable to the media, academics, or the public, but only to traders on trading floors. There were no visible lines of creditors at banks that could be seen publicly. The media and academics focused on the effects of the crisis, firms in trouble and then the bailouts.

The crisis was detected late and action came late. The Livingston doctrine had already become confused because of Continental Illinois, and so it seems that Lehman had to be allowed to fail for political reasons (though the alternative may well have been worse). The complications of Continental Illinois haunt analyses of the crisis that still focus on "moral hazard" and "too-big-to-fail."

The confused response to the crisis in Dodd-Frank reflects what Treasury Secretary Geithner called the paradox of financial crises, the problem that saving the banking system also saves the bankers, so that "what feels just and fair is the opposite of what's required for a just and fair outcome."

And economists did little to contribute to understanding what happened.

XIV. THE THEORY
AND PRACTICE
OF SEEING

In theory there is no difference between theory and practice. In practice there is.

—Yogi Berra

When we look at the world, what do we "see"? The reality of the financial crisis ought to sharpen our vision. Richard Stone's diagram from chapter 7 shows the place of Experience in the economic-knowledge production process. To really understand a financial crisis one needs to be an eyewitness, to *see* it. There is no substitute for Experience. Yale economist James Tobin (1918–2002; 1981 Nobel Prize winner) explained this in an interview with Robert Shiller, also of Yale:

> I do stress [the experience of having been brought up in the Great Depression] because I think that a lot of contemporary economists who have never had any experience with that catastrophe regard it as some kind of aberration so that they don't have to worry about accommodating it in their theories of macroeconomics. They just dismiss it as something that didn't happen or that they can't explain. But for people who did grow up in the depression, it was an obsession. (Shiller 1999, 869)

At some level, everyone has some experience of the current financial crisis. You might not be unemployed; your house may not be in foreclosure. But everyone can understand something of the effects of the current financial crisis. For the country as a whole those effects are such that it seems safe to say that understanding financial crises is the most important task facing economists today. It ought to be an obsession. There is no larger problem. The human toll from crises makes this so.

Experience is one way of seeing. Constructing models of a complex reality should aid the process of seeing, like a telescope aided Galileo. Seeing in the social sciences is complicated—there are no Michelson-Morley experiments. That is, there is never a single experimental result that once and for all demonstrates that a theory is dead, or alters how the world is seen.[1] There is no telescope of Galileo to confirm the ideas of Copernicus. In the social sciences there is never an empirical result that causes the world suddenly to be seen differently. That only happens over a long period of time. But there are events that may sometimes serve the same purpose. The financial crisis is such an event.

However economics changes in response to the crisis, the paramount goal should be to prevent crises. To prevent crises, bank regulation must stop them for a significant period of time. A goal would be to reproduce a period like the Quiet Period, but currently that goal seems unreachable. One reason is economists fail to understand crises, so there is no consensus on policy recommendations—quite the opposite. But this problem can be overcome. I am confident that economists will make progress. But, now that we have just had a crisis, there is another problem. The second reason that this goal seems beyond us is that we need to overcome the paradox of financial crises. That has never happened—the National Bank Acts and federal deposit insurance were not adopted by design. The Main Street/Wall Street battle is not conducive to conversation about financial policy, and it is the root of our inability to build banking systems that are immune to crisis. Overcoming this paradox is a matter of education.

THE ARGUMENT REPRISED

What explains the intellectual failure of economists? The problem with economics is not economic models per se. And the problem is not the use of mathematics. There are good models and there are bad models. The problem is that there was a lack of understanding that a crisis could occur in the United States. Macroeconomists mostly studied a short recent period of time—the

Quiet Period. The view was that models did not need to include crises, so they didn't. They matched the reality of the Quiet Period. If the Quiet Period was the future, the end of history, then there was no need to be interested in economic history or institutional details. The financial crisis showed through practice that this theory is wrong. The difference between theory and practice couldn't be clearer.

There is also a conceptual confusion. Conceptually, there is a very significant difference between tackling the underlying problem of the vulnerability of bank debt and addressing the problems caused by trying to solve the underlying problem. Because they were confused about the expectations of firms and people, economists can't tell the difference. This is why the Quiet Period was thought to be permanent. The problem is that people don't act as they would if the government was not expected to act. The government acts to keep people and firms from behaving in a certain way, and it may be more or less successful. The economist then sees how the government acted, and not how people and firms would have acted. The government's actions then become the focus, even though the government would have no reason to act if the underlying problem was solved. The problem is misidentified as being the government.

Remember the radar gun story from chapter 7? Suppose we study drivers today. We observe that drivers speed quite frequently, but in a volatile manner. That is, they speed for a while and then slow down, only to speed up again. In fact, our study would show that the faster a speeding vehicle is traveling, the more likely it is that it occasionally slows down. And, overall, there is quite a lot of speeding. One such study actually concluded that "over half of all tractor-trailers and more than one quarter of all vehicles travelling over 70 mph had speed reductions suggesting the use of radar detectors." Another study by the Maryland State Police found that of 1,190 commercial vehicles stopped for speeding, 79% had radar detectors—and those were the ones who were caught. Radar detectors actually encouraged speeding. We could conclude that the state police are *causing* speeding, and the government exacerbated the problem of highway deaths.

So what, as economists, should we do differently? We must see things differently.

SEEING THE PLUMBING

All market economies have a technology for trading, but banking and transactions are missing from macroeconomic models. They were simply viewed as unimportant. Further, the technology for trading, clearing, settlement, and regulations involves myriad institutional details, and the plumbing of market economies is hidden within them. But no one, including economists, cares about the details of the plumbing until the toilets back up. The details themselves are not the point. But buried in these details is the structure of market economies. Without a transaction technology, macroeconomic models have nothing to say about financial crises. I have tried to outline some of these details above to elucidate the common structure of private money.

Without attention to the details of the plumbing, we did not see the transformation of the financial system, the decline of traditional banking, the advent of loan sales, securitization, the rise of repo, the rise of institutional investors, and so on, all of which happened before our very eyes. In the end, perhaps it is an inability to understand change—change at its most basic level, real change, happening during our lifetimes. Henry Adams, in *The Education of Henry Adams*, concludes in the last chapter, after describing the impact of changes to the U.S., that "a nineteenth-century education was as useless ... as an eighteenth-century education had been to the child of 1838." It seems that a twentieth-century education may not be so useful for the twenty-first century.

Transactions technology and banking must be included in macroeconomic models.

"SEEING" EXPECTATIONS AND BELIEFS: THE WHAT-IF PROBLEM

A central point I made earlier is that the very *existence* of the Federal Reserve System changed the behavior of households, so that there was no bank run in June 1920 or October 1929. And the runs of the Great Depression came late. Those statements were based on a study of how the timing of panics worked in the National Banking Era. Many models can be constructed to explain why households ran on banks during the National Banking Era. At the core of any such model are the beliefs or expectations of people in the economy.

Macroeconomic models and game-theoretic models depend on some statement about how people form their beliefs about what is going to happen. One reason these mathematical models are rarely tested is that there is a basic problem: we cannot measure households' or firms' beliefs, and we do not know what information they have, where they get their information, or how they process their information. Rational expectations is one way to model beliefs theoretically. But we have not been very successful at taking rational expectations from theory to data, from theory to practice. Chicago economist James Heckman (2000 Nobel Prize winner) explains:

> [Rational expectations] became a kind of tautology that had enormously powerful policy implications, in theory. But the fact is, it didn't have any empirical content. When Tom Sargent, [Chicago economist] Lars Hansen, and others tried to test it using cross equation restrictions, and so on, the data rejected the theories. (interview with John Cassidy, *Rational Irrationality* blog, *New Yorker*, January 14, 2010, http://www. newyorker.com/online/blogs/johncassidy/2010/01/interview-with-james-heckman.html)

A better approach in a particular context may be more fruitful. In my study of the panics in the National Banking Era, I guessed what information the households would be looking at to form their beliefs and to decide if they should run. Burns and Mitchell had identified the liabilities of failed nonfinancial firms as a leading indicator of recessions. And panics tended to happen at business cycle peaks. Putting those two observations together led to the idea that public news arriving about this could be a proxy for how households changed their beliefs and came to question the backing collateral of bank money.

That idea was the basis for the counterfactual about what would have happened during the period after the Federal Reserve came into being, had it not come into being. So I was able to answer the question of what the timing of panics would have been if the clearinghouse system had continued without the Federal Reserve. The point is not that we want to go back to the clearinghouse system; it is that the construction of the counterfactual requires being able to measure a proxy for beliefs—in this case, the information at the root of the formation of beliefs.

If I had not been able to construct the counterfactual, I would not have been able to make the argument about the existence of the Federal Reserve changing people's beliefs such that there was no panic in June 1920 and that the panics of the Great Depression were delayed.

Beliefs and expectations are central to the discussion. We do not know how people in the 1920s came to believe that there was no need to run to the banks in June 1920 because of the existence of the Federal Reserve System. And we do not know why there was no bank run in October 1929, but there was later. What were people thinking? Think of Franklin Roosevelt's first fireside chat. It was words, and promised actions, that led depositors to change their views (though it did not end the Great Depression). How did that happen? We do not know for sure what inference bankers and others drew from watching Continental Illinois get bailed out. Was the failure of Lehman a devastating event because of the real effects of Lehman failing, or was it expectations that other large firms would be allowed to fail during the crisis? Or was it induced pessimism about the future of the economy? Why is the economy languishing now?

Figure 14.1 is the Index of Consumer Sentiment, calculated at the University of Michigan.[2] It is derived from the following five questions:

- We are interested in how people are getting along financially these days. Would you say that you (and your family living there) are better off or worse off financially than you were a year ago?
- Now looking ahead—do you think that a year from now you (and your family living there) will be better off financially, or worse off, or just about the same as now?
- Now turning to business conditions in the country as a whole—do you think that during the next twelve months we'll have good times financially, or bad times, or what?
- Looking ahead, which would you say is more likely—that in the country as a whole we'll have continuous good times during the next five years or so, or that we will have periods of widespread unemployment or depression, or what?
- About the big things people buy for their homes—such as furniture, a refrigerator, stove, television, and things like that. Generally speaking, do you think now is a good or bad time for people to buy major household items?

The index is not a measure of specific expectations about the future, but perhaps it is a measure of people's general attitude about the future. The index moves around over time.

We do not know why. One view is that sentiment just reflects the realities of the macroeconomy. When times are good, people are happy and optimistic, and sentiment rises, and vice versa when times are bad. We do not know why people are optimistic or pessimistic, or why they change their states of mind. Without these details economic models admit "multiple equilibria" of the following sort: If everyone is pessimistic, firms don't hire or invest, people stop looking for work, and the pessimism is confirmed. If everyone is optimistic, the opposite happens. Such a model is completely useless, because it says nothing about why people and firms are optimistic or pessimistic. No policy recommendations flow from such a model.

Some economists make a virtue of multiple equilibria, or the indeterminacy of beliefs. They claim it is a feature of reality. But in fact it is not a problem with reality but with certain models. Reality is exactly one outcome. A model with multiple equilibria is an incomplete model—if it were complete it would tell us why people have one set of beliefs and not another. The economics profession spent several decades working on the existence and uniqueness of equilibrium. These were huge achievements. But it is hard at this point to see how indeterminacy in a model is a virtue. Of course, economic theorists can choose a way to select a single equilibrium as being "natural," but this is largely ad hoc and unsatisfactory. It would be better to study "information" and how it is processed in detailed empirical settings.

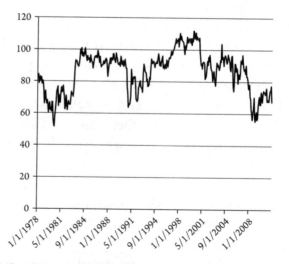

Figure 14.1 The Index of Consumer Sentiment
Source: University of Michigan/Thomson Reuters.

There are many questions about information. For example, does information aggregate over time—is there a straw-that-broke-the-camel's-back effect? I am often asked why the crisis began on August 9, 2007. One view is to see what news was announced that day and attribute the onset to that information. But a lot of news arrived all through the first part of 2007, and many market participants anticipated problems in subprime mortgage markets as early as late 2005 and 2006. There were many rumors about, and much discussion of, the Bear Stearns hedge funds long before they got into trouble. There is a great deal of information aggregation that seems to occur before it affects prices. That is, over-the-counter markets seem to aggregate information very differently than in stock markets.

In over-the-counter markets there is no centralized exchange, like the New York Stock Exchange, where everyone sees the prices. "Over-the-counter" refers to bilateral trade, transactions between two parties, such as two traders at different banks. There is no centralized exchange, and no one except the parties to the transaction see the prices. The idea of "efficient markets" is that dispersed market participants trade based on their information, and the outcome of the aggregate of their different pieces of information is the price. The dispersed participants in the stock market do not all know each other, but they trade in the centralized market. Over-the-counter markets are not like this. Information aggregation to a large extent takes place *before* two parties transact. Traders talk and they solicit bid and ask prices, which can be quoted truthfully or strategically. Of course, traders have beliefs when they trade, but the information aggregation process and price formation process seem fundamentally different than the usual "efficient markets" idea. But we know very little about this.

The formation of expectations and the meaning and processing of information are very important for understanding counterfactuals. And policy questions depend on knowing about counterfactuals—a choice of policies is a completely counterfactual exercise. Without credible models it is difficult for policymakers to be able to argue that the alternative would have been worse. This is an issue at the root of the bank bailouts. Would things have been worse if…? Would there have been a financial crisis if Continental Illinois had not been bailed out? Could a credible counterfactual have resulted in a possibly extralegal bailout of Lehman Brothers?

These "what if"-type questions are not questions that economists can currently answer, because the models are inadequate for understanding the expectations and beliefs of people and firms. Such models are needed to build a social consensus about the solutions to crises. This is the task for economists. It needs to encompass a broad array of approaches, surveys, textual analysis, and narrow settings. It must be empirical.

SEEING THE WORLD: DATA AND TRUTH

We economists have a lot of work to do. Like Richard Stone twenty years ago, I hope there will be change in emphasis:

> I hope [economists] will become more empirical because, while theory is essential, its purpose is to help us to interpret and understand the world we live in. Spinning theories is good fun, especially when they are expressed mathematically; testing them quantitatively is a swot but is the only way of finding out whether they have any validity. I know that theorizing is considered a nobler pursuit than number crunching and is therefore held up as the highest achievement to all who aspire to fame. As a consequence, thousands of theoretical papers are published every year. I doubt whether thousands of worthwhile theories are produced every year. (Stone and Pesaran 1991, 112)

Becoming more empirical is not easy when studying financial crises. And the difficulties suggest methodological issues with economics. Earlier I said that crises are frequent. This is a relative term. They occur more often than most people think. But for economic research there are relatively few data sets on crises—there are not that many crises. Most of the time the economy is in a quiet period, so there are a lot more data about quiet periods. One data set on crises is that of Laeven and Valencia (2008), which covers the years 1970–2007 and has 124 crisis episodes from thirty-seven countries. This data set builds on Caprio, Klingbiel, Laeven, and Noguera (2005). But there is usable data for only forty-two crises, so that is the sample size. The only other period of study, currently, is the U.S. National Banking Era, during which there were seven panics (though some researchers argue that there were more). Of course, there are many individual episodes that have been studied. But for addressing the most important questions—Are crises manifestations of bank runs? Do these events have structural similarities involving bank debt? What explains the cross-section variation in crisis costs? To what extent is the financial crisis paradox a problem? and so on—this is not much to go on.

This raises an obvious issue. How can we study financial crises with such a small number of observations? In fact, the counterfactual that I constructed was based on seven observations because there were *seven* banking panics during the National Banking Era. In recent work with my Yale colleague Guillermo Ordoñez we used U.S. business cycles as the unit of observation, and we had twenty-six observations. So the fact is that there is little data to go on. "Little data" means it is often not possible to use formal econometric testing. Then what should be done? Should we not study crises? And this is not just about financial crises. Many important problems in economics are like this. For example, what are the effects of peacetime fiscal stimulus programs?

"Identification" is another problem when studying crises. Suppose two variables, x and y, are correlated. Identification refers to the problem of determining whether the relationship between two variables is causal (x causes y), or is it reverse causality (y causes x), or is there some third variable, z, that drives both x and y? Obviously, this is an important problem for economists. Now, think of a question like this: Did the Troubled Asset Relief Program (TARP), introduced during the crisis, have positive effects? TARP was a law passed on October 3, 2008, that allocated $700 billion for use during the financial crisis. The problem is that the government chose certain banks for TARP allocations, so it is difficult to cleanly sort out the causality. Was TARP a cause or, because of the nonrandom selection of banks, was it an effect, or did some other variable during the crisis cause both TARP and the banks' behavior? Identification is hard and not likely to be clear-cut. So do we just not try to answer this question?

There are many examples of this problem. I noted in the preface that the economic history of the last century or so in Argentina is in large part due to bad economic policies. This kind of statement must be based on a narrative of what happened. It is difficult to test such a complicated question. Partly, it is the path dependence—the effectiveness of one policy depends also on past policies. This is another example of something that is hard to test formally. Do we not study the history of policy over a lengthy time period? These, however, are the questions one must confront.

The answer is not to forget about statistical significance and identification. But the requirements for purity in this regard severely limit the questions that can be addressed, not to mention what can get published. Adhering to a purist position in the name of "science" makes economics irrelevant. The trade-off between rigor and relevance has traditionally favored rigor, resulting in a decrease in relevance. Many formally correct but uninteresting papers are published, while the more interesting papers are ignored or rejected because they are on questions that encounter these problems. I advocate a tipping of the balance toward relevance. We can still learn a lot from small samples, especially if other methods are admitted—for instance, historical methods. One example is simple narrative. For understanding the crisis, this strikes me as a very reasonable approach, but then one must invest in learning the details of what happened and find some new data to buttress the narrative.

The financial crisis dramatically revealed the shortcomings of the data that are currently collected. Understanding the crisis was difficult for academics and regulators because there was a paucity of relevant data. I spent enormous amounts of time trying to obtain data from banks (none would help) and from trader friends (who did help). It is astounding how limited we are.

Currently, the major measurement systems consist of the Federal Reserve System's Flow of Funds data, which collects a balance sheet of assets and liabilities for sectors of the economy; the Federal Deposit Insurance Corporation's Reports of Condition and Income, which collects balance-sheet and income-statement information for U.S. banks; and the National Income and Product Accounts, which is the main measure of economic activity for the nation as a whole. What is not measured is "risk" and "liquidity," the two variables most closely related to the financial crisis. In fact, more generally in a world of derivative securities, the idea of measuring cash instruments or using accounting concepts is simply no longer adequate. There has been no serious updating of measurement systems in the last fifty years or so.

My colleagues Markus Brunnermeier (of Princeton) and Arvind Krishnamurthy (of Northwestern) and I have proposed a new system of measurement for financial firms that aims to measure their sensitivity to changes in risk variables (Brunnermeier, Gorton, and Krishnamurthy, forthcoming). We propose a measurement system that can answer questions like: How much would your firm gain or lose if house prices were to fall by 5%, 10%, 15%, and so on? In other words, we propose collecting measures of the sensitivity of firm values to movements in a large number of such risk factors. We propose collecting a fairly large amount of data like this at regular intervals; every quarter, for example. In addition, we propose a measure of liquidity.

Such data would be useful for many purposes, but two are paramount. First, government regulators would be better informed, immediately. Regulators could also solicit responses to specific scenarios, in addition to the standard set of data. This would not prevent crises, but it would make for better understanding of risk buildups. Second, eventually, as these data are collected over time, economists would have a rich picture of *risk*: how it builds up, where it is concentrated, its cyclical variation, and the interaction of different risks. A new research agenda would emerge, and new classes of models for understanding systemic risk and financial crises would result. Current macroeconomics is a conceptual child of the collection of national income data. New data would result in a new macroeconomics.

Our proposal is for a new information infrastructure. This cannot be built by academics. Fortunately, however, there is a way to begin such a project. The Dodd-Frank legislation establishes an "Office of Financial Research" (OFR) as part of the Treasury Department to improve the quality of financial data available to policymakers. The OFR has awesome power. It has subpoena power, so it can order firms to produce information, such as trading positions, transactions, human resources records, and bonus amounts. It has the power to tax financial firms to make up its budget. And the law says that when the head of the OFR testifies before Congress, no one can review the testimony. So there is enormous autonomy. The OFR should build this information infrastructure. The OFR should mandate collecting historical data as well, so that a more comprehensive data set of financial crises could be studied.

Economics has come to a fork in the road. I think that this is ultimately the point of the critics, the point of Krugman and Volcker, and others. And I agree. We can either embrace reality—through history, institutional details, and measurement—or we can choose to ignore the lessons of the financial crisis, of our failure, and languish in irrelevancy.

BIBLIOGRAPHIC NOTES

These notes are not an exhaustive survey of the academic literature, but only a road-map to some of the relevant literature. In the text I do not provide citations to many statements. Instead, here I cite and sometimes briefly discuss the relevant papers, and other material that may have been implicitly referred to in the main text.

PREFACE

Argentina is worthy of more attention than I give it in the preface, because of its apparently long history of policy failures. I only mention it in this regard, though Argentina pops up elsewhere in the text. On Argentina, see, for example, della Paolera and Taylor (2001), Taylor (1994), the Joint Economic Committee, United States Congress (2003), and Mundlak, Cavallo, and Domenech (1989). The statement about the number of central bank governors in Argentina comes from the data set of Dreher, Sturm, and De Haan (2010).

I. INTRODUCTION

The "Great Moderation" literature in macroeconomics is about a short period of time, starting in the mid-1980s. Economists were struggling with the question of how to evaluate policy, and in particular monetary policy; could changes in monetary policy explain the decline in macroeconomic volatility over a roughly twenty-year period? This is an important question and one I return to in the last chapter. The question is how policy can be evaluated when there is not much data. It is similar to the point about Argentina above.

There is a large literature on the Great Moderation. For a survey of the literature, see Stock and Watson (2002). For a survey of some of the empirical evidence, see Summers (2005). The most common explanations for the Great Moderation fall into one of three categories: better monetary policy, changes in inventory management, and good luck. See Gali and Gambetti (2008). My point here and elsewhere in the text is that it was precisely during the Great Moderation that the shadow banking system developed. Macroeconomists, focusing on limited data and unable to "see" financial intermediation as relevant, did not see the buildup of risk or the transformation of the banking system. I think they misinterpreted what they saw. These issues, of "seeing" and data, also come up again in chapter 14.

2. THE QUIET PERIOD

Diamond and Dybvig (1983) highlight and emphasize the mismatch between the transaction horizon and the length of time of real investments. This is a central point about financial intermediation—that it is this mismatch that creates the vulnerability of bank debt. This point is the key to understanding that bank debt vulnerability is an inherent feature of economies with private bank money.

Free Banking

Almost all U.S. banking history books cover the Free Banking Era. See Knox (1900), Hepburn (1915), or Dewey (1918) for examples. Redlich (1952), Sumner (1896), Dwyer (1996), and Bodenhorn (2000) give different overviews of the Free Banking Era. Lanier (1922) focuses on the history of banking in New York State.

Hugh Rockoff, and later Art Rolnick and Warren Weber, overturned many of the long-held beliefs about the Free Banking Era being chaos. Rockoff (1974, 1975) started the modern literature on the Free Banking Era. Rolnick and Weber (1983, 1984) revisit the issue of "wild cat banking" and argue that this was not really an issue. They argue that free banks failed because the bond collateral sometimes declined in value. I follow them on this point. See Rockoff (1985) for a rejoinder. The data discussed in the text about which bonds were owned by New York free banks is from Rolnick and Weber (1984). Also see Jaremski (2010).

In Gorton (1996, 1999) I studied banknote prices to show that banknote markets were efficient in the financial economics sense; the notes were priced correctly on average. In a formal sense, the further away from the issuing bank that the bank's notes circulate, the higher the value of the put option that the noteholder is short. Increasing distance becomes increasing maturity.

However, while there may have been few wildcat banks, and the secondary markets for free banknotes may have been efficient (in the finance sense), this transaction technology was still inefficient in the economics sense. (On the relationship between "economic efficiency" and "market efficiency" see Dow and Gorton [1997]). Dillistin (1949) gives an overview of the difficulties of transacting with private banknotes. The contemporary sources, some of which I quote, suggest that transacting with banknotes was costly.

Other related studies on free banking include Economopoulos and O'Neill (1995), Hasan and Dwyer (1994), and Ng (1988).

State Debt Defaults
Between 1839 and 1843 nine U.S. states defaulted on their debt, and five repudiated all or part of their debt. On state defaults on their debt see English (1996), Kim (2003), Wallis (2004), Wallis, Sylla, and Grinath (2004), and Dove (n.d.).

National Bank Acts
Background on the National Bank Acts is found in many books on the Civil War, but more detailed information is found in biographies of Salmon P. Chase, the U.S. secretary of the Treasury at the time and architect of the acts. See, e.g., Niven (1995). Gould (1904) provides details on the various National Bank Acts and their amendments. Also see Bolles (1910). Million (1894) discusses the debates on the National Bank Act of 1863 prior to its passage.

Business Cycle Dating
With regard to the dating of business cycles, see Davis (2006, 2004) and Romer (1988). Fels (1951), speaking of the Panic of 1893, wrote: "There are many reasons for not accepting the Bureau's [the National Bureau for Economic Research] dates in blind faith. Not the least of which is the scarcity of monthly data for the 1870's" (336). Miron and Romer (1990) point out that "these differences in the timing of real output movements around financial panics could have large effects in studies that seek to identify the direction of causation between panics and recessions" (332). Burns and Mitchell (1946) provide the original dating.

Checks
On the rise of checks, there are a few articles from the nineteenth century; see Dunbar (1887) and Fisher (1895). Fisher (1895) discusses the comptroller's survey of fifty-two national banks; see p. 394. Also, on measuring the use of checks, see Kinley (1910, 1897). Gorton (1984, 1985b) discusses the role of clearinghouses in the rise of checks. Gilbert (2000) discusses the role of the Federal Reserve System in payments system.

National Banking Era Panics
Overall, see the U.S. banking histories of Sumner (1896) and Redlich (1968). Specifically on the National Banking Era, see O. Sprague (1910), Gorton (1988), Calomiris

and Gorton (1991), Grossman (1993), and Wicker (2000). There are many books and articles on individual panics. Some are mentioned here.

Deposit Insurance

There were state deposit insurance systems that were experimented with early on, and then later, after the Panic of 1907. The early systems are discussed by Golembe (1960) and Calomiris (1989, 1990, 1992). Cooke (1909) is about the early nineteenth-century systems, including Oklahoma. Also see Robb (1921, 1934).

The literature on the passage of federal deposit insurance includes Calomiris and White (1994) and Flood (1992). Also see Gayer (1935).

Deposit insurance systems around the world have been studied in a number of papers. Looking at insurance systems around the world, Demirgüç-Kunt and Detragiache (1998) find that "the presence of an explicit deposit insurance scheme makes bank unsoundness more likely" (83). The design issues matter, but perhaps the most important factors are the presence of sound legal systems and strict oversight of banks. Also see Laeven (2002), Demirgüç-Kunt (1992a, 1992b), Demirgüç-Kunt and Kane (2002), and Demirgüç-Kunt, Kane, and Laeven (2008).

Beck, Demirgüç-Kunt, and Levine (2006) found that more concentrated banking systems are less likely to experience crises in an empirical study of a panel of sixty-nine countries over the period 1980–97. As mentioned earlier, the massive bank merger wave of the 1980s and 1990s has increased the concentration of the U.S. banking system.

Canada

On Canada, see Johnson (1910) and Bordo, Rockoff, and Redish (2010). Grossman (1994) looks at the stability of banking systems of Britain, Canada, and ten other countries during the Great Depression. Beck (2002) discusses the club-like arrangements of large banks with the central bank in Germany.

3. FINANCIAL CRISES

There are a number of very important practical issues with regard to measuring crises. The most important concerns whether an event is a "crisis" or not. Clearly, this issue affects the frequency of crises. Another important issue concerns the practical matter of determining the start date and the end date of a crisis. There is significant disagreement about the dating of crises and about whether some events constitute a "crisis." Boyd, De Nicolò, and Loukoianova (2011) look at the four crisis classifications in the literature, all of which build on Caprio and Kingebiel (1996, 1999). The four classifications are those given by: (1) Demirgüç-Kunt and Detragiache (2002, 2005); (2) Caprio, Klingebiel, Laeven, and Noguera (2005); (3) Reinhart and Rogoff (2009a); and (4) Laeven and Valencia (2008). Boyd, De Nicolò, and Loukoianova (2011) show that these classifications differ in significant ways. This problem is likely due to the fact that the start date of crises is usually an observable government intervention. This occurs *after* the crisis has already begun, because something had to have already happened for the government to intervene. But the intervention may be confused or piecemeal, and since the crisis dating is based on annual data, the start date can shift a year or so forward or backward. End dates are even more problematic. How do we determine when a crisis has ended? These questions raise issues for future research.

Frequency of Crises

The frequency of crises is not a settled question. Laeven and Valencia (2008) identify 124 systemic banking crises over the period 1970–2007. Reinhart and Rogoff (2008a) note that "*for the advanced economies during the full sample, the picture that emerges is one of serial banking crises. The world's financial centers, the United Kingdom, the United States and France stand out in this regard, with 12, 13, and 15 banking crises episodes, respectively*" (14; emphasis in original). They go on to note that the frequency of crises declines in the post–World War II era until the current crisis. Looking at 120 years, 1880–2000, Bordo, Eichengreen, Klingebiel, and Martinez-Peria (2001), however, argue that the frequency of crises has doubled since 1973.

Eichengreen and Bordo (2002) identify thirty-eight financial crises between 1945 and 1973 and 139 between 1973 and 1997. Caprio and Klingebiel (1997) identified 112 banking crises in ninety-three countries (and fifty-one borderline crises in forty-six countries) between the late 1970s and 1997. Also see Reinhart and Rogoff (2009a). Kaminsky and Reinhart (1999), Caprio and Klingebiel (1996, 1997), and Bordo and Murshid (2001), among others, also provide lists and evidence on the frequency of crises. Schularick and Taylor (2009, 12) note that "the frequency of banking crises in the 1945–71 period was virtually zero; but since 1971 ... crises became much more frequent." This suggests that the Quiet Period was worldwide and may have been due to good luck. We do not know for sure. This is another important topic for research.

Laeven and Valencia (2008, 19) also note the frequency of bank runs during these crises:

> Bank runs are a common feature of banking crises, with 62 percent of crises experiencing momentary sharp reductions in total deposits. The largest one-month drop in the ratio of deposits to GDP averages about 11.2 percent for countries experiencing bank runs, and is as high as 26.7 percent in one case. Severe runs are often system-wide, but it is also common to observe a flight to quality effect within the system from unsound banks to sound banks that implies no or moderate systemic outflows. During the Indonesian crisis in 1997, for instance, private national banks lost 35 trillion Rupiah in deposits between October and December 2007, while state-owned banks and foreign and joint-venture banks gained 12 and 2 trillion respectively (Batunanggar, 2002). A similar situation occurred in Paraguay following the intervention of the third and

fourth largest banks and the uncovering of unrecorded deposits. Depositors migrated from these banks to those perceived as more solid.

While bank runs are quite common features of crises, the question of the timing remains—that is, are the crises in the modern era due to information arrival about the government's or central bank's actions, rather than news about a recession? This too is a topic for research.

Definition of a Financial Crisis or Banking Panic

Calomiris and Gorton (1991, 96) say: "A banking panic occurs when bank debt holders at all or many banks in the banking system suddenly demand that banks convert their debt claims into cash (at par) to such an extent that the banks suspend convertibility of their debt into cash or, in the case of the United States, act collectively to avoid suspension of convertibility by issuing clearing-house loan certificates."

Reinhart and Rogoff (2008a) say: "We mark a banking crisis by two types of events: (1) bank runs that lead to the closure, merging, or takeover by the public sector of one or more financial institutions; and (2) if there are no runs, the closure, merging, takeover, or large-scale government assistance of an important financial institution (or group of institutions) that marks the start of a string of similar outcomes for other financial institutions" (table A2, p. 58). Part 2 of this definition is necessitated by the presence of the government and its possible intervention.

Laeven and Valencia (2008):

> We start with a definition of a systemic banking crisis. Under our definition, in a systemic banking crisis, a country's corporate and financial sectors experience a large number of defaults and financial institutions and corporations face great difficulties repaying contracts on time. As a result, non-performing loans increase sharply and all or most of the aggregate banking system capital is exhausted. This situation may be accompanied by depressed asset prices (such as equity and real estate prices) on the heels of run-ups before the crisis, sharp increases in real interest rates, and a slowdown or reversal in capital flows. In some cases, the crisis is triggered by depositor runs on banks, though in most cases it is a general realization that systemically important financial institutions are in distress.

Bordo, Eichengreen, Klingbiel, and Martinez-Peria (2001, 4) define financial crises as "episodes of financial-market volatility marked by significant problems of illiquidity and insolvency among financial-market participants and/or by official intervention to contain those consequences."

The definition in the main text includes as crises events in which holders of short-term bank debt *"would have engaged in such a mass run had not explicit or implicit government intervention been in place or been expected."* This counterfactual is exactly the point.

In chapter 14, I discuss the necessity of measuring beliefs for understanding such counterfactuals. Some of the above definitions are empirically based, such as situations where there is a sudden increase in nonperforming loans and large-scale government assistance to the banking sector. These seem like fine workable definitions, though as discussed above, applying definitions is difficult. But to understand the root causes of these events I focus on bank runs and emphasize the counterfactual.

4. LIQUIDITY AND KEEPING SECRETS

That the output of banks is debt is the logic of Diamond and Dybvig (1983) and Gorton and Pennacchi (1993a). Gorton and Pennacchi follow Diamond and Dybvig in adopting the fundamental view that transactions happen at shorter frequencies than the horizon of real investment in the economy. Diamond and Dybvig and Gorton and Pennacchi assume debt is the optimal contract. The two papers have different notions of "liquidity." In Diamond and Dybvig bank debt helps people smooth consumption. There is no interim trading of the short-term debt and so no prices. If people in the model want to transact early, they withdraw from the bank rather than write checks to other agents. Debt in Gorton and Pennacchi is designed to be riskless so that uninformed people do not lose to better informed counterparties when they trade at the interim date. The issue of the existence of a price, or discount from par, that is discussed in the main text, requires trade at the interim date. Such trade coordinates beliefs via the price.

The ideas in the text that debt is designed to be "secretless" or "information-insensitive" have their origin in Holmström (2008) and are further developed in Holmström (2012). Dang, Gorton, and Holmström (2011) also develop this idea and argue that debt is the best instrument for trading purposes, "providing liquidity." A main point is that debt is "least information-sensitive," meaning that it minimizes the incentive for agents to produce private information, creating adverse selection, and that debt maintains the most value in the presence of aggregate shock. This is not the same as "riskless." Dang, Gorton, and Holmström propose that a "crisis" corresponds to a public shock that causes secretless debt to become information-sensitive. This creates the rational fear of adverse selection—the idea that you might meet a better informed counterparty in the market who takes advantage of you. The crisis then results in a decline in trade as people and firms mark down the value of the debt, or there is in fact adverse selection. In either case, there is an event resembling a crisis.

Clearinghouses

Clearinghouses, starting in New York City in 1853 with the rise of checks, were an integral part of the U.S. banking system until the existence of the Federal Reserve System. Clearinghouses are so integral to U.S. banking history that discussing banking without discussing clearinghouses is not really possible. The classic sources are J. Cannon (1910a) and Gibbons (1859). More recent work on U.S. clearinghouses includes

Timberlake (1984), Gorton (1984, 1985b), and Gorton and Mullineaux (1987). Gorton and Huang (2003, 2006) present a theory explaining how clearinghouses work. These works all emphasize the central bank–like aspects of the clearinghouses.

On clearinghouse loan certificates see J. Cannon (1910b). Redlich (1968) provides details on the clearinghouse loan certificate and its evolution, and on George S. Coe. See chapter 17 of Redlich. Redlich also contains a biography of Coe in an appendix, pp. 424–47. Swanson (1908a, 1908b) discusses the first issue of clearinghouse loan certificates in the crisis of 1860.

Sources on the Term Securities Lending Facility (TSLF) are discussed below.

5. CREDIT BOOMS AND MANIAS

The idea that financial crises are the result of credit booms is in both Minsky (1982) and Kindleberger (2005). Gorton and Ordoñez (2011) present a formal model of crises and credit booms.

Schularick and Taylor (2009) study fourteen developed countries over the period 1870–2008. Their summary is: "All forms of the model show that a credit boom over the previous five years is indicative of a heightened risk of a financial crisis" (20). Schularick and Taylor look at credit in the previous five years, measuring credit in different ways (real total assets of banks, or real total bank loans). Laeven and Valencia (2008, 9) say that a credit boom is "defined as three-year pre-crisis average growth in private credit to GDP in excess of 10 percent per annum." They study forty-two crises over the period 1970–2007 and conclude:

> Banking crises are also often preceded by credit booms, with pre-crisis rapid credit growth in about 30 percent of crises. Average annual growth in private credit to GDP prior to the crisis is about 8.3 percent across crisis countries, and is as high as 34.1 percent in the case of Chile. (19)

Demirgüç-Kunt and Detragiache (1998) find evidence supporting the idea that lending booms precede banking crises. Hardy and Pazarbaşioğlu (1998) find that there is robust evidence that credit to the private sector follows a boom-and-bust pattern ahead of banking crises. Gourinchas, Valdes, and Landerretche (2001) examine a large number of episodes characterized as lending booms and find that the probability of having a banking crisis significantly increases after such episodes. There are other papers as well.

One issue concerns the definition of a "credit boom." Some authors define a credit boom as a given annual percentage change in the ratio of private credit to GDP. Other authors study the growth in private credit relative to trend. For various examples, see Demirgüç-Kunt and Detragiache (1998), Kaminsky and Reinhart (1999), Collyns and Senhadji (2002), Eichengreen and Mitchener (2003), Hume and Sentence (2009), and Mendoza and Terrones (2008).

The Mexican Tequila Crisis
I only touch on the Mexican Tequila Crisis as an example of a credit boom leading to a crisis. There is much, much more that could be said about this important crisis. See, for example, Folkerts-Landau and Ito (1995), Gil-Diaz and Carstens (1996), Sachs, Tornell, and Velasco (1996), Whitt (1996), Gil-Diaz (1998), and McQuerry (1999).

Securitization
The statistics on securitization are from the statement of Tom Deutsch before the House Financial Services Committee, Subcommittee on Capital Markets and Government Sponsored Enterprises, April 14, 2011, and from the Federal Reserve Board of Governors, "G19: Consumer Credit," (September 2009), http://www.federalreserve.gov/releases/g19/current/g19.htm. On securitization in general see Gorton and Metrick (forthcoming a) and Gorton and Souleles (2006).

Credit Booms and Property Prices
There appears to be an association between a credit boom and an increase in property prices. Reinhart and Rogoff (2008b) look at a sample of crises in developed economies and shows a striking similarity in that there is a run-up in real housing prices prior to each crisis. Hilbers, Lei, and Zacho (2001) analyze eleven banking crises and find that in all these cases "residential real estate prices surged sharply (on average by more than 20 percent in real terms) and then began falling (by more than 15 percent in two years) before the beginning of financial sector distress. After that, real estate prices continue to fall.... On average, residential property prices dropped by a total of 35 percent.... A broadly similar development can be observed for commercial property prices" (29). Reinhart and Rogoff (2009a, 2009b) show that the six major historical episodes of banking crises in advanced economies since the mid-1970s were all associated with a housing bust. They document that this pattern can also be found in many emerging market crises, including the Asian financial crisis of 1997–98, with the magnitude of house price declines being broadly similar in both advanced and emerging market countries.

What is not clear is whether the banks fuel the rise in property prices by lending or whether banks lend against increasingly valuable property that is going up in value for other reasons. Rajan and Ramcharan (2012) tackle this question of whether credit availability causes asset price rises. They study the boom and bust in agricultural commodity prices in the United States during 1917–20. At the county level there is a large variation in the effects of the exogenous movements in commodity prices because different counties produced different crops. They find that credit availability did cause an inflation in land prices.

Earlier Credit Booms
Narratives of earlier U.S. history often discuss this link between credit and property prices. Hibbard (1965) and Sakolski (1932) discuss early American land booms.

Hibbard is a history of public land policies; Sakolski records narratives of early land-related price booms.

Railroads

The role of railroads in the development of the United States is a long-studied subject; see Jenks (1944), Chandler (1965), Fishlow (1965), Fogel (1971, 1964), and R. White (2011). R. White (2011) is a revisionist counterpoint to Chandler's view of the railroad companies as the modern efficient corporate form. Fogel (1971) is a classic work arguing that the railroad was not a uniquely necessary industry for driving nineteenth-century American growth to "take off." The issue of whether railroad bond financing facilitated growth by creating a large amount of debt for collateral has not been studied, partly due to issues with determining the outstanding amount of railroad debt. So we do not know, for example, whether railroad bonds played the role of high-quality collateral for financial transactions or for insurance company portfolios.

The Florida Land Boom of the 1920s

See Frazer and Guthrie (1995), Vanderblue (1927a, 1927b), Vickers (1994), and E. White (2009).

Other Land Booms

Hoyt (1933) covers one hundred years of Chicago land prices. Van Dyke (1890) tells the story of the late-nineteenth-century land price boom in southern California.

Taking the Punch Bowl Away

The source for the quote from William McChesney Martin is "Business: The Martin Era," *Time* magazine, February 2, 1970.

6. CAUSES OF CRISES

How do agents form beliefs or expectations and decide to run on banks? Perhaps an easier question is: How and when do beliefs change? The empirical evidence discussed in the main text is from Gorton (1988). Gorton (1988) studies the National Banking Era and argues that people in the economy receive news about the liabilities of failed nonfinancial firms, a leading indicator of recession, and runs on their banks. This study is the basis for a large part of this chapter.

There are also interesting studies of runs on specific banks, which provides a glimpse of the richness of panic dynamics. For example, see Kelley and Ó Gráda (e), and Ó Gráda and White (2003). These authors examined detailed records from the Emigrant Industrial Savings Bank in New York City in studying the panics of 1854 and 1857.

Financial crises in the era of central banks are also empirically associated with a weakening of the macroeconomy and with currency crises. For example, Demirgüç-Kunt and Detragiache (1998) examine the period 1980–94 and "find that low GDP growth, excessively high real interest rates, and high inflation significantly increase the likelihood of systemic problems in our sample" (83). Also see, e.g., Kaminsky and Reinhart (1999).

Pre-Fed Period

Overviews are provided by Redlich (1968), Sumner (1896), O. Sprague (1910), Gorton (1988), Calomiris and Gorton (1991), and Wicker (2000). These sources also cover the individual panics, listed below, particularly Wicker (2000). In addition, on individual U.S. panic episodes, an incomplete list includes the following:

Panics of 1837 and 1839: See McGrane (1924), Temin (1969), Rousseau (2002), Wallis (2005, 2002).

Panic of 1857: See Callender (1858), Gibbons (1859), Van Vleck (1943), Huston (1983, 1987), Calomiris and Schweikart (1991), Kelley and Ó Gráda (2000), Ó Gráda and White (2003).

Panic of 1873: See Journalist (1873), Fels (1951).

Panic of 1884: See Fels (1952).

Panic of 1890: See Wirth (1893).

Panic of 1893: See Lauck (1907), Stevens (1894), Warner (1895), Carlson (2005).

Panic of 1907: See Andrew (1908a, 1908b), O. Sprague (1908), Noyes (1909), Moen and Tallman (1992, 2000, 2010), Bruner and Carr (2009).

Panic of 1914: See O. Sprague (1915), Silber (2007a, 2007b).

For the GNP fall with regard to the NBER business cycle with the peak of the cycle at January 1920 and the trough at July 1921, see Romer (1988).

Post-Fed Period

Gorton (1988) argues that the introduction of the Federal Reserve System in 1914 fundamentally altered depositor behavior, compared to the National Banking Era. On the effects of the Federal Reserve System on interest rates see Shiller (1980), Miron (1986), and Mankiw, Miron, and Weil (1987).

On the bank failures of the 1920s and the Great Depression, see Calomiris (1990), Calomiris and Mason (1997, 2003), Wheelock (1992), Alston, Grove, and Wheelock (1994), and Saunders and Wilson (1996).

Ohanian (2010) emphasizes the oddity of the Great Depression, but for other reasons. He argues, among other things, that the Great Depression was severe, or "Great," prior to the panics.

On the Reconstruction Finance Corporation, see Sprinkel (1952), Nash (1959), and Mason (2003).

The issue of "stigma" from a bank going to the discount window is a well-known problem, but one that is mostly based on anecdote. This is necessarily so if it is counterfactual. That is, if banks don't go to the discount window because of stigma, then we never see the stigma. In the financial crisis of 2007–8, however, there was an opportunity to measure this stigma. See Armantier, Ghysels, Sarkar, and Shrader (2011). This research paper is the source of the thirty-seven-basis-points figure that banks would pay to avoid the discount window.

Penn Central

Penn Central was the first default of an investment-grade company in the postwar period (see Kidwell and Trzcinka [1979]). Between June 24 and July 15, 1970, outstanding commercial paper dropped almost 10% (see Stojanovic and Vaughn [1998]). Also see Calomiris (1994) and Brimmer (1989).

Crises and Recessions

It is difficult to distinguish real effects of a recession from the effects of problems in the financial sector. Does a financial crisis make the recession worse? Is a financial crisis an inherent part of worse recessions? The evidence suggests that severe financial crises are associated with prolonged and severe downturns and may make them worse. See Reinhart and Rogoff (2009a).

It has been difficult to formally demonstrate that the panics in the National Banking period made the recessions worse. Grossman (1993) and Jalil (2009) provide some evidence. Grossman (1993) studies the National Banking Era. He concludes that "bank failures during the National Banking era had a substantial negative impact on aggregate economic activity" (317). Dell'Ariccia, Detragiache, and Rajan (2008) get at the issue using panel data from forty-one countries from 1980 to 2000. The identification strategy is based on the idea that industries that are more dependent on bank finance will be hurt more after a banking crisis. They find that this is the case. Another interesting study is Peek and Rosengren (2000). They show that U.S. firms were affected when their lenders were Japanese banks in crisis.

On the post-Fed period, see, e.g., Bernanke (1983) and Cerra and Saxena (2008). Bernanke (1983) studies the Great Depression. Cerra and Saxena (2008) analyze recoveries of countries' economies from large negative shocks. They study 190 countries over the years 1960–2001 and find large output losses associated with financial crises. But whether the severity and length is due to the financial crisis still seems like an open question. We don't know the details of the channels of effects. Moreover, it is difficult to distinguish whether costs emanating from the financial sector are from costs due to uncertainty concerning the presence of a central bank or government, institutions that might intervene in the financial sector or from effects due to expectations that the government might intervene.

7. ECONOMIC THEORY WITHOUT HISTORY

The Stone diagram was first used by Stone (1963) and was used again in Stone's Nobel lecture (Stone [1997]).

My summary of the development of modern macroeconomics is very, very brief. Lucas and Sargent (1981) and Miller (1994) collect many of the seminal papers in the Rational Expectations–revolution literature. Chari (1998) provides an overview of Robert Lucas's work. Greenwood (1994) summarizes methodology.

On the Phillips curve see Fuhrer (1995).

The problem of short time series for analysis is pervasive in macroeconomics. Researchers subsequent to Kydland and Prescott, like Stock and Watson (1999), for example, updated the stylized business cycle facts studying the period 1941–96 or fifty-five years.

8. DEBT DURING CRISES

The Suffolk Bank System

The Suffolk Bank, of Boston, acted as a quasi-central bank in the Northeast prior to the Civil War. On the Suffolk System, see Whitney (1878), Lake (1947), Mullineaux (1987), Calomiris and Kahn (1996), and Rolnick, Smith, and Weber (1998).

Legal History of Debt and Crises

My legal history of debt and crises is very brief; there are many more cases that could be reviewed, though without changing the basic narrative of the main text. For example, another important case that I omitted for the sake of brevity in the main text comes from South Carolina and came to be known as "the Bank Case." South Carolina was not a free banking state. In South Carolina bank charters did not have a provision for a grace period of suspension. The banks in South Carolina suspended convertibility on May 18, 1837, and continued until September 1, 1838. However, they again suspended from October 1839 until July 21, 1840. In 1840, the state legislature passed a law that required all banks that remained in suspension to pay the state a penalty of 5% interest on the outstanding amounts of notes in circulation. The legislation also required the banks to make monthly reports of their condition and allow the state comptroller general to examine them. Otherwise a bank would lose its charter and would have to wind down its business. Clark (1922) explains what happened next:

> Every bank in the state with the exception of the Bank of Georgetown had suspended specie payment from May, 1837, until September, 1838, and that five banks in Charleston suspended specie payments from October, 1839, to July, 1840. Of the five banks which had suspended specie payment in Charleston in 1839, three accepted the terms of the Act and exempted themselves from forfeiture under the above statute. Under the terms of the Act above referred to, proceedings had been instituted on behalf of the state by the Attorney General against

all of the offending banks and a test case made in the name of the The State vs. The Bank of South Carolina. It will be observed that this test case was aimed at the oldest and possibly the most prominent bank at that time in South Carolina. It was this bank which, prior to 1801, had engaged in banking business in Charleston under the management of the very officers who became its incorporators under the state in 1801, and as such had issued bills and put them in circulation. (152)

The history of this case is discussed by Clark (1922) and Lesesne (1970). The case was so closely followed, and seen as of such importance, that the state ordered the trial transcripts published; see South Carolina Court of Errors (1844).

The Livingston Doctrine

The *Livingston* case seems to me to be the first clear articulation of the idea that the banking system should not be liquidated during a crisis, and it defines a crisis as an event where there is a general suspension of convertibility. I first read of *Livingston v. Bank of New York* in Hammond (1957). In fact, my first published paper is an attempt to make sense of the *Livingston* case, although I didn't mention the case in that paper— I probably should have. See Gorton (1985a), titled "On Bank Suspension of Convertibility." Hammond only mentions the case in one paragraph, but he clearly recognized the importance of the case:

> Traditionally and in principle, a debtor who openly and flatly refused to pay an obligation was culpable, and the legislature had evidently adopted the law under some conviction. The court, however, took a different view. It would not admit the refusal [to pay specie] to be evidence that the bank was insolvent, especially when all the banks were united in action. This was tantamount to judicial recognition of the fact long established in practice and accepted by all but the most conservative business men, agrarians, and die-hard theorists, that bank notes were money and no longer simply promissory notes to be dealt with as individual obligations between debtor and creditor. (693)

Bolles, in his exhaustive *A Treatise on the Modern Law of Banking* (1907), summarizes *Ferry v. Bank* as follows:

> Temporary inability to command money to meet a bank's obligations does not mean insolvency. As banks lend the larger portion of their deposits, occasions happen when they cannot immediately repay on demand. If they are wisely lent, and in due time are likely to be repaid, so that neither depositors nor stockholders will lose anything, the lending bank is not insolvent. (794)

Another example is Zane (1900).

Solvency/Insolvency of Banks
Braver (1936) provides an overview of the legal history. Bliss and Kaufman (2007) compare U.S. corporate insolvency procedures with the different procedures for banks. Also see Hüpkes (2005).

The Bank Holidays during the Great Depression
The banking holidays of the Great Depression and subsequent legislation are described by almost any book on the history of the Great Depression; see, e.g., Preston (1933). Also see "The Emergency Banking Relief Act of 1933," U.S. *Statutes at Large* (73rd Congress, 1933).

President Roosevelt's fireside chat is discussed by Silber (2009).

The Trading with the Enemy Act is discussed by Lourie (1943) and Bishop (1949).

Section 13(3) of the Federal Reserve Act
See Fettig (2008) and Mehra (2010).

State Debt Moratoria
Coleman (1974) presents the history of interactions between debtors and creditors in America and discusses the history of stay laws.

Alston (1983, 1984) and Wheelock (2008a, 2008b) discuss the conditions of American farmers during the Great Depression. Feller (1933) provides a history of debt moratoria and, in an appendix, a tabulation of moratoria legislation in the United States. Prosser (1934), Rogers (1933–34), and Amundson and Rotman (1984) focus on Minnesota. Amundson and Rotman (1984) also briefly discuss the 1983 Minnesota mortgage moratorium. Knapp (1983) provides more detail on the recent legislation. Skilton (1943) discussed mortgage moratoria after 1933. The legal issues are discussed by Rogers (1933–34), Levy (1997–98), and Roots (2000).

Spector (2008) discusses the effect of the U.S. *Blaisdell* decision on certain court decisions in Argentina during crises there.

9. THE END OF THE QUIET PERIOD, OR WHY WAS THERE NO CRISIS DURING 1934–2007?
The decline of traditional banking has been much written about, and there is a large literature on this topic. Still, it is hard to unravel the effects of competition from outside the banking industry from the effects of deregulation. This is a topic for research.

Changes in Traditional Banking
Berger, Kashyap, and Scalise (1995) exhaustively document the changes in the United States regulated banking sector, summarizing the changes this way: "Virtually all aspects of the U.S. banking industry have changed dramatically over the last fifteen years" (55).

They describe the 1980s and the first half of the 1990s as "undoubtedly the most turbulent period in U.S. banking history since the Great Depression" (57). In 1992 D'Arista and Schlesinger also observed the changes, writing: "Over the last two decades, the U.S. [banking] system has been reshaped by the spread of multifunctional financial conglomerates and the emergence of an unregulated parallel banking system. Along with powerful trends like securitization, these events have broken down the carefully compartmentalized credit and capital marketplace established in New Deal legislation 60 years ago" (1992, 2). Also see Bryan (1988), Barth, Brumbaugh, and Litan (1990, 1992), Boyd and Gertler (1993, 1994), and Edwards and Mishkin (1995), among many others.

Change in banking was largely spurred by innovation by nonbank competitors. On the growth of money market mutual funds, see Cook and Duffield (1979) and Gorton and Pennacchi (1993b). On the asset side of bank balance sheets there were also competitors, namely, commercial paper and junk bonds. On the subject of junk bonds, see Taggart (1988), Perry and Taggart (1988), Loeys (1990), Benveniste, Singh, and Wilhelm (1993), and Molyneux and Shamroukh (1996). The figures on the growth of junk bonds in the text are from Taggart (1988) and Perry and Taggart (1988). Benveniste, Singh, and Wilhelm (1993) provide evidence that junk bonds and bank loans are substitutes. On commercial paper see, e.g., Post, Schoenbeck, and Payne (1992), Hurley (1977), Becketti and Morris (1992), and Calomiris, Himmelberg, and Wachtel (1995).

Banks responded to these changes, and rates of return returned to the pre-deregulations levels only in the early 1990s. See Humphrey and Pulley (1997) and Keeley and Zimmerman (1984). The competition from junk bonds and MMMFs, as well as deregulation (e.g., of interest rate ceilings), caused bank charter values to decline, which in turn caused banks to increase risk and reduce capital. This has been documented by Keeley (1990), Gorton and Rosen (1995), and Demsetz, Saidenberg, and Strahan (1996), among others.

Bank regulation also changed dramatically during this period. These changes are summarized by Berger, Kashyap, and Scalise (1995).

One response of banks to the decline of the traditional business model was the innovation of securitization. On securitization see Gorton and Souleles (2006) and Gorton and Metrick (forthcoming a). Banks, both regulated depository institutions and other financial intermediaries, created the supply of asset-backed securities. Pozsar (2011) describes how the rise of institutional money management led to a demand for asset-backed securities. On the rise of institutional investors see Fender (2008), Gonnard, Kim, and Ynesta (2008), and Davis and Steil (2001).

The cash held by U.S. nonfinancial firms has increased significantly over the last twenty-five years. The statement in the text that "from 1980 to 2006 the ratio of cash to assets for U.S. industrial firms more than doubled from 10.5% to 23.2%" is from Bates, Kahle, and Stulz (,2008). Also see Foley, Hartzell, Titman, and Twite (2006).

Rise of Shadow Banks

On the rise of shadow banking, see Gorton (2010) and Gorton and Metrick (2010b). They also discuss the size of the repo market.

The view that the Quiet Period was in large part due to the design of bank regulation and the design of deposit insurance is closely related to the research on the decline in charter value in the late 1970s and early 1980s. Charter value is not observable, so the evidence is somewhat indirect. More research is need here to understand the Quiet Period.

Financial innovation

On the evolution of repo, see Garbade (2006). On GCF Repo, see Fleming and Garbade (2003). On the evolution of bankruptcy law, see Krimminger (2006). Innovation in the structuring of special purpose vehicles for securitization is discussed by Gorton and Metrick (forthcoming a).

10. MORAL HAZARD AND TOO-BIG-TO-FAIL

Marcus (1984) pointed out that the logic of moral hazard in banking does not work when bank charter value is high enough. That is, the logic that the shareholders should take more risk because they get the "upside" at the expense of the government is altered when bankruptcy would result in the loss of a license to valuable monopoly profits—the bank charter. Empirically it has also been hard to find evidence of moral hazard as a general phenomenon in banking. Some studies of the S and L crisis claim to have found some evidence, but even there it is not so clear whether the evidence is about looting, as described by Akerlof and Romer (1993), or "moral hazard." So an argument—"moral hazard"—that has become an accepted truth in the last twenty-five years seems to stand on rather wobbly empirical legs.

Deposit Insurance Internationally

Above, I mentioned that deposit insurance systems around the world have been studied by a number of researchers. See Demirgüç-Kunt and Detragiache (1998), Laeven (2002), Demirgüç–Kunt (1992a), Demirgüç-Kunt and Kane (2002), and Demirgüç-Kunt, Kane, and Laeven (2008).

Early Deposit Insurance Schemes

Even before the state deposit insurance plans of the early 20th century, there were experiences with pre–Civil War state insurance schemes. These included the New York Safety Fund System; see Chaddock (1910). Also see Calomiris (1990) and Weber (2010).

The state insurance schemes of the early 20th century were mostly in the Midwest and reflected the influence of the populist movement, the largest mass movement in U.S. history (see Goodwin [1978]). Kniffin (1916, 329 and 159) is the source for the information about the Kansas City Country Clearing House.

Continental of Illinois

William Isaac, who was the chairman of the Federal Deposit Insurance Corporation (FDIC) from 1981 through 1985, argued that the failure of Continental Illinois would cause other, more widespread bank runs in his statement to the House of Representatives (Isaac 1984). Volcker's view that Continental should be bailed out is mentioned in passing in Volcker (1984b). Also see Volcker (1984a).

The Continental Illinois bailout is the subject of Swary (1986) and Wall and Peterson (1990). On too-big-to-fail more generally, see Kaufman (1985), O'Hara and Shaw (1990), and Morgan and Stiroh (2005).

The takeover of Continental occurred in 1984. Seven years later the bank was sold to Bank of America. The old shareholders lost everything; the creditors and preferred shareholders lost nothing. The FDIC lost $1.6 billion. See Isaac (2009).

Panics of 1884 and 1890—Clearinghouse Rescues of Banks

The point about the New York City Clearing House bailing out banks during the Panic of 1884 and the Panic of 1890 is drawn from Wicker (2000). R. Barnett (1884) provides a narrative of what happened in 1884. Also see O. Sprague (1910). Other contemporaneous material is Coe (1884), H. Cannon (1884), and the New York Clearing House Association (1884).

Panic of 1907

Wicker (2000) also discusses J. P. Morgan and the decision not to bailout the Knickerbocker Trust. The Panic of 1907 is discussed by O. Sprague (1910), Wicker (2000), Bruner and Carr (2009), and Moen and Tallman (1992). Neal (1971) discusses the rise of trust companies in the late nineteenth century, a kind of shadow banking system at that time.

II. BANK CAPITAL

Background on bank capital is provided by Morgan (1992).

The U.S. Banking Act of 1933 required that regulators consider the "adequacy of the capital structure," but there was no attempt to enforce explicit capital requirements until 1982. Risk-based capital requirements became effective in 1990, and the passage of the Federal Deposit Insurance Corporation Improvement Act (FDICIA) in 1991 explicitly required regulators to force bank compliance. Similar trends held internationally. Some history of capital standards is provided by Keeley (1988), Morgan (1992), Baer and McElravey (1992), and Gilbert, Stone, and Trebing (1985).

In 1988 bank regulators of the G10 countries plus Switzerland and Luxembourg coordinated their policies, focusing on risk-based capital requirements. This was the "Basel Accord"; see Committee on Banking Regulations and Supervisory Practices (1987); also see Kapstein (1991). Wagster (1996, 1999) investigates the effects of the Basel standards on banks. Goodhart (2011) surveys the Basel Committee history from 1975 to 1997.

Some papers on the effects of capital requirements include Keeley (1988), Baer and McElravey (1992), and Gropp and Heider (2010). Gorton, Lewellen, Metrick (2011) discuss capital ratios in the context of the recent financial crisis.

Diamond and Rajan (2000) and Gorton and Winton (2000) discuss the theory of bank capital.

I first saw the figure showing the decline in capital ratios since 1834 in Berger, Herring, and Szegö (1995). I speculate why there has been this downward trend, which also appears to be true internationally. But research needs to be done to explain this trend. The figures showing the downward trend internationally are due to Grossman (2007), who also presents some ideas about why this might be. Brewer, Kaufman, and Wall (2008) investigate bank capital ratios around the world in the more recent period.

The idea that the long decline in bank capital ratios is due to technological change has not been formally studied. There are many aspects to the technological progress in banking that may help explain the decline in capital ratios. I only mention a few. See Redlich (1952) on the evolution of bank administration over the period 1780–1914. Carter (1992) discusses the evolution of bank liquidity and discretionary reserve management over the period 1863–1913. Prendergast (1906) discusses the evolution of credit analysis. As he puts it: "During the last ten years credit men of banks and business concerns have exhibited much interest in the study of credit" (v). He discusses the function of the credit department and the sources of information, among other topics. He also discusses the sharing of information: "Credit interchange is the latest significant development of credit economy" (203). Other aspects include the development of bankruptcy law, which makes the collection of debt easier; the development of accounting methods; etc. There are many other aspects to bank technological progress; I have only given a sense of the research on various aspects of this. There is no overall study.

12. FAT CATS, CRISIS COSTS, AND THE PARADOX OF FINANCIAL CRISES

Indonesia during the Asian Crisis

Indonesia's crisis, part of the Asian Crisis, came after thirty years of continuous growth. The crisis was devastating and is the best example of the costs of a crisis in the modern era, although if we could calculate costs more accurately, I suspect the prolonged nature of the crisis-related stagnation in Japan might also be high. On the experience of Indonesia during the Asian Crisis, see, for example, Enoch, Baldwin, Frécaut, and Kovanen (2001), Hill (1999), Batunanggar (2002), Friend (2003), and Djiwandono (2005).

Crisis Costs

There are no good measures of crisis costs, at least for a reasonable sample of countries. The literature on crisis costs focuses on gross fiscal costs and the output loss as measures of "costs." As discussed in the text, both of these measures are problematic conceptually and as a practical matter. Nevertheless, for lack of anything else, researchers have converged on these measures. There are other issues as well. A crisis must be defined and its beginning and end must be determined. Determining the end point is particularly hard. Many papers discuss these issues.

In the main text I presented bar charts showing crisis costs as the gross fiscal costs as a percentage of GDP and the output loss as a percentage of GDP. These bar charts are based on data from Laeven and Valencia (2008), who have the most extensive data. Laeven and Valencia explain:

> Gross fiscal costs are computed over the first five years following the start of the crisis using data from Hoelscher and Quintyn (2003), Honohan and Laeven (2003), IMF Staff reports, and publications from national authorities and institutions. Output losses are computed by extrapolating trend real GDP, based on the trend in real GDP growth up to the year preceding the crisis, and taking the sum of the differences between actual real GDP and trend real GDP expressed as a percentage of trend real GDP for the first four years of the crisis (including the crisis year). Minimum real GDP growth rate is the lowest real GDP growth rate during the first three years of the crisis. (6)

Other studies are in the same range of costs, but almost all are based on World Bank data, so the major differences concern the definitions of "output loss." Hoggarth, Reis, and Saporta (2001) found that the cumulative output losses incurred during crisis periods were large, estimated on the order of 15–20%, on average, of annual GDP. They study twenty-four crises reported by Caprio and Klingebiel (1999) and Barth, Caprio, and Levine (2000). Hoggarth, Reis and Saporta (2001) write:

> We find that the cumulative output losses incurred during crisis periods are large, roughly 15%–20%, on average, of annual GDP. In contrast to previous research, we also find that output losses incurred during crises in developed countries are as high, or higher, on average, than those in emerging market economies. Moreover, output losses during crisis periods in developed countries also appear to be significantly larger—10%–15%—than in neighboring countries that did not at the time experience severe banking problems.

In the main text I mention the idea of trying to match a crisis country with a similar, neighboring country that had a downturn in economic activity but no banking crisis. This is from Hoggarth, Reis, and Saporta (2001), who undertake such matching.

Also see Boyd, Kwak, and Smith (2005).

Social, Medical, and Psychic Costs

On the harder to measure, but very important, costs in this category see Currie and Tekin (2011), Hurd and Rohwedder (2010), and Deaton (2011). Currie and Tekin look at data on emergency room visits and hospital discharges in three states that have been hard hit by foreclosures. They find that in proximity foreclosed property in zip code areas of Arizona, Florida, and New Jersey there is a higher incidence of medical visits for anxiety and suicide attempts, and also of hypertension and other physical complaints. The effect is larger for blacks than whites. Hurd and Rohwedder (2010) using survey data found widespread effects of the crisis between November 2008 and April 2010. People, based on the survey, are pessimistic about the future. Similarly, Deaton (2011) finds that

> in the fall of 2008, around the time of the collapse of Lehman Brothers, and lasting into the spring of 2009, at the bottom of the stock market, Americans reported sharp declines in their life evaluation, sharp increases in worry and stress, and declines in positive affect. By the end of 2010, in spite of continuing high unemployment, these measures had largely recovered, though worry remained higher and life evaluation lower than in January 2008.

Sources of Losses: The U.S. S&L Example

There is an enormous literature on the U.S. S and L crisis. In my view, the best examples of that literature are two books, one by Black (2005) and the other by Pizzo, Fricker, and Muolo (1989); the third is a paper by Akerlof and Romer (1993). Curry and Shibut (2000) provide estimates of the cost of cleaning up the S and L crisis. A regulator's perspective is provided by Seidman (1993), who was the head of the Federal Deposit Insurance Corporation during the S and L crisis. Also see Kane (1989) and Barth (1991).

The general point that fiscal costs are related to how a crisis is resolved is also discussed and documented by Dziobek and Pazarbasioglu (1997), Frydl (1999), Hoggarth, Reis, and Saporta (2001), and Honohan and Klingebiel (2003). Also see Kaufman (1985) and Kaufman and Seelig (2002).

Acting Late: Political Problems in Reacting to Crises

In emerging markets, for example, failing banks are less likely to be taken over by the government before elections. This point is drawn from Brown and Dinç (2005). Also see Brown and Dinç (2011). Evidence on the effects of forbearance in Japan is provided by Caballero, Hoshi, and Kashyap (2008) in a classic paper. There are also problems of political interference: "Of the 86 episodes of bank insolvency (1980–94) in the Caprio-Klingebiel dataset, at least 20 of these featured 'cronyism,' meaning excessive political interference, connected lending, or similar labels" (Caprio [1998, 9]). Premature financial liberalization can also lead to problems; see Caprio (1998). Laeven and Valencia (2008) write:

> Existing empirical research has shown that providing assistance to banks and their borrowers can be counterproductive, resulting in increased losses to banks, which often abuse forbearance to take unproductive risks at government expense. The typical result of forbearance is a deeper hole in the net worth of banks, crippling tax burdens to finance bank bailouts, and even more severe credit supply contraction and economic decline than would have occurred in the absence of forbearance. (4)

For more empirical evidence on this forbearance, see Demirguc-Kunt and Detragiache (2002), Honohan and Klingebiel (2003), and Claessens, Klingebiel, and Laeven (2003). For example, Batunanggar (2008) writes:

> The inability to take fast and decisive actions in restructuring the banking system, when combined with political intervention, make the resolution of the banking crisis ineffective and costlier [De Luna-Martinez (2000), Batunanggar (2002 and 2004)]. Failure to gauge the magnitude of the problems or delays in its resolution invariably compounds the problems and costs involved (Sheng, 1992). Furthermore, in the case of Indonesia, Batunanggar (2002 and 2004) found that the absence of financial safety nets and a crisis-management framework and guidelines as well as political intervention were among the culprits behind the ineffective, prolonged, and costly resolution of its banking crisis. (citations in the original)

Also related to this topic are the works of Alesina and Drazen (1991) and Rodrik (1999).

Benefits of Crises?
Might there be benefits to allowing economies to develop fragility over time, or should governments always act to prevent credit booms? Another way to pose the question is to ask whether financial liberalization and innovation is better for economic growth than financial repression. This issue is raised by Rancière, Tornell, and Westermann (2008). They suggest that it might be the case that

> in a financially liberalized economy, systemic risk taking reduces the effective cost of capital and relaxes borrowing constraints. This allows greater investment and growth as long as a crash does not occur. Of course, when a crash does occur the short-term effects of the sudden collapse in financial intermediation are severe.

Gorton and Ordoñez (2011) present a formal model of credit booms in which it may be optimal to have fragility and crises. We simply do not yet know enough about this important topic.

13. THE PANIC OF 2007–8

More detail on the Panic of 2007–8 can be found in Bernanke (2009, 2010), the Bank for International Settlements *Annual Report* (2009), Brunnermeier (2009), Gorton (2010), Gorton and Metrick (2010a, 2010b, forthcoming b), Hördahl and King (2008), and Krishnamurthy (2010), among many other articles. Wessel (2010) provides a narrative of the crisis. Gorton (2010) and Gorton and Metrick (2010b, forthcoming b) provide empirical descriptions of the run on repo. The run in the asset-backed commercial paper market is described by Covitz, Liang, and Suarez (2009).

There are many aspects of the crisis that we do not understand because there is only scanty data. It is unfortunate that the data are not being collected, or cannot be collected, so that we can understand the crisis better.

There have been estimates of the size of the repo market, but they are just that— estimates. This is discussed in Gorton and Metrick (forthcoming b). Given that the runs were concentrated among a small group of firms—the dealer banks—perhaps repo did not need to be too large to precipitate a crisis. We do not know. Also, although we know to a fair extent the vulnerability of the dealer banks to repo, we know almost no details about what happened at each bank. One source of information is the interviews conducted by the Financial Crisis Inquiry Commission, available online at http://cybercemetery.unt.edu/archive/fcic/20110310171826/http://fcic.gov/resource/interviews.

There is, however, other evidence that helps confirm the basic story of the run on repo. Some such evidence comes from studying the Term Securities Lending Facility (TSLF), one of the Federal Reserve facilities made available during the crisis. It was adopted on March 11, 2008, specifically to address the problem that dealer banks were having with ABS, namely, that it had become difficult to use as collateral. The haircuts on this type of collateral were rising. Keep in mind that repo haircuts rising means that money is being withdrawn from banks. The TSLF was unique in that a dealer bank could borrows U.S. Treasury bonds from the Fed, posting agency bonds, ABS, or investment-grade corporate bonds as collateral. All the other facilities involve posting collateral in exchange for cash. The TSLF was the only facility where there was an exchange of one type of bond for another. Fleming, Hrung, and Keane (2010a, 2010b) and Hrung and Seligman (2011) describe and analyze the TSLF.

Hrung and Seligman focus on the unique Treasury bond for private bond exchange feature of the TSLF. But they also keep track of all the various lending programs that were changing the overall amount of Treasuries in the economy. Their main finding is that an increase in collateral due to the TSLF narrows the Fed funds–repo spread.

In other words, it helped relieve the pressure on the dealer banks by trading higher-quality collateral for lower-quality collateral.

Another type of evidence is provided by Beltratti and Stulz (forthcoming), who study two samples of large banks in thirty countries, one sample that is 165 banks with assets in excess of $50 billion and the other with 386 banks with assets in excess of $10 billion. Most of these banks are universal banks—that is, they combine depository banking with broker-dealer activities, like JP Morgan or Citi. The period analyzed is July 1, 2007, to December 31, 2008. They have many findings; here is one of their summaries: "Our evidence is inconsistent with the argument that poor governance of banks made the crisis worse, but it is supportive of theories that emphasize the fragility of banks financed with short-run capital market funding."

In the text I focused on the bilateral repo market, in which two parties privately contract. A smaller, but still very significant, part of the repo market is the triparty repo market, in which there is an intermediary, a triparty bank. See Copeland, Martin, and Walker (2010). Copeland, Martin, and Walker (2010) document that in the triparty market there weren't really successive increases in haircuts; rather, there was a precipitous withdrawal of depositors. Also see Duffie (2010).

He, Khang, and Krishnamurthy (2010, 118) is the source for the data on the increase in the balance sheets of commercial banks during the financial crisis. There are many other interesting findings as well. Overall, they find that "sectors that substantially use repo financing—in particular, the hedge fund and broker-dealer sector—have reduced asset holdings, while the commercial banking sector, which has had access to more stable funding sources, has increased asset holdings."

In discussing the lessons of the crisis, I talk about the role of the central bank. There is much that has been written about the role of the central bank. Interesting work includes Flandreau and Ugolini (2011) and Bignon, Flandreau, and Ugolini (2012). It will no doubt take years to assess the central bank interventions during the recent crisis. But in that regard see Tucker (2009), Madigan (2009), and Goodhart (2010).

14. THE THEORY AND PRACTICE OF SEEING
Gorton (1988), Calomiris and Gorton (1991), Donaldson (1992), and Grossman (1993) study the National Banking Era.

Information and the Formation of Beliefs
We don't know much empirically about how beliefs are formed. In terms of learning and measuring about beliefs, an example of what I have in mind is my paper with Ping He (Gorton and He 2008). That paper studies an infinitely repeated game with many equilibria, depending on economic agents' beliefs. In the paper, the "economic agents" are banks. Banks' beliefs depend on other banks' beliefs, and banks' beliefs about other banks' beliefs depend also on current and past information. As a theory paper, it does not have much to say with regard to policy, so one could try to theoretically narrow

down the equilibria somehow. But how? We don't know enough about how beliefs are formed.

Instead, we *empirically* determine the equilibrium, i.e., "test" the model, by parameterizing the public information that is the basis for banks' beliefs about their rivals' strategies, and we then use such measures as proxies for beliefs. In other words, we look at the information that is available to banks, and reason that, in fact, that is what banks do look at to form their beliefs. We then construct a proxy measure of beliefs that is suggested by the model. We show that the empirical behavior of U.S. bank credit card lending, commercial and industrial lending, and bank profitability is consistent with the model. Bank credit cycles are a systematic risk. Further, we found that, consistent with this, our belief proxy, called the performance difference index (PDI), is a priced factor in an asset pricing model of bank stock returns. Most importantly, the PDI is a priced factor for nonfinancial firms as well, and increasingly so as firm size declines.

The point is that "beliefs" can be studied empirically. It is not always easy to find suitable settings, and there is the necessary step of guessing at what information would be used to form beliefs. But you can get a sense of how an otherwise useless model for policy—with multiple equilibria—can become useful. A regulator can now ask what change in the information environment would help prevent the type of credit crunches that happen in the model.

But other avenues seem potentially fruitful as well. Surveys may be useful. For example, Case and Shiller (2003) use surveys to try to determine whether house prices were a bubble. Textual analysis may also be very useful. Tetlock, Saar-Tsechansky, and Macskassy (2008) quantify the language used in financial news stories and show how such a quantitative measure of language can predict individual firms' accounting earnings and stock returns. Also see Tetlock (2007).

The general question of how information production is organized in the economy and whether that effects the formation of beliefs is slowly being explored empirically. Gomes, Gorton, and Madureira (2007) show how the adoption of a particular Securities and Exchange Commission regulation resulted in an endogenous reallocation of equity analysts, away from small firms. Small firms ended up with a higher cost of capital.

NOTES

PREFACE

Epigraph: Sumner, William Graham. *A History of Banking in the United States.* (New York: Journal of Commerce and Commercial Bulletin, 1896), 415.

CHAPTER I

Epigraph: Commercial and Financial Chronicle, August 7, 1875.

1. This dating does not consider the Savings and Loans crisis as a systemic event. Although it was very expensive to close thousands of S and Ls, the crisis was contained to that category of institutions. A definition of a "financial crisis" is given below.

2. Wesley Mitchell (1874–1948) had a PhD in economics from the University of Chicago and was the founder of modern business cycle research. He was also one of the founders of the National Bureau of Economic Research and was president of the American Economic Association in 1923–24.

3. A sale and repurchase agreement (repo) is essentially the deposit of money for a short period of time in exchange for interest. Repo is collateralized with bonds, at market value. That is, the depositor takes physical possession of the collateral, but

the return on the collateral belongs to the bank, which is borrowing the money. The collateral is present to make the deposit safe.

4. After Hyman Minsky's (1982) book *Can "It" Happen Again?*

CHAPTER 2

Epigraph: Ricardo, David. *The Works of David Ricardo: With a Notice of the Life and Writings of the Author.* (London: J. Murray, 1876), 397.

1. David Ricardo (1772–1823), one of the most famous economists in history, was a member of the English Parliament, as well as a businessman. He is one of the economists credited with establishing classical economics, notably the principle of comparative advantage in trade.

2. "Greenbacks" had been issued during the Civil War just prior to the National Banking Acts. See Mitchell (1903). Also, during the American Revolution the Continental dollar was issued, but it did not trade at par.

3. The *Legal Tender* cases determined the constitutionality of the federal government issuing money. But before the *Legal Tender* cases came the case of *Veazie Bank v. Fenno* (8 Wall. 533 [1969]). The National Banking System was established in 1863, but state banknotes continued to circulate until 1865, when a federal tax of 10% was levied on state banknotes. This tax was intended to eliminate the use of private banknotes. Veazie Bank of Maine fought this to the U.S. Supreme Court, where the legality of the tax was upheld by none other than Chief Justice Samuel P. Chase, who had in fact introduced the National Bank Act legislation when he was the treasury secretary during the Civil War. Private banknotes were taxed out of existence. The Supreme Court decision upholding this was also written by Chief Justice Chase. Ironically, in the first of the *Legal Tender* cases, *Hepburn v. Griswold* (8 Wall. 603 [1870]), Chief Justice Chase, writing for the majority, held that it was unconstitutional for Congress to issue money, invalidating the legislation that he had supported. Then, in May 1871, the Court decided *Knox v. Lee* (79 U.S. 457 [1871]), which reversed Hepburn v. Griswold. See Dam (1981).

4. The timing of the panics in the table is subject to two caveats. First, the table is based on U.S. Comptroller of the Currency bank call reports, so the date of the panic is given as the nearest call report date. Also, the National Bureau of Economic Research business cycle dating is not without controversy, as the dates have been revised based on more recent—but annual—data.

CHAPTER 3

Epigraph: Gilman, Theodore. *Federal Clearing Houses.* (Boston: Houghton Mifflin, 1899), 183.

1. William N. Parker (1919–2000) had a long distinguished career at Yale, from 1963 to 1989. During World War II his studies were interrupted and he worked in the mobilization effort at the Office of Production Management and then the U.S.

Army Ordnance Corps. Parker was among the first economic historians to make systematic use of quantitative and statistical methods in economic history.

2. Unless they happened to have had a deposit at IndyMac or Washington Mutual (WaMu) "Citing a massive run on deposits, regulators shut its main branch three hours early, leaving customers stunned and upset" ("Federal Regulators Seize Crippled IndyMac Bank," *Los Angeles Times*, July 12, 2008). According to the Office of Thrift Supervision, "an outflow of deposits began on September 15, 2008, totaling $16.7 billion. With insufficient liquidity to meet its obligations, WaMu was in an unsafe and unsound condition to transact business" (OTS Press Release 08-046, "Washington Mutual Acquired by JPMorgan Chase," September 25, 2008).

CHAPTER 4

Epigraph: Robb, Thomas Bruce. *The Guaranty of Bank Deposits*. (Boston: Houghton Mifflin, 1921), ix.

1. Stock market crashes are not systemic crises. Think of the 1987 crash or the crash of the tech bubble. These were losses of enormous wealth, but they were not systemic; the financial system was not insolvent as a result.

CHAPTER 5

Epigraph: *The Nation*, September 25, 1873.

1. Hugh McCulloch (1808–95), a lawyer and banker, was the first comptroller of the currency, starting in 1863. Later, he was appointed secretary of the Treasury by President Abraham Lincoln in 1865 and continued in that role under President Andrew Johnson after the assassination of Lincoln. Later, in 1884, he again served as U.S. Treasury secretary under President Chester A. Arthur.

2. Davis Rich Dewey, the younger brother of John Dewey, the famous philosopher and educational reformer, was a professor of economics at the Massachusetts Institute of Technology and was the managing editor of the *American Economic Review* in 1911.

3. Bogue earned a PhD from Cornell and was the president of many associations, including the Economic History Association, the Agricultural History Society, and the Organization of American Historians. He was one of only three historians ever elected to the National Academy of Sciences.

4. Calvin Brice (1845–98) was born in Ohio, served in the Union Army, and got a law degree from the University of Michigan. He later became president of the Lake Erie and Western Railroad, and famously became very rich.

5. Leland H. Jenks (1892–1976) was a professor of economics and sociology at Wellesley College and also taught economic history at Columbia University.

6. Carroll Wright (1840–1909) was a lawyer who served as the first U.S. commissioner of labor from 1885 to 1905, and was in charge of the Eleventh Census in 1893.

CHAPTER 6

Epigraph: Bayles, W. Harrison. 1916. "A History of the Origin and Development of Banks and Banking and of Banks and Banking in the City of New York." *McMaster's Commercial Cases* 19:289.

1. Wesley Mitchell and Arthur Burns found an average lead of nine months. Their analysis covered twelve business cycles (1961). Arthur Burns (1904–87) was a student of Wesley Mitchell's at Columbia, where he earned his PhD in economics. He taught at Columbia, was the president of the National Bureau of Economic Research, and was chairman of the Federal Reserve System from 1970 to 1985.

2. Victor Zarnowitz fled Poland to escape the Nazis, eventually coming to the United States in 1952 and teaching at the University of Chicago. He became a leading expert on business cycles.

3. W. Jett Lauck (1879–1949) was an economist who taught at Washington and Lee University and was Secretary of the National War Labor Board, established by President Woodrow Wilson to keep disputes between workers and employers to a minimum during World War I.

4. The data are based on call reports, reports from banks to regulators on their "condition and income" that was collected five times annually at different (randomly selected months). The December shock would coincide with the 1929 stock market crash, because October 1929 was not a call report data collection month.

5. The two numbers given for bank failure percentages during the Great Depression correspond to two definitions of "failure." The first number is based on the Federal Reserve's definition of suspension; the second number is the number of banks in receivership that were closed during 1930–33 that did not reopen after the March 1933 banking holiday. The two numbers can be thought of as upper and lower bounds.

6. The nine banks were Goldman Sachs, Morgan Stanley, JPMorgan Chase, Citigroup Inc., Wells Fargo, State Street Corp., Bank of New York Mellon, and Bank of America Corp., including the soon-to-be-acquired Merrill Lynch. The CEOs present at the October 13 meeting were Vikram Pandit of Citigroup, Jamie Dimon of JP Morgan, Richard Kovacevich of Wells Fargo, John Thain of Merrill Lynch, John Mack of Morgan Stanley, Lloyd Blankfein of Goldman Sachs, Robert Kelly of Bank of New York, and Ronald Logue of State Street Bank.

7. Former U.S. Treasury secretary Hank Paulson's "CEO Talking Points" were obtained under a Freedom of Information Act request by Judicial Watch; see http://www.judicialwatch.org/files/documents/2009/Treasury-CEO-TalkingPoints.pdf

8. Available online at http://info.worldbank.org/etools/Bspan/PresentationView.asp?PID=940&EID=328.

9. Dody Tsiantar, *CNNMoney*, "Fears of a Greek Bank Run," March 9, 2010. Available online at http://money.cnn.com/2010/03/09/news/international/greece_money.fortune/index.htm.

CHAPTER 7

Epigraph: Clews, Henry. 1891. "The Late Financial Crisis." *North American Review* 152:103–13.

1. Henry Clews (1836–1923) was a cofounder of Livermore, Clews, and Company, which became the second largest marketer of federal bonds during the Civil War.

2. Richard Stone is probably one of the least known economists to have won the Nobel Prize. Few economists today could explain what he did to deserve the prize. And Stone himself seems to have been quite modest, explaining that in this diagram he rarely left the box labeled "Facts." He mostly studied the measurement of economic activity, the basic starting point for understanding economic reality.

3. Alan Turing (1912–54) was an English mathematician and cryptographer who is most famous for his foundational work in computer science and for breaking the German code during World War II.

4. The models could have included financial intermediation and security markets (1) if there had been a desire to include these aspects of reality, and (2) if there had been some consensus model(s) that were suited to being incorporated. But there are no such consensus models, and there was no desire to include them.

CHAPTER 8

Epigraph: Feller, A. H. 1933. "Moratory Legislation: A Comparative Study." *Harvard Law Review* 46:1061.

1. Henry Wysham Lanier (1873–1958) was the son of the poet Sydney Lanier and a writer in his own right. He founded Golden Book Magazine, which published 22 volumes from 1925–1939.

2. Richard Hildreth (1807-65) graduated from Harvard College in 1826 and became a lawyer and a journalist.

3. See *Laws of the State of New York, passed at the Sixty-Fourth Session of the Legislature* (1841, 347).

4. See Ohio v. Commercial Bank of Cincinnati (10 Ohio 535, 1841 WL 39 [Ohio]); Supreme Court of Ohio, In Bank. The State of Ohio, Ex Rel. The Prosecuting Attorney of Hamilton County v. The Commercial Bank of Cincinnati; The Same v. The Lafayette Bank of Cincinnati; The Same v. The Franklin Bank of Cincinnati; December Term, 1841.

5. The Commercial Bank of Natchez v. The State of Mississippi, high Court of Errors and Appeals of Mississippi, January Term, 1846 (6 Smedes & M. 599, 14 Miss. 599 [Miss. Err. & App.], 1846 WL 1659 [Miss. Err. & App.]).

6. Following the Emergency Banking Relief Act of 1933 was the Banking Act of 1933, enacted on June 16 and popularly known as the Glass-Steagall Act. It established the Federal Deposit Insurance Corporation.

7. Although in his inaugural address on March 4, 1933, Roosevelt had talked about the "money changers."

8. The speech can be heard on YouTube: http://www.youtube.com/watch?v=z9 CBpbuV3ok.

9. Ben Bernanke, chairman of Federal Reserve System, did provide a narrative in his speech at the Federal Reserve Bank of Kansas City's annual conference at Jackson Hole, Wyoming, on August 21, 2009. But his response was complicated and late, and Chairman Bernanke is not exactly part of the administration.

10. This was the same act that created the Reconstruction Finance Corporation.

11. Home Building and Loan Association v. Blaisdell (290 U.S. 398, 54 Sup.Ct. 231, 78 L.Ed. [Adv. Ops.] 255 [1934]).

CHAPTER 9

Epigraph: William Blaylock, Christopher Redman, Adam Zagorin, and Stephen Koep, "Banking Takes a Beating," *Time*, December 3, 1984.

1. Money market funds are registered investment companies that are regulated by the Securities and Exchange Commission (SEC) in accordance with Rule 2a-7 adopted pursuant to the Investment Company Act of 1940.

2. The category "mortgage-related" includes agency (GNMA, FNMA, and FHLMC) mortgage-backed securities and CMOs, CMBS, and private-label MBS/CMOs.

CHAPTER 10

Epigraph: Sprague, Irvine H. *Bailout: An Insider's Account of Bank Failures and Rescues.* (New York: Basic Books, 1986), 245.

1. The firm was notable because former president Ulysses S. Grant (the eighteenth U.S. president) and his son were involved with the firm, though Grant's name apparently only appeared for show.

2. *Inquiry Into the Continental Illinois Corp. and Continental Illinois National Bank: Hearings Before the Subcommittee on Financial Institutions Supervision, Regulation, and Insurance of Committee on Banking, Finance and Urban Affairs*, U.S. House of Representatives, 98th Cong., 2nd Sess., September (1994), 98–111; emphasis added.

3. Ibid., 288.

4. Ibid., 206.

5. Ibid., 67.

6. Ibid., 208.

7. Ibid., 300.

8. Paul Volcker, "Panel 4: The 1980s in Retrospect," in Federal Deposit Insurance Corporation (1997).

CHAPTER 11

Epigraph: Ricardo, David. *The Works of David Ricardo: With a Notice of the Life and Writings of the Author.* (London: J. Murray, 1876), 406.

1. The membership of the Basel Committee has changed over the years. Currently, it consists of Argentina, Australia, Belgium, Brazil, Canada, China, France, Germany, Hong Kong SAR, India, Indonesia, Italy, Japan, Korea, Luxembourg, Mexico, the Netherlands, Russia, Saudi Arabia, Singapore, South Africa, Spain, Sweden, Switzerland, Turkey, the United Kingdom, and the United States.

CHAPTER 12

Epigraph: John Schoen, MSNBC.com, March 29, 2009.

1. *Southern Mercury* (Dallas, TX), official journal of the Farmers' State Alliance, quoted in *Bankers' Magazine* 52 (January–June 1896): 647.

2. Quoted in Arthur Delaney, "White House Adviser: AIG Deserves 'Nobel Prize for Evil,'" *Huffington Post*, April 16, 2009, http://www.huffingtonpost.com/2009/03/16/white-house-advisor-aig-d_n_175408.html.

3. *Savings and Loan Policies in the Late 1970's and 1980's: Hearings before the House Committee on Banking, Finance, and Urban Affairs*, 101st Cong., 2d Sess., Ser. No. 101–176 (1990), 227.

4. Ed Kane has an economics PhD from MIT and is a past president of the American Finance Association.

5. http://www.ggdc.net/MADDISON/oriindex.htm.

CHAPTER 13

Epigraph: Kathleen McBride, "Dodd Delivers Vivid Speech on Financial Crisis at fi 360 Conference," *AdvisorOne*, May 5, 2011.

1. 100 basis points equals 1%.

2. A dealer bank, or broker-dealer, operates as a securities dealer by underwriting and trading publicly registered securities. Investment banks are dealer banks that do not have any depository function. Some regulated depository banks also have broker-dealer subsidiaries. Examples are Citigroup, Bank of America, and JP Morgan. Prior to the financial crisis broker-dealer banks were regulated by the Securities and Exchange Commission.

3. JP Morgan is not included because they do not report their data in a manner consistent with the other banks. Also, in the year 2000 only three of the banks reported. These data are not required to be reported, but starting in 2000 most of the dealer banks reported. There are no available data for foreign dealer banks, such as Deutsche Bank or Société General.

4. This number is unaffected by the acquisitions of Bear Sterns by JP Morgan, Merrill Lynch by Bank of America, and Wachovia by Wells Fargo, or by the Lehman failure.

5. See "Regulating the Shadow Banking System," *Brookings Papers on Economic Activity*, Fall 2010, 261–312, available at: http://papers.ssrn.com/sol3/papers.cfm? abstract_id=1676947.

CHAPTER 14

Epigraph: DeVito, Carlo. 2008. *Yogi: The Life and Times of an American Original.* Chicago: Triumph Books.

1. In 1887 Albert Michelson and Edward Morley (of what is now Case Western Reserve University) showed that the theory of luminous ether was not supported by experimental evidence and instead favored Einstein's not-yet-devised theory of special relativity. The experiment showed that light takes the same time to travel a given distance along the direction parallel to the velocity of the frame as in the transverse direction. This was the beginning of a new epoch in physics.

2. See http://www.sca.isr.umich.edu/main.php.

REFERENCES

Akerlof, George A., and Paul M. Romer. 1993. "Looting: The Economic Underworld of Bankruptcy for Profit." *Brookings Papers on Economic Activity* 2:1–73.

Alesina, Alberto, and Allan Drazen. 1991. "Why Are Stabilizations Delayed?" *American Economic Review* 82:1170–88.

Alston, Lee. 1983. "Farm Foreclosures in the United States during the Interwar Period." *Journal of Economic History* 43:885–903.

Alston, Lee. 1984. "Foreclosure Moratorium Legislation: A Lesson from the Past." *American Economic Review* 74:445–57.

Alston, Lee, Wayne Grove, and David Wheelock. 1994. "Why Do Banks Fail? Evidence from the 1920s." *Explorations in Economic History* 31:409–31.

Amundson, Roland, and Lewis Rotman. 1984. "Depression Jurisprudence Revisited: Minnesota's Moratorium on Mortgage Foreclosure." *William Mitchell Law Review* 10:805–50.

Andrew, A. Piatt. 1908a. "Substitutes for Cash in the Panic of 1907." *Quarterly Journal of Economics* 22 (2): 290–99.

Andrew, A. Piatt. 1908b. "Hoarding in the Panic of 1907." *Quarterly Journal of Economics* 22 (4): 497–516.

Andrew, A. Piatt. 1913. "The Crux of the Currency Question." *Yale Review* 2 (4): 595–620.

Angly, Edward. 1931. *Oh, Yeah?* New York: Viking.

Armantier, Olivier, Eric Ghysels, Asani Sarkar, and Jeffrey Shrader. 2011. "Stigma in Financial Markets: Evidence from Liquidity Auctions and Discount Window Borrowing during the Crisis." New York Federal Reserve Bank Staff Report 483.

Baer, Herbert, and John McElravey. 1992. "The Changing Impact of Capital Requirements on Bank Growth: 1975 to 1991." Working paper, Federal Reserve Bank of Chicago.

Bailey, Dudley. 1890. *The Clearing House System.* New York: Homans.

Bank for International Settlements. 2009. *79th Annual Report.* Basel, Switzerland: Bank for International Settlements.

Barnett, George E. 1911. "Recent Tendencies in State Banking Regulation." In "The Reform of the Currency," ed. Henry Mussey. Special issue, *Proceedings of the Academy of Political Science* 1 (2): 270–84.

Barnett, Robert. 1884. "On the Action of the New York Clearing House Association during the Recent Crisis." *Journal of the Institute of Bankers* 4 (7): 481–503.

Barth, James R. 1991. *The Great Savings and Loan Debacle.* Washington, DC: American Enterprise Institute Press.

Barth, James, Dan Brumbaugh, and Robert Litan. 1990. *Banking Industry in Turmoil: A Report on the Condition of the U.S. banking Industry and the Bank Insurance Fund.* Washington, DC: Government Printing Office.

Barth, James R., R. Dan Brumbaugh, Jr., and Robert E. Litan. 1992. *The Future of American Banking.* London: Sharpe.

Barth, James, Gerard Caprio, and Ross Levine. 2000. "Banking Systems Around the Globe: Do Regulation and Ownership Affect Performance and Stability?" In *Prudential Supervision: What Works and What Doesn't*, ed. Frederick Mishkin, 31–96. Chicago: University of Chicago Press.

Bates, Thomas, Kathleen Kahle, and René Stulz. 2008. "Why do U.S. Firms Hold So Much More Cash than They Used To?" Working paper, Ohio State University.

Batunanggar, Sukarela. 2002. "Indonesia's Banking Crisis Resolution: Lessons and the Way Forward." Working paper, Bank of Indonesia.

Batunanggar, Sukarela. 2008. *Comparison of Problem Bank Identification, Intervention and Resolution in the SEACEN Countries.* Kuala Lumpur: South East Asian Central Banks [SEACEN] Research and Training Centre.

Bayles, W. Harrison. 1916. "A History of the Origin and Development of Banks and Banking and of Banks and Banking in the City of New York." *McMaster's Commercial Cases* 19:127–328.

Beck, Thorsten. 2002. "Deposit Insurance as Private Club: Is Germany a Model?" *Quarterly Review of Economics and Finance* 42:701–19.

Beck, Thorsten, Asli Demirgüç-Kunt, and Ross Levine. 2006. "Bank Concentration, Competition, and Crises: First Results." *Journal of Banking and Finance* 30:1581–1603.

Becketti, S., and C. Morris. 1992. "Are Bank Loans Still Special?" *Economic Review* 77 (3): 71–84.

Beltratti, Andrea, and René M. Stulz. Forthcoming. "The Credit Crisis Around the Globe: Why Did Some Banks Perform Better?" *Journal of Financial Economics.*

Benveniste, Lawrence, Manoj Singh, and William Wilhelm. 1993. "The Failure of Drexel Burnham Lambert: Evidence on the Implications for Commercial Banks." *Journal of Financial Intermediation* 3:104–37.

Berger, Allen N., Richard J. Herring, and Giorgio P. Szegö. 1995. "The Role of Capital in Financial Institutions." *Journal of Banking and Finance* 19:393–430.

Berger, Allen, Anil Kashyap, and Joseph Scalise. 1995. "The Transformation of the U.S. Banking Industry: What a Long Strange Trip It's Been." *Brookings Papers on Economic Activity* 2:55–218.

Bernanke, Ben. 1983. "Non-Monetary Effects of the Financial Crisis in Propagation of the Great Depression." *American Economic Review* 73:257–76.

Bernanke, Ben. 2007. "Inflation Expectations and Inflation Forecasting." Speech at the Monetary Economics Workshop of the National Bureau of Economic Research Summer Institute, Cambridge, MA, July 10, 2007.

Bernanke, Ben. 2009. "Reflections on a Year of Crisis." Speech at the Federal Reserve Bank of Kansas City's Annual Economic Symposium, Jackson Hole, WY, August 21, 2009.

Bernanke, Ben S. 2010. "Causes of the Recent Financial and Economic Crisis." Testimony before the Financial Crisis Inquiry Commission. September 2, 2011, Washington, DC. Available online, http://www.federalreserve.gov/newsevents/testimony/bernanke20100902a.htm.

Bignon, Vincent, Marc Flandreau, and Stefano Ugolini. 2012. "Bagehot for Beginners: The Making of Lending of Last Resort Operations in the Mid-19th Century." *Economic History Review* 65:580–608.

Bishop, Joseph. 1949. "Judicial Construction of the Trading with the Enemy Act." *Harvard Law Review* 62:721–59.

Black, William K. 2005. *The Best Way to Rob a Bank Is to Own One.* Austin: University of Texas Press.

Bliss, Robert, and George Kaufman. 2007. "U.S. Corporate and Bank Insolvency Regimes: A Comparison and Evaluation." *Virginia Law and Business Review* 2:143–77.

Bodenhorn, Howard. 2000. *A History of Banking in Antebellum America: Financial Markets and Economic Development in an Era of Nation-Building.* New York: Cambridge University Press.

Bogue, Allan. 1955. *Money at Interest: The Farm Mortgage on the Middle Border.* Lincoln: University of Nebraska Press.

Bolles, Albert S. 1907. *A Treatise on the Modern Law of Banking.* Philadelphia: George T. Bisel.

Bolles, Albert S. 1910. *The National Bank Act and its Judicial Meaning*. 4th ed. Philadelphia: George T. Bisel.

Bordo, Michael, Barry Eichengreen, Daniela Klingbiel, and Maria Soledad Martinez-Peria. 2001. "Is the Crisis Problem Growing More Severe?" *Economic Policy* 16:51–82.

Bordo, Michael, and Antu Panini Murshid. 2001. "Are Financial Crises Becoming More Contagious?" In *International Financial Contagion*, ed. Stijn Claessens and Kristin Forbes, 367–403. Boston: Kluwer Academic.

Bordo, Michael, Angela Redish, and Hugh Rockoff. 2010. "Why Canada Didn't Have a Banking Crisis in 2008." Working paper, Rutgers University.

Boyd, John, Gianni De Nicolò, and Elena Loukoianova. 2011. "Banking Crises and Crisis Dating: Theory and Evidence." Working paper, University of Minnesota.

Boyd, John, and Mark Gertler. 1993. "U.S. Commercial Banking: Trends, Cycles, and Policy." *NBER Macroeconomics Annual* 8:319–77.

Boyd, John, and Mark Gertler. 1994. "Are Banks Dead? Or Are the Reports Greatly Exaggerated?" *Federal Reserve Bank of Minneapolis Quarterly Review* 18:1–27.

Boyd, John, Sungkyu Kwak, and Bruce Smith. 2005. "The Real Output Losses Associated with Modern Banking Crises." *Journal of Money, Credit and Banking* 37:977–999.

Braver, Hirsch. 1936. *Liquidation of Financial Institutions*. Indianapolis: Bobbs-Merrill.

Brewer, Elijah, III, George Kaufman, and Larry Wall. 2008. "Bank Capital Ratios across Countries: Why Do They Vary?" *Journal of Financial Services Research* 34:177–201.

Brimmer, Andrew. 1989. "Distinguished Lecture on Economics in Government: Central Banking and Systemic Risks in Capital Markets." *Journal of Economic Perspectives* 3 (2): 3–16.

Brown, Craig O., and I. Serdar Dinç. 2005. "The Politics of Bank Failures: Evidence from Emerging Markets." *Quarterly Journal of Economics* 120 (4): 1413–44.

Brown, Craig O., and I. Serdar Dinç. 2011. "Too Many to Fail? Evidence of Regulatory Forbearance when the Banking Sector is Weak." *Review of Financial Studies* 24:1378–1405.

Bruner, Robert F., and Sean D. Carr. 2009. *The Panic of 1907: Lessons Learned from the Market's Perfect Storm*. Hoboken, NJ: Wiley.

Brunnermeier, Markus. 2009. "Deciphering the Liquidity and Credit Crunch." *Journal of Economic Perspectives* 23:77–100.

Brunnermeier, Markus, Gary Gorton, and Arvind Krishnamurthy. Forthcoming. "Risk Topography." *NBER Macroeconomics Annual* 26.

Bryan, Lowell L. 1988. *Breaking Up the Bank: Rethinking an Industry Under Siege*. Homewood, IL: Dow Jones-Irwin.

Burns, Arthur, and Wesley Mitchell. 1961. "Statistical Indicators of Cyclical Revivals." In *Business Cycle Indicators*, ed. Geoffrey Moore, 162–83. New York: National Bureau of Economic Research.

Burns, Arthur, and Wesley Mitchell. 1946. *Measuring Business Cycles*. New York: National Bureau of Economic Research.

Caballero, Ricardo, Takeo Hoshi, and Anil Kashyap. 2008. "Zombie Lending and Depressed Restructuring in Japan." *American Economic Review* 98 (5): 1943–77.

Callender, William. 1858. *The Commercial Crisis of 1857: Its Causes and Results*. London: Longman.

Calomiris, Charles. 1989. "Deposit Insurance: Lessons from the Record." *Economic Perspectives—Federal Reserve Bank of Chicago*, May/June, 10–30.

Calomiris, Charles. 1990. "Is Deposit Insurance Necessary? A Historical Perspective." *Journal of Economic History* 50 (2): 283–95.

Calomiris, Charles W. 1992. "Getting the Incentives Right in the Current Deposit Insurance System: Successes from the Pre-FDIC Era." In *The Reform of Deposit Insurance: Disciplining Government and Protecting Taxpayers*, ed. James Barth and R. Dan Brumbaugh, 13–35. New York: Harper Collins.

Calomiris, Charles. 1994. "Is the Discount Window Necessary? A Penn Central Perspective." *Review—Federal Reserve Bank of St. Louis* 76 (3): 31–56.

Calomiris, Charles, and Gary Gorton. 1991. "The Origins of Banking Panics: Models, Facts, and Bank Regulation." In *Financial Markets and Financial Crises*, ed. Glenn Hubbard, 93–163. Chicago: University of Chicago Press.

Calomiris, Charles, Charles Himmelberg, and Paul Wachtel. 1995. "Commercial Paper, Corporate Finance, and the Business Cycle: A Microeconomic Perspective." *Carnegie-Rochester Conference Series on Public Policy* 42:203–50.

Calomiris, Charles, and Charles Kahn. 1996. "The Efficiency of Self-Regulated Payments Systems: Learning from the Suffolk System." *Journal of Money, Credit and Banking* 28:766–97.

Calomiris, Charles, and Joseph Mason. 1997. "Contagion and Bank Failures during the Great Depression: The June 1932 Chicago Banking Panic." *American Economic Review* 87:863–83.

Calomiris, Charles, and Joseph Mason. 2003. "Consequences of Bank Distress during the Great Depression." *American Economic Review* 93:937–47.

Calomiris, Charles, and Larry Schweikart. 1991. "The Panic of 1857: Origins, Transmission, and Containment." *Journal of Economic History* 51:807–34.

Calomiris, Charles, and Eugene White. 1994. "The Origins of Federal Deposit Insurance." In *The Regulated Economy: A Historical Approach to Political Economy*, ed. Claudia Goldin and Gary Libecap, 145–88. Chicago: University of Chicago Press.

Cannon, Henry. 1884. *Annual Report of the Comptroller of the Currency*. Washington, DC: Government Printing Office.

Cannon, James Graham. 1910a. *Clearing Houses*. Washington, DC: Government Printing Office.

Cannon, James Graham. 1910b. *Clearing House Loan Certificates, and Substitutes for Money Used During the Panic of 1907*. New York: Trow Press.

Caprio, Gerard. 1998. "Banking on Crises: Expensive Lessons from Recent Financial Crises." Working paper, World Bank.

Caprio, Gerard, and Daniela Klingebiel. 1996. "Bank Insolvencies: Cross Country Experience." Policy Research Working Paper 1620, World Bank.

Caprio, Gerard, Jr., and Daniela Klingebiel. 1997. "Bank Insolvency: Bad Luck, Bad Policy, or Bad Banking?" *Annual World Bank Conference on Development Economics 1996.*

Caprio, Gerard, and Daniela Klingebiel. 2000. "Bank Insolvencies: Cross Country Experience," Policy Research Discussion Paper 1620.

Caprio, Gerard, and Daniela Klingebiel. 2003. "Episodes of Systemic and Borderline Financial Crises." World Bank Dataset. Available online, http://go.worldbank.org/5DYGICS7B0.

Caprio, Gerard, Daniela Klingebiel, Luc Laeven, and Guillermo Noguera, comps. 2005. "Appendix: Banking Crisis Database." In *Systemic Financial Crises: Containment and Resolution,* ed. Patrick Honohan and Luc Laeven, 307–40. Cambridge, UK: Cambridge University Press.

Carlson, Mark. 2005. "Causes of Bank Suspensions in the Panic of 1893." *Explorations in Economic History* 42:56–80.

Carter, J. M. 1992. *Commercial Bank Liquidity Management, Discretionary Reserve Behavior, and the Allocation of Credit, 1863–1913.* New York: Garland.

Caruana, Jaime. 2010. "Basel III: Towards a Safer Financial System." Speech at the Third Santander International Banking Conference, Madrid, September 15, 2010. Available online, http://www.bis.org/speeches/sp100921.pdf.

Case, Karl, and Robert Shiller. 2003. "Is There a Bubble in the Housing Market?" *Brookings Papers on Economic Activity,* no. 2, 299–342.

Cerra, Valerie, and Sweta Chaman Saxena. 2008. "Growth Dynamics: The Myth of Economic Recovery." *American Economic Review* 98 (1): 439–57.

Chaddock, Robert E. 1910. *The Safety Fund Banking System in New York State, 1829–1866.* Washington, DC: Government Printing Office.

Chandler, Alfred, ed. 1965. *The Railroads: The Nation's First Big Business.* New York: Harcourt, Brace & World.

Chari, V. V. 1998. "Nobel Laureate Robert E. Lucas, Jr.: Architect of Modern Macroeconomics." *Journal of Economic Perspectives* 12:171–86.

Chevalier, Michael. 1839. *Society, Manners and Politics in the United States.* Boston: Weeks, Jordan.

Claessens, Stijn, Daniela Klingebiel, and Luc Laeven. 2003. "Financial Restructuring in Banking and Corporate Sector Crises: What Policies to Pursue?" In *Managing Currency Crises in Emerging Markets,* ed. Michael Dooley and Jeffrey Frankel, 147–80. Chicago: University of Chicago Press.

Clark, Washington Augustus. 1922. *The History of the Banking Institutions Organized in South Carolina Prior to 1860.* Columbia: Historical Commission of South Carolina.

Clews, Henry. 1891. "The Late Financial Crisis." *North American Review* 152:103–13.

Coe, George S. 1884. "Address of George S. Coe." *Bankers' Magazine*, July, 44–51.

Coleman, Peter. 1974. *Debtors and Creditors in America*. Madison: State Historical Society of Wisconsin.

Collyns, Charles, and Abdelhak Senhadji. 2002. "Lending Booms, Real Estate Bubbles, and the Asian Financial Crisis." IMF Working Paper 02/20. Washington, DC: International Monetary Fund.

Committee on Banking Regulations and Supervisory Practices. 1987. *Proposals for International Convergence of Capital Measurement and Capital Standards*. Basel, Switzerland: Bank for International Settlements.

Cook, Timothy, and Jeremy Duffield. 1979. "Money Market Mutual Funds: A Reaction to Government Regulations or a Lasting Financial Innovation?" *Economic Review—Federal Reserve Bank of Richmond*, July/August, 15–31.

Cooke, Thornton. 1909. "The Insurance of Bank Deposits in the West." *Quarterly Journal of Economics* 24:85–108.

Copeland, Adam, Antoine Martin, and Michael Walker. 2010. *The Tri-Party Repo Market before the 2010 Reforms*. Federal Reserve Bank of New York Staff Report 477.

Covitz, Daniel, Nellie Liang, and Gustavo Suarez. 2009. "The Evolution of a Financial Crisis: Runs in the Asset-Backed Commercial Paper Market." Working Paper 2009–36, Board of Governors of the Federal Reserve System.

Currie, Janet, and Erdal Tekin. 2011. "Is the Foreclosure Crisis Making Us Sick?" Working Paper 17310, National Bureau of Economic Research.

Curry, Timothy, and Lynn Shibut. 2000. "The Cost of the Savings and Loan Crisis: Truth and Consequences." *FDIC Banking Review* 13:26–35.

Dam, Kenneth. 1981. "The Legal Tender Cases." *Supreme Court Review* 1981:367–412.

Dang, Tri Vi, Gary Gorton, and Bengt Holmström. 2011. "Ignorance and the Optimality of Debt." Working paper, Yale and MIT.

D'Arista, Jane W., and Tom Schlesinger. 1992. "The Parallel Banking System." Unpublished paper, Economic Policy Institute, Washington, DC.

Davis, E. Philip, and Benn Steil. 2001. *Institutional Investors*. Cambridge, MA: MIT Press.

Davis, Joseph H. 2004. "An Annual Index of U.S. Industrial Production, 1790–1915." *Quarterly Journal of Economics* 119 (4): 1177–1215.

Davis, Joseph. 2006. "An Improved Annual Chronology of U.S. Business Cycles since the 1790s." *Journal of Economic History* 66:103–21.

Deaton, Angus. 2011. "The Financial Crisis and the Well-Being of Americans." Working Paper 17128, National Bureau of Economic Research.

della Paolera, Gerardo, and Alan Taylor. 2001. *Straining at the Anchor: The Argentine Currency Board and the Search for Macroeconomic Stability, 1880–1935*. Chicago: University of Chicago Press.

Dell'Ariccia, Giovanni, Enrica Detragiache, and Raghuram Rajan. 2008. "The Real Effects of Banking Crises." *Journal of Financial Intermediation* 17:89–112.

Demirgüç–Kunt, Asli. 1992a. "Do 'Vulnerable' Economies Need Deposit Insurance?: Lessons from U.S. Agriculture in the 1920s." In *If Texas Were Chile: A Primer on Banking Reform*, ed. Philip L. Brock, 237–314. San Francisco: Institute for Contemporary Studies Press.

Demirgüç–Kunt, Asli. 1992b. "Response." In *If Texas Were Chile: A Primer on Banking Reform*, ed. Philip L. Brock, 319–28. San Francisco: Institute for Contemporary Studies Press.

Demirgüç-Kunt, Asli, and Enrica Detragiache. 1998. "The Determinants of Banking Crises: Evidence from Developing and Developed Countries." *IMF Staff Papers* 45 (1): 81–109.

Demirgüç-Kunt, Asli, and Enrica Detragiache. 2002. "Does Deposit Insurance Increase Banking System Stability? An Empirical Investigation." *Journal of Monetary Economics* 49:1373–1406.

Demirgüç-Kunt, Asli, and Enrica Detragiache. 2005. "Cross-Country Empirical Studies of Systemic Bank Distress: A Survey." *National Institute of Economic Review* 192.

Demirgüç-Kunt, Asli, and Edward Kane. 2002. "Deposit Insurance around the Globe: Where Does It Work?" *Journal of Economic Perspectives* 16 (2): 175–95.

Demirgüç-Kunt, Asli, Edward Kane, and Luc Laeven. 2008. *Deposit Insurance around the World*. Cambridge, MA: MIT Press.

Demirgüç-Kunt, Asli, Baybars Karacaovali, and Luc Laeven. 2005. "Deposit Insurance around the World: A Comprehensive Data Base." World Bank Working Paper WPS 3628.

Demsetz, Rebecca, Marc Saidenberg, and Philip Strahan. 1996. "Banks with Something to Lose: The Disciplinary Role of Franchise Value." *FRBNY Economic Policy Review* 2 (2): 1–14.

DeVito, Carlo. 2008. *Yogi: The Life and Times of an American Original*. Chicago: Triumph Books.

Dewey, Davis Rich. 1918. *Financial History of the United States*. New York: Longmans, Green.

Diamond, Douglas, and Philip Dybvig. 1983. "Bank Runs, Deposit Insurance, and Liquidity." *Journal of Political Economy* 91:401–19.

Diamond, Douglas W., and Raghuram G. Rajan. 2000. "A Theory of Bank Capital." *Journal of Finance* 55:2431–65.

Dillistin, William. 1949. *Bank Note Reporters and Counterfeit Detectors, 1826–1866*. American Numismatic Notes and Monographs 114. New York: American Numismatic Society.

Djiwandono, J. Soedradjad. 2005. *Bank Indonesia and the Crisis: An Insider's View*. Singapore: Institute of Southeast Asian Studies.

Donaldson, R. Glen. 1992. "Sources of Panics, Evidence from the Weekly Data." *Journal of Monetary Economics* 29:277–305.

Donaldson, R. Glen. 1993. "Financing Banking Crises: Lessons from the Panic of 1907." *Journal of Monetary Economics* 31:69–95.

Dove, John. n.d. "Credible Commitments and Constitutional Constraints: State Debt Repudiation and Default in 19th Century America." Working paper, West Virginia University.

Dow, James, and Gary Gorton. 1997. "Stock Market Efficiency and Economic Efficiency: Is There a Connection?" *Journal of Finance* 52 (3): 1087–1130.

Dreher, Axel, Jan-Egbert Sturm, and Jakob De Haan. 2010. "When Is a Central Bank Governor Replaced? Evidence Based on a New Data Set." *Journal of Macroeconomics* 32:766–81.

Duffie, Darrell. 2010. *How Big Banks Fail and What to Do About It.* Princeton, NJ: Princeton University Press.

Dunbar, Charles. 1887. "Deposits as Currency." *Quarterly Journal of Economics* 1:401–19.

Dwyer, Gerald. 1996. "Wildcat Banking, Banking Panics, and Free Banking in the United States." *Economic Review—Federal Reserve Bank of Atlanta*, December, 1–20.

Dwyer, Gerald P., and R. Alton Gilbert. 1989. "Bank Runs and Private Remedies." *Review—Federal Reserve Bank of St. Louis*, May/June, 43–61.

Dziobek, Claudia, and Ceyla Pazarbasioglu. 1997. "Lessons from Systemic Bank Restructuring: A Survey of 24 Countries." IMF Working Paper 97/161.

Eccles, George S. 1982. *The Politics of Banking.* Salt Lake City: University of Utah, Graduate School of Business.

Economopoulos, Andrew, and Heather O'Neill. 1995. "Bank Entry during the Antebellum Period." *Journal of Money, Credit and Banking* 27:1071–85.

Edwards, Franklin, and Frederic Mishkin. 1995. "The Decline of Traditional Banking: Implications for Financial Stability and Regulatory Policy." *FRBNY Economic Policy Review*, July, 27–45.

Eichengreen, B., and M. Bordo. 2002. "Crises Now and Then: What Lessons from the Last Era of Financial Globalization." NBER Working Paper 8716, National Bureau of Economic Research, Cambridge, MA.

Eichengreen, Barry, and Kris Mitchener. 2003. "The Great Depression as a Credit Boom Gone Wrong." Bank for International Settlements Working Paper 137.

English, William B. 1996. "Understanding the Costs of Sovereign Default: American State Debts in the 1840's." *American Economic Review* 86:259–75.

Enoch, Charles, Barbara Baldwin, Olivier Frécaut, and Arto Kovanen. 2001. "Indonesia: Anatomy of a Banking Crisis, Two Years of Living Dangerously, 1997–99." Working Paper WP/01/52, International Monetary Fund.

Federal Deposit Insurance Corporation. 1997. *History of the 80s: Lessons for the Future.* Vol. 1, *An Examination of the Banking Crises of the 1980s and Early 1990s.* Washington, DC: Federal Deposit Insurance Corporation.

Federal Reserve Bank of Boston. n.d. *Closed for the Holiday: The Bank Holiday of 1933.* Boston: Federal Reserve Bank of Boston.

Feller, A. H. 1933. "Moratory Legislation: A Comparative Study." *Harvard Law Review* 46:1061–85.

Fels, Rendigs. 1951. "American Business Cycles, 1865–79." *American Economic Review* 41 (3): 325–49.

Fels, Rendigs. 1952. "The American Business Cycle of 1879–85." *Journal of Political Economy* 60:60–75.

Fender, Ingo. 2008. "Institutional Asset Managers: Industry Trends, Incentives and Implications for Market Efficiency." *Bank for International Settlements Quarterly Review,* September, 75–86.

Fettig, David. 2008. "The History of a Powerful Paragraph." *The Region,* June, 33–34.

Financial Crisis Inquiry Commission. 2011. *Report.* New York: Public Affairs.

Fisher, Willard. 1895. "Money and Credit Paper in the Modern Market." *Journal of Political Economy* 3:391–413.

Fishlow, Albert. 1965. *American Railroads and the Transformation of the American Economy.* Cambridge, MA: Harvard University Press.

Flandreau, Marc, and Stefano Ugolini. 2011. "Where It All Began: Lending of Last Resort and the Bank of England during the Overend, Gurney Panic of 1866." Geneva Graduate Institute of International and Development Studies Working Paper 04/2011.

Fleming, Michael, and Kenneth Garbade. 2003. "The Repurchase Agreement Refined: GCF Repo." *Current Issues in Economics and Finance* 9 (6): 1–7.

Fleming, Michael J., Warren B. Hrung, and Frank M. Keane. 2010a. *Repo Market Effects of the Term Securities Lending Facility.* Federal Reserve Bank of New York Staff Report 426.

Fleming, Michael J., Warren B. Hrung, and Frank M. Keane. 2010b. "Repo Market Effects of the Term Securities Lending Facility." *American Economic Review Papers and Proceedings* 100:591–96.

Flood, Mark. 1992. "The Great Deposit Insurance Debate." *Review—Federal Reserve Bank of St. Louis,* July/August, 51–77.

Fogel, Robert. 1964. *Railroads and American Economic Growth: Essays in Econometric History.* Baltimore: Johns Hopkins University Press.

Fogel, Robert. 1971. "Railroads and American Economic Growth." In *The Reinterpretation of American Economic History,* ed. Robert Fogel and Stanley Engerman, 187–207. New York: Harper & Row.

Foley, C. Fritz, Jay Hartzell, Sheridan Titman, and Garry Twite. 2006. "Why Do Firms Hold So Much Cash? A Tax-Based Explanation." NBER Working Paper 12649.

Folkerts-Landau, David, and Takatoshi Ito. 1995. "Evolution of the Mexican Crisis." *IMF International Capital Markets: Developments, Prospects and Policy Issues, International Monetary Fund,* October, 53–69.

Frazer, William, and John J. Guthrie, Jr. 1995. *The Florida Land Boom: Speculation, Money and the Banks.* Westport, CT: Quorum.

Friedman, Milton, and Anna Schwartz. 1963. *A Monetary History of the United States, 1867–1960.* Princeton, NJ: Princeton University Press.

Friend, Theodore. 2003. *Indonesian Destinies.* Cambridge, MA: Belknap Press of Harvard University Press.

Frydl, Edward. 1999. "The Length and Cost of Banking Crises." IMF Working Paper 99/30.

Fuhrer, Jeffrey. 1995. "The Phillips Curve is Alive and Well." *New England Economic Review—Federal Reserve Bank of Boston,* March/April, 41–56.

Gali, Jordi, and Luca Gambetti. 2008. "On the Sources of the Great Moderation." Working Paper 14171, National Bureau of Economic Research.

Garbade, Kenneth. 2006. "The Evolution of Repo Contracting Conventions in the 1980s." *FRBNY Economic Policy Review,* May, 27–42.

Gayer, A. D. 1935. "The Banking Act of 1935." *Quarterly Journal of Economics* 50:97–116.

Gibbons, J. S. 1859. *The Banks of New York, Their Dealers, the Clearing House, and the Panic of 1857.* New York: D. Appleton.

Gilbert, R. Alton. 2000. "The Advent of the Federal Reserve and the Efficiency of the Payments System: The Collection of Checks, 1915–1930." *Explorations in Economic History* 37:121–48.

Gilbert, R. Alton, Courtenay Stone, and Michael Trebing. 1985. "The New Bank Capital Adequacy Standards." *Review—Federal Reserve Bank of St. Louis,* May, 12–20.

Gil-Diaz, Francisco. 1998. "The Origins of Mexico's 1994 Financial Crisis." *Cato Journal* 17:303–13.

Gil-Diaz, Francisco, and Agustín Carstens. 1996. "One Year of Solitude: Some Pilgrim Tales about Mexico's 1994–1995 Crisis." *American Economic Review* 86:164–69.

Gilman, Theodore. 1899. *Federal Clearing Houses.* Boston: Houghton, Mifflin.

Ginzberg, Eli. 2004. *The Illusion of Economic Stability.* New Brunswick, NJ: Transaction. First published 1939.

Golembe, Carter. 1960. "The Deposit Insurance Legislation of 1933: An Examination of Its Antecedents and its Purposes." *Political Science Quarterly* 75:181–200.

Gomes, Armando, Gary Gorton, and Leonardo Madureira. 2007. "SEC Regulation FD, Information, and the Cost of Capital." *Journal of Corporate Finance* 13:300–334.

Gonnard, Eric, Eun Jung Kim, and Isabelle Ynesta. 2008. *Recent Trends in Institutional Investors Statistics.* Financial Market Trends (OECD).

Goodhart, Charles. 2010. "The Changing Role of Central Banks," Bank for International Settlements Working Paper 326.

Goodhart, Charles. 2011. *The Basel Committee on Banking Supervision: A History of the Early Years, 1974–1997*. Cambridge, UK: Cambridge University Press.

Goodwin, Lawrence. 1978. *The Populist Movement: A Short History of the Agrarian Revolt in America*. New York: Oxford University Press.

Gorton, Gary. 1984. "Private Bank Clearinghouses and the Origins of Central Banking." *Business Review—Federal Reserve Bank of Philadelphia*, January/February, 3–12.

Gorton, Gary. 1985a. "Bank Suspension of Convertibility." *Journal of Monetary Economics* 15:177–93.

Gorton, Gary. 1985b. "Clearinghouses and the Origin of Central Banking in the United States." *Journal of Economic History* 45 (2): 277–83.

Gorton, Gary. 1988. "Banking Panics and Business Cycles." *Oxford Economic Papers* 40 (4): 751–81.

Gorton, Gary. 1996. "Reputation Formation in Early Bank Note Markets." *Journal of Political Economy* 104 (2): 346–97.

Gorton, Gary. 1999. "Pricing Free Bank Notes." *Journal of Monetary Economics* 44:33–64.

Gorton, Gary. 2010. *Slapped by the Invisible Hand: The Panic of 2007*. New York: Oxford University Press.

Gorton, Gary, and Ping He. 2008. "Bank Credit Cycles." *Review of Economic Studies* 75:1181–1214.

Gorton, Gary, and Lixin Huang. 2003. "Banking Panics and the Origin of Central Banking." In *Evolution and Procedures in Central Banking*, ed. David Altig and Bruce Smith, 181–219+. Cambridge, UK: Cambridge University Press.

Gorton, Gary, and Lixin Huang. 2006. "Banking Panics and Endogenous Coalition Formation." *Journal of Monetary Economics* 53 (7): 1613–29.

Gorton, Gary, Stefan Lewellen, and Andrew Metrick. 2011. "Bank Capital and Survival during the Financial Crisis." Working paper, Yale School of Management.

Gorton, Gary, and Andrew Metrick. 2010a. "Haircuts." *Review—Federal Reserve Bank of St. Louis* 92 (6), 507–20.

Gorton, Gary, and Andrew Metrick. 2010b. "Regulating the Shadow Banking System." *Brookings Papers on Economic Activity*, Fall, 261–97.

Gorton, Gary, and Andrew Metrick. Forthcoming a. "Securitization." In *Handbook of the Economics of Finance*, vol. 2, edited by George M. Constantinides, Milton Harris, and René M. Stulz. Amsterdam: Elsevier.

Gorton, Gary, and Andrew Metrick. Forthcoming b. "Securitized Banking and the Run on Repo," *Journal of Financial Economics*.

Gorton, Gary, and Don Mullineaux. 1987. "The Joint Production of Confidence: Endogenous Regulation and Nineteenth Century Commercial Bank Clearinghouses." *Journal of Money, Credit, and Banking* 19 (4): 458–68.

Gorton, Gary, and Guillermo Ordoñez. 2011. "Collateral Crises." Working paper, Yale.

Gorton, Gary, and George Pennacchi. 1993a. "Financial Intermediaries and Liquidity Creation." *Journal of Finance* 45:49–72.

Gorton, Gary, and George Pennacchi. 1993b. "Money Market Funds and Finance Companies: Are They the Banks of the Future?" In *Structural Change in Banking,* ed. Michael Klausner and Lawrence White, 173–214. Homewood, IL: Irwin.

Gorton, Gary, and Richard Rosen. 1995. "Corporate Control, Portfolio Choice, and the Decline of Banking." *Journal of Finance* 50 (5): 1377–1420.

Gorton, Gary, and Nicholas S. Souleles. 2006. "Special Purpose Vehicles and Securitization." In *The Risks of Financial Institutions,* ed. Rene Stulz and Mark Carey, 549–602. Chicago: University of Chicago Press.

Gorton, Gary B., and Andrew Winton. 2000. "Liquidity Provision, Bank Capital, and the Macroeconomy." Working paper; abstract online at http://papers.ssrn.com/sol3/papers.cfm?abstract_id=253849.

Gould, John. 1904. *The National Bank Act, with All Its Amendments Annotated and Explained.* Boston: Little, Brown.

Gourinchas, Pierre-Olivier, Rodrigo Valdes, and Oscar Landerretche. 2001. "Lending Booms: Latin America and the World." *Economia* 1:47–99.

Greenwood, Jeremy. 1994. "Modern Business Cycle Analysis." Unpublished paper.

Gropp, Reint, and Florian Heider. 2010. "The Determinants of Bank Capital Structure." *Review of Finance* 14:1–36.

Grossman, Richard. 1993. "The Macroeconomic Consequences of Bank Failures under the National Banking System." *Explorations in Economic History* 30:294–320.

Grossman, Richard. 1994. "The Shoe That Didn't Drop: Explaining Banking Stability During the Great Depression." *Journal of Economic History* 54:654–82.

Grossman, Richard S. 2007. "Other People's Money: The Evolution of Bank Capital in the Industrialized World." In *The New Comparative Economic History: Essays in Honor of Jeffrey G. Williamson,* ed. Tim Hatton, Kevin O'Rourke, and Alan Taylor, 141–63. Cambridge, MA: MIT Press.

Hagerty, James. 1913. *Mercantile Credit.* New York: Henry Holt.

Hammond, Bray. 1957. *Banks and Politics in America, from the Revolution to the Civil War.* Princeton, NJ: Princeton University Press.

Hardy, Daniel, and Ceyla Pazarbaşioğlu. 1998. "Leading Indicators of Banking Crises: Was Asia Different?" International Monetary Fund Working Paper WP/98/91.

Hasan, Iftekhar, and Gerald Dwyer. 1994. "Bank Runs in the Free Banking Period." *Journal of Money, Credit and Banking* 26:271–88.

He, Zhiguo, In Gu Khang, and Arvind Krishnamurthy. 2010. "Balance Sheet Adjustments during the 2008 Crisis." *IMF Economic Review* 58:118–56.

Hepburn, A. Barton. 1915. *A History of Currency in the United States.* New York: Macmillan.

Herrick, Myron T. 1908. "The Panic of 1907 and Some of Its Lessons." In "Lessons of the Financial Crisis (1908)." Special issue, *ANNALS of the American Academy of Political and Social Science* 31 (2): 8–25.

Hibbard, Benjamin Horace. (1924) 1965. *A History of the Public Land Policies*. Madison: University of Wisconsin Press.

Hilbers, Paul, Qin Lei, and Lisbeth Zacho. 2001. "Real Estate Market Developments and Financial Sector Soundness." IMF Working Paper WP/01/129.

Hildreth, Richard. 1840. *Banks, Banking and Paper Currencies*. Boston: Whipple & Damrell.

Hill, Hal. 1999. *The Indonesian Economy in Crisis: Causes, Consequences and Lessons*. Singapore: Institute of Southeast Asian Studies.

Hoelscher, David, and Marc Quintyn. 2003. "Managing Systemic Banking Crises." IMF Occasional Paper 224. Washington, DC: International Monetary Fund.

Hoggarth, Glenn, Ricardo Reis, and Victoria Saporta. 2001. "Costs of Banking System Instability: Some Empirical Evidence." Working paper, Bank of England.

Holmström, Bengt. 2008. "Commentary: The Panic of 2007." In *Maintaining Stability in a Changing Financial System*. Proceedings of the 2008 Jackson Hole Conference, Federal Reserve Bank of Kansas City. Available online, http://www.kc.frb.org/publicat/sympos/2008/Holmstrom.03.12.09.pdf.

Holmström, Bengt. 2010. "Comment on 'The Credit Rating Crisis,' by Efraim Benmelech and Jennifer Dlugosz." *NBER Macroeconomics Annual* 24:215–22.

Holmström, Bengt. 2012. "The Nature of Liquidity Provision: When Ignorance is Bliss," Presidential Address, Econometric Society, ASSA Meetings, Chicago, January 5–8. Slides available online, http://economics.mit.edu/files/7500.

Honohan, Patrick, and Daniela Klingebiel. 2003. "Controlling the Fiscal Costs of Banking Crises." *Journal of Banking and Finance* 27:1539–60.

Honohan, Patrick, and Luc Laeven, eds. 2005. *Systemic Financial Crises: Containment and Resolution*. Cambridge, UK: Cambridge University Press.

Hördahl, Peter, and Michael King. 2008. "Developments in Repo Markets during the Financial Turmoil." *BIS Quarterly*, December, 37–53.

House of Commons, Treasury Committee. 2008, *The Run on the Rock*. 2 vols. Fifth Report of Session 2007–8, HC 56-I.

Hoyt, Homer. 1933. *One Hundred Years of Land Values in Chicago*. New York: Arno.

Hrung, Warren, and Jason Seligman. 2011. "Responses to the Financial Crisis: Treasury Debt, and the Impact on Short-Term Money Markets." Federal Reserve Bank of New York Staff Report 481.

Hume, Michael, and Andrew Sentence. 2009. "The Global Credit Boom: Challenges for Macroeconomics and Policy." Discussion Paper 27, Bank of England.

Humphrey, David, and Lawrence Pulley. 1997. "Banks' Responses to Deregulation: Profits, Technology, and Efficiency." *Journal of Money, Credit and Banking* 29:73–93.

Hüpkes, Eva. 2005. "Insolvency—Why a Special Regime for Banks." *Current Developments in Monetary and Financial Law* 3:471–514.

Hurd, Michael, and Susann Rohwedder. 2010. "Effects of the Financial Crisis and Great Recession on American Households." RAND Labor and Population Working Paper 810.

Hurley, Evelyn. 1977. "The Commercial Paper Market." *Federal Reserve Bulletin* 63:525–27.

Huston, James. 1983. "Western Grains and the Panic of 1857." *Agricultural History* 57:14–32.

Huston, James. 1987. *The Panic of 1857 and the Coming of the Civil War*. Baton Rouge: Louisiana State University Press.

International Capital Market Association. 2007. *European Repo Market Survey* 13.

Investment Company Institute. 2011. *2011 Investment Company Fact Book*, 51st ed. http://www.icifactbook.org/.

Isaac, William. 1984. "Statement on Federal Assistance to Continental Illinois Corporation and Continental Illinois National Bank," presented to the Subcommittee on Financial Institutions Supervision, Regulation and Insurance of the Committee on Banking, Finance and Urban Affairs, House of Representatives, Washington, DC, October 4.

Isaac, William. 2009. "Bank Nationalization Isn't the Answer." *Wall Street Journal*, February 24, 2009.

Jalil, Andrew. 2009. "A New History of Banking Panics in the United States, 1825–1929: Construction and Implications." Working paper, University of California, Berkeley.

Jaremski, Matthew. 2010. "Free Bank Failures: Risky Bonds versus Undiversified Portfolios." *Journal of Money, Credit and Banking* 42:1565–87.

Jenks, Leland H. 1944. "Railroads as an Economic Force in American Development." *Journal of Economic History* 4:1–20.

Johnson, Joseph. 1910. "The Canadian Banking System and Its Operation under Stress." *Annals of the American Academy of Political and Social Science* 36:60–84.

Joint Economic Committee, United State Congress. 2003. *Argentina's Economic Crisis: Causes and Cures*. Washington, DC: Joint Economic Committee.

Journalist, A [pseud.]. 1873. *The Terrible Panic of 1873*. Chicago: Western News.

Kagan, Robert. 1984. "The Routinization of Debt Collection: An Essay on Social Change and Conflict in the Courts." *Law and Society Review* 18:323–72.

Kaminsky, Graciela, and Carmen Reinhart. 1999. "The Twin Crises: The Causes of Banking and Balance-of-Payments Problems." *American Economic Review* 89 (3): 473–500.

Kane, Edward J. 1989. *The S & L Insurance Mess: How Did It Happen?* Washington, DC: Urban Institute Press.

Kapstein, Ethan B. 1991. *Supervising International Banks: Origins and Implications of the Basle Accord*. Princeton Essays in International Finance. Princeton, NJ: International Finance Section, Dept. of Economics, Princeton University.

Kaufman, George G. 1985. "Implications of Large Bank Problems and Insolvencies for the Banking System and Economic Policy." Staff Memoranda 85–3, Federal Reserve Bank of Chicago.

Kaufman, George, and Steven Seelig. 2002. "Minimizing Post-Resolution Costs in Bank Failures." Working paper, Loyola University Chicago.

Keefer, Philip. 2007. "Elections, Special Interests, and Financial Crisis." *International Organization* 61 (3): 607–41.

Keeley, Michael C. 1988. "Bank Capital Regulation in the 1980s: Effective or Ineffective?" *Economic Review—Federal Reserve Bank of San Francisco*, Winter, 3–20.

Keeley, Michael. 1990. "Deposit Insurance, Risk, and Market Power in Banking." *American Economic Review* 80 (5): 1183–1200.

Keeley, Michael, and Gary Zimmerman. 1984. "Competition for Money Market Deposit Accounts." *Federal Reserve Bank of San Francisco Weekly Letter*, July 13.: 5-27.

Kelley, Morgan, and Cormac Ó Gráda. 2000. "Market Contagion: Evidence from the Panics of 1854 and 1857." *American Economic Review* 90 (5): 1110–24.

Keynes, John Maynard. 1930. *A Treatise on Money.* Vol. 2, *The Applied Theory of Money.* London: Macmillan.

Kidwell, David, and Charles Trzcinka. 1979. "The Risk Structure of Interest Rates and the Penn-Central Crisis." *Journal of Finance* 34 (3): 751–60.

Kindleberger, Charles. 1986. "A Further Comment." In *Economic History and the Modern Economist*, ed. William N. Parker, 83–92. Oxford: Blackwell.

Kindleberger, Charles. 2005. *Manias, Panics, and Crashes: A History of Financial Crises.* 5th ed. Hoboken, NJ: John Wiley.

Kinley, David. 1897. "Credit Instruments in Business Transactions." *Journal of Political Economy* 5:157–74.

Kinley, David. 1910. *The Use of Credit Instruments in Payments in the United States.* Washington, DC: National Monetary Commission.

Knapp, John. 1983. "Minnesota Foreclosure Relief Act: How It Works." *Minnesota Real Estate Law Journal* 1:190–200.

Kniffin, William Henry. 1916. *The Practical Work of a Bank.* 2nd ed. New York: Bankers Publishing.

Knox, John Jay. 1900. *A History of Banking in the United States.* New York: Bradford Rhodes.

Krimminger, Michael. 2006. "The Evolution of U.S. Insolvency Law for Financial Market Contracts." Working paper, FDIC.

Krishnamurthy, Arvind. 2010. "How Debt Markets Have Malfunctioned in the Crisis." *Journal of Economic Perspectives* 24:3–28.

Krugman, Paul. 2009. "How Did Economists Get It So Wrong?" *New York Times*, September 6.

Kydland, Finn, and Edward Prescott. 1982. "Time to Build and Aggregate Fluctuations." *Econometrica* 50:1345–70.

Kydland, Finn, and Edward Prescott. 1990. "Business Cycles: Real Facts and a Monetary Myth." *Federal Reserve Bank of Minneapolis Quarterly Review*, Spring, 1–17.

Kydland, Finn E., and Edward C. Prescott. 1996. "The Computational Experiment: An Econometric Tool." *Journal of Economic Perspectives* 10:69–85.

Laeven, Luc. 2002. "International Evidence on the Value of Deposit Insurance." *Quarterly Review of Economics and Finance* 42:721–32.

Laeven, Luc, and Fabian Valencia. 2008. "Systemic Banking Crises: A New Database." International Monetary Fund Working Paper WP/08/224.

Lake, Wilfred. 1947. "The End of the Suffolk System." *Journal of Economic History* 7:183–207.

Lanier, Henry Wysham. 1922. *A Century of Banking in New York, 1822–1922.* New York: Gilliss.

Lauck, W. Jett. 1907. *The Causes of the Panic of 1893.* Boston: Houghton.

Laws of the State of New York, passed at the Sixty-Fourth Session of the Legislature. 1841. Albany: Thurlow Weed.

Lesesne, J. Maudlin. 1970. *The Bank of the State of South Carolina.* Columbia: University of South Carolina Press.

Levy, Daniel. 1997–98. "A Legal History of Irrational Exuberance." *Case Western Reserve Law Review* 48:799–863.

Lincoln, Charles Z., ed. 1909. *Messages from the Governors, State of New York.* Vol. 5, *1857–1858.* Albany, NY: J. B. Lyon.

Loeys, Jan. 1990. "What Explains the Growth of High Yield Debt?" In *The High Yield Debt Market*, ed. Ed Altman, 243–48. Homewood, IL: Dow Jones-Irwin.

Lord, William Blair, comp. 1863. *Arguments of Counsel in the Court of Appeals of the State of New York.* New York: Wm. C. Bryant.

Lourie, Samuel Anatole. 1943. "The Trading with the Enemy Act." *Michigan Law Review* 42:205–34.

Lucas, Robert E., Jr. 1976. "Econometric Policy Evaluation: A Critique." *Carnegie-Rochester Conference Series on Public Policy* 1:19–46.

Lucas, Robert E., Jr. 1977. "Understanding Business Cycles." *Carnegie-Rochester Conference Series on Public Policy* 5:7–29.

Lucas, Robert E., Jr. 1980. "Methods and Problems in Business Cycle Theory." *Journal of Money, Credit and Banking* 12:696–715.

Lucas, Robert E., Jr. 2005. "Present at the Creation: Reflections on the 2004 Nobel Prize to Finn Kydland and Edward Prescott." *Review of Economic Dynamics* 8:777–79.

Lucas, Robert E., Jr., and Thomas Sargent. 1981. *Rational Expectations and Econometric Practice.* 2 vols. Minneapolis: University of Minnesota Press.

Madigan, Brian F. 2009. "Bagehot's Dictum in Practice: Formulating and Implementing Policies to Combat the Financial Crisis." Speech at the Federal Reserve Bank of Kansas City's Annual Economic Symposium, Jackson Hole, WY, August 12, 2009, http://www.federalreserve.gov/newsevents/speech/madigan20090821a.htm.

Madison, James H. 1974. "The Evolution of Commercial Credit Reporting Agencies in Nineteenth-Century America." *Business History Review* 48:164–86.

Mankiw, Gregory, Jeffrey Miron, and David Weil. 1987. "The Adjustment of Expectations to a Change in Regime: A Study of the Founding of the Federal Reserve." *American Economic Review* 77:358–74.

Marcus, Alan. 1984. "Deregulation and Bank Financial Policy." *Journal of Banking and Finance* 8:557–65.

Mason, Joseph R. 2003. "The Political Economy of Reconstruction Finance Corporation Assistance during the Great Depression." *Explorations in Economic History* 40:101–21.

McCloskey, Donald. 1976. "Does the Past Have Useful Economics?" *Journal of Economic Literature* 14:434–61.

McCulloch, Hugh. 1888. *Men and Measures of Half a Century*. New York: Charles Scribner's Sons.

McGrane, Reginald. 1924. *The Panic of 1837*. Chicago: University of Chicago Press.

McQuerry, Elizabeth. 1999. "The Banking Sector Rescue in Mexico." *Economic Review—Federal Reserve Bank of Atlanta*, third quarter, 14–29.

Mehra, Alexander. 2010. "Legal Authority in Unusual and Exigent Circumstances: The Federal Reserve and the Financial Crisis." *University of Pennsylvania Journal of Business Law* 13:221–73.

Mendelsohn, M. S. 1984. "Continental Seen as Biggest Banking Setback Since 1931: Run Was the First Instance of Large-Scale Withdrawals of Credit Lines in the International Interbank Market." *American Banker*, May 21, 1.

Mendoza, Enrique, and Marco Terrones. 2008. "An Anatomy of Credit Booms: Evidence from Macro Aggregates and Micro Data." IMF Working Paper WP/08/226.

Miller, Preston. 1994. *The Rational Expectations Revolution: Readings from the Front Line*. Cambridge, MA: MIT Press.

Million, John Wilson. 1894. "The Debate on the National Bank Act of 1863." *Journal of Political Economy* 2:251–80.

Minsky, Hyman P. 1982. *Can "It" Happen Again?: Essays on Instability and Finance*. Armonk, NY: M. E. Sharpe.

Miron, Jeffrey. 1986. "Financial Panics, the Seasonality of the Nominal Interest Rate, and the Founding of the Fed." *American Economic Review* 76:125–40.

Miron, Jeffrey A., and Christina D. Romer. 1990. "A New Monthly Index of Industrial Production, 1884–1940." *Journal of Economic History* 50 (2): 321–37.

Mitchell, Wesley Clair. 1903. *A History of the Greenbacks: With Special Reference to the Economic Consequences of Their Issue, 1862–65*. Chicago: University of Chicago Press.

Mitchell, Wesley Clair. 1913. *Business Cycles*. Berkeley: University of California Press.

Mitchell, Wesley C. 1922. "The Crisis of 1920 and the Problem of Controlling Business Cycles." *American Economic Review* 12:20–32.

Mitchell, Wesley Clair. 1941. *Business Cycles and Their Causes.* Berkeley: University of California Press.

Moen, Jon, and Ellis Tallman. 1992. "The Bank Panic of 1907: The Role of Trust Companies." *Journal of Economic History* 52 (3): 611–30.

Moen, Jon, and Ellis Tallman. 2000. "Clearinghouse Membership and Deposit Contraction during the Panic of 1907." *Journal of Economic History* 60:145–63.

Moen, Jon, and Ellis Tallman. 2010. "Liquidity Creation Without a Lender of Last Resort: Clearing House Loan Certificates in the Banking Panic of 1907." Federal Reserve Bank of Cleveland Policy Discussion Paper 2010–10.

Molyneux, Phil, and Nidal Shamroukh. 1996. "Diffusion of Financial Innovations: The Case of Junk Bonds and Note Issuance Facilities." *Journal of Money, Credit, and Banking* 28 (3): 502–22.

Morgan, Donald, and Kevin Stiroh. 2005. "Too Big to Fail after All These Years." Federal Reserve Bank of New York Staff Report 220.

Morgan, George. 1992. "Capital Adequacy." In *The New Palgrave Dictionary of Money and Finance,* ed. Peter Newman, Murray Milgate, and John Eatwell. London: Macmillan.

Mullineaux, Donald. 1987. "Competitive Monies and the Suffolk Bank System: A Contractual Perspective." *Southern Economic Journal* 53:884–98.

Mundlak, Yair, Domingo Cavallo, and Roberto Domenech. 1989. *Agriculture and Economic Growth in Argentina, 1913–84.* Research Report 76, International Food Policy Institute.

Nadler, Marcus, and Jules Bogen. 1933. *The Banking Crisis: The End of an Epoch.* New York: Dodd, Mead.

Nash, Gerald D. 1959. "Herbert Hoover and the Origins of the Reconstruction Finance Corporation." *Mississippi Valley Historical Review* 46:455–68.

Neal, Larry. 1971. "Trust Companies and Financial Innovation, 1897–1914." *Business History Review* 45 (1): 35–51.

New York Clearing House Association. 1884. "Report of the Committee of the New York Clearing House Association." *Bankers' Magazine,* August, 129–33.

New York State Bankers' Association. 1901. *Eight Annual Convention of the New York State Bankers' Association, Buffalo June 21–22, 1901.* New York: Bankers' Magazine Press.

Ng, Kenneth. 1988. "Free Banking Laws and Barriers to Entry in Banking, 1838–1860." *Journal of Economic History* 48:877–89.

Niven, John. 1995. *Salmon P. Chase: A Biography.* New York: Oxford University Press.

Noyes, Alexander. 1894. "The Banks and the Panic of 1893." *Political Science Quarterly* 9 (1): 12–30.

Noyes, Alexander. 1909. "A Year after the Panic of 1907." *Quarterly Journal of Economics* 23:185–212.

Ó Gráda, Cormac, and Eugene White. 2003. "The Panics of 1854 and 1857: A View from the Emigrant Industrial Savings Bank." *Journal of Economic History* 63 (1): 213–40.

Ohanian, Lee. 2010. "The Economic Crisis from a Neoclassical Perspective." *Journal of Economic Perspectives* 24 (4): 45–66.

O'Hara, Maureen, and Wayne Shaw. 1990. "Deposit Insurance and Wealth Effects: The Value of Being 'Too Big to Fail.'" *Journal of Finance* 45:1587–1600.

Park, Sunyoung. 2012. "The Safeness of AAA-Rated Subprime MBS." PhD diss., Yale University.

Parker, Randall E. 2002. *Reflections on the Great Depression.* Cheltanham, UK: Elgar.

Parker, William N., ed. 1986. *Economic History and the Modern Economist.* Oxford: Blackwell.

Paulson, Henry. 2008. *Remarks by Secretary Henry M. Paulson, Jr. at the Ronald Reagan Presidential Library.* HP-1285. Washington DC: Press Room of U.S. Department of the Treasury.

Peek, Joe, and Eric Rosengren. 2000. "Collateral Damage: Effects of the Japanese Bank Crisis on Real Activity in the United States." *American Economic Review* 90:30–45.

Perry, Kevin J., and Robert A. Taggart. 1988. "The Growing Role of Junk Bonds in Corporate Finance." *Journal of Applied Corporate Finance* 1 (1): 37–45.

Pizzo, Stephen, Mary Fricker, and Paul Muolo. 1989. *Inside Job: The Looting of America's Savings and Loans.* New York: McGraw-Hill.

Post, Mitchell, Michael Schoenbeck, and Joyce Payne. 1992. "The Evolution of the U.S. Commercial Paper Market since 1980." *Federal Reserve Bulletin* 78:879–91.

Pozsar, Zoltan. 2011. "Institutional Cash Pools and the Triffin Dilemma of the U.S. Banking System." IMF Working Paper WP/11/190.

Prendergast, William. 1906. *Credit and Its Uses.* New York: D. Appleton.

Preston, Howard. 1933. "The Banking Act of 1933." *American Economic Review* 23:585–607.

Price, Bonamy. 1876. *Currency and Banking.* New York: D. Appleton.

Prosser, Wiliam. 1934. "The Minnesota Mortgage Moratorium." *Southern California Law Review* 7:353–71.

Rajan, Raghuram, and Rodney Ramcharan. 2012. "The Anatomy of a Credit Crisis: The Boom and Bust in Farm Land Prices in the United States in the 1920s." National Bureau of Economic Research Working Paper 18027.

Rancière, Romain, Aaron Tornell, and Frank Westermann. 2008. "Systemic Crises and Growth." *Quarterly Journal of Economics* 123:359–406.

Redlich, Fritz. 1952. "American Financial Institutions: Bank Administration, 1780–1914." *Journal of Economic History* 12:438–53.

Redlich, Fritz. 1968. *The Molding of American Banking.* New York: Johnson Reprint Company.

Reinhart, Carmen, and Kenneth Rogoff. 2008a. "Banking Crises: An Equal Opportunity Menace." NBER Working Paper 14587.

Reinhart, Carmen, and Kenneth Rogoff. 2008b. "Is the 2007 U.S. Sub-prime Financial Crisis So Different?" *American Economic Review* 98:339–44.

Reinhart, Carmen, and Kenneth Rogoff. 2009a. *This Time Is Different: Eight Centuries of Financial Folly*. Princeton, NJ: Princeton University Press.

Reinhart, Carmen, and Kenneth Rogoff. 2009b. "The Aftermath of Financial Crises." *American Economic Review* 99:466–72.

Rezneck, Samuel. 1950. "Distress, Relief, and Discontent in the United States during the Depression of 1873–78." *Journal of Political Economy* 58 (6): 494–512.

Ricardo, David. 1876. *The Works of David Ricardo: With a Notice of the Life and Writings of the Author*. London: J. Murray.

Robb, Thomas Bruce. 1921. *The Guaranty of Bank Deposits*. Boston: Houghton Mifflin.

Robb, T. Bruce. 1934. "Safeguarding the Depositor." *Annals of the American Academy of Political and Social Science* 171:54–62.

Rockoff, Hugh. 1974. "The Free Banking Era: A Reexamination." *Journal of Money, Credit and Banking* 6:141–67.

Rockoff, Hugh. 1975. *The Free Banking Era: A Reexamination*. New York: Arno.

Rockoff, Hugh. 1985. "New Evidence on Free Banking in the United States." *American Economic Review* 75:886–89.

Rodrik, Dani. 1999. "Where Did All the Growth Go? External Shocks, Social Conflict, and Growth Collapses." *Journal of Economic Growth* 4:385–412.

Rogers, Daniel. 1933–34. "Constitutional Law—Impairment of Contract—Moratory Legislation for the Relief of Mortgagors." *Minnesota Law Review* 18:319–46.

Rolnick, Arthur J., Bruce D. Smith, and Warren E. Weber. 1998. "Lessons from a Laissez-Faire Payments System: The Suffolk Banking System (1825–58)." *Federal Reserve Bank of Minneapolis Quarterly Review* 22 (3): 105–16.

Rolnick, Arthur, and Warren Weber. 1983. "New Evidence on the Free Banking Era." *American Economic Review* 73:1080–91.

Rolnick, Arthur, and Warren Weber. 1984. "The Causes of Free Bank Failures." *Journal of Monetary Economics* 14:267–91.

Romer, Christina. 1988. "World War I and the Postwar Depression: A Reinterpretation Based on Alternative Estimates of GNP." *Journal of Monetary Economics* 22:91–115.

Roots, Roger. 2000. "Government by Permanent Emergency: The Forgotten History of the New Deal Constitution." *Suffolk University Law Review* 33:259–96.

Rousseau, Peter. 2002. "Jacksonian Monetary Policy, Specie Flows, and the Panic of 1837." *Journal of Economic History* 62:457–88.

Sachs, Jeffrey, Aaron Tornell, and Andrés Velasco. 1996. "The Collapse of the Mexican Peso: What Have We Learned?" *Economic Policy* 11:13–63.

Sakolski, Aaron. 1932. *The Great American Land Bubble*. New York: Harper & Brothers.

Saunders, Anthony, and Berry Wilson. 1996. "Contagious Bank Runs: Evidence from the 1929–1933 Period." *Journal of Financial Intermediation* 5:409–23.

Schularick, Moritz, and Alan Taylor. 2009. "Credit Booms Gone Bust: Monetary Policy, Leverage Cycles and Financial Crises, 1870–2008." NBER Working Paper 15512.

Seidman, L. William. 1993. *Full Faith and Credit: The Great S & L Debacle and Other Washington Sagas.* New York: Times Books.

Shiller, Robert. 1980. "Can the Federal Reserve Control Real Interest Rates?" In *Rational Expectations and Economic Policy,* ed. Stanley Fischer, 117–67. Chicago: University of Chicago Press.

Shiller, Robert J. 1999. "The ET Interview: Professor James Tobin." *Econometric Theory* 15:867–900.

Shiller, Robert J. 2005. *Irrational Exuberance.* 2nd ed. Princeton, NJ: Princeton University Press.

Silber, William. 2007a. "The Great Financial Crisis of 1914: What Can We Learn from Aldrich-Vreeland Emergency Currency?" *American Economic Review Papers and Proceedings* 97 (2): 285–89.

Silber, William. 2007b. *When Washington Shut Down Wall Street: The Great Financial Crisis of 1914 and the Origins of America's Monetary Supremacy.* Princeton, NJ: Princeton University Press.

Silber, William. 2009. "Why Did FDR's Bank Holiday Succeed?" *Economic Policy Review—Federal Reserve Bank of New York,* July, 19–30.

Skilton, Robert. 1943. "Mortgage Moratoria since 1933." *University of Pennsylvania Law Review and American Law Register* 92:53–90.

Smith, Tynan, and Raymond Hengren. 1947. "Bank Capital: The Problem Restated." *Journal of Political Economy* 55:553–66.

South Carolina Court of Errors. 1844. *The Bank Case: A Report of the Proceedings in the Cases of the Bank of South Carolina, and the Bank of Charleston, Upon Scire Facias to Vacate.* Charleston, SC: W. Riley.

Spector, Horacio. 2008. "Constitutional Transplants and the Mutation Effect." *Chicago-Kent Law Review* 83:129–45.

Sprague, Irvine H. 1986. *Bailout: An Insider's Account of Bank Failures and Rescues.* New York: Basic Books.

Sprague, O. M. W. 1908. "The American Crisis of 1907." *Economic Journal* 18 (71): 353–72.

Sprague, O. M. W. 1910. *History of Crises under the National Banking System.* Senate Document 538. Washington DC: Government Printing Office.

Sprague, O. M. W. 1915. "The Crisis of 1914 in the United States." *American Economic Review* 5 (3): 499–533.

Sprinkel, Beryl. 1952. "Economic Consequences of the Operations of the Reconstruction Finance Corporation." *Journal of Business of the University of Chicago* 25 (4): 211–24.

Stevens, Albert C. 1894. "Analysis of the Phenomena of the Panic in the United States in 1893." *Quarterly Journal of Economics* 8 (2): 117–48.

Stock, James, and Mark Watson. 1999. "Business Cycle Fluctuations in U.S. Macroeconomic Time Series." In *Handbook of Macroeconomics,* vol. 1, ed. John B. Taylor and Michael Woodford, 3–64. Amsterdam: Elsevier Science.

Stojanovic, Dusan, and Mark Vaughn. 1998. "The Commercial Paper Market: Who's Minding the Shop?" *Regional Economist—Federal Reserve Bank of St. Louis*, April, 5–9.

Stone, Richard. 1963. "Models of the National Economy for Planning Purposes." *OR* 14:51–59.

Stone, Richard. 1997. "The Accounts of Society: Nobel Memorial Lecture, 8 December 1984." *American Economic Review* 87:17–29.

Stone, Richard, and Hashem Pesaran. 1991. "The ET Interview: Professor Richard Stone." *Econometric Theory* 7:85–123.

Summers, Peter. 2005. "What Caused The Great Moderation? Some Cross-Country Evidence." *Economic Review—Federal Reserve Bank of Kansas City*, third quarter, 6–32.

Sumner, William Graham. 1896. *A History of Banking in the United States*. New York: Journal of Commerce and Commercial Bulletin.

Suryahadi, Asep, Sudarno Sumarto, and Lant Pritchett. 2003. "The Evolution of Poverty during the Crisis in Indonesia," Working paper, SMERu Research Institute, Jakarta.

Swanson, William Walker. 1908a. "The Crisis of 1860 and the First Issue of Clearing-House Certificates: I." *Journal of Political Economy* 16 (2): 65–75.

Swanson, William Walker. 1908b. "The Crisis of 1860 and the First Issue of Clearing-House Certificates: II." *Journal of Political Economy* 16 (4): 212–26.

Swary, Itzhak. 1986. "Stock Market Reaction to Regulatory Action in the Continental Illinois Crisis." *Journal of Business* 59:451–73.

Taggart, Robert. 1988. "The Growth of the 'Junk' Bond Market and its Role in Financing Takeovers." In *Mergers and Acquisitions*, ed. A. J. Auerbach, 5–24. Chicago: University of Chicago Press.

Taylor, Alan. 1994. "Three Phases of Argentine Economic Growth." Historical Paper 60, National Bureau of Economic Research.

Temin, Peter. 1969. *The Jacksonian Economy*. New York: W. W. Norton.

Tetlock, Paul. 2007. "Giving Content to Investor Sentiment: The Role of Media in the Stock Market." *Journal of Finance* 62:1139–68.

Tetlock, Paul, Maytal Saar-Tsechansky, and Sofus Macskassy. 2008. "More Than Words: Quantifying Language to Measure Firms' Fundamentals." *Journal of Finance* 62:1437–67.

Timberlake, Richard. 1984. "The Central Banking Role of Clearinghouse Associations." *Journal of Money, Credit and Banking* 16:1–15.

Tucker, Paul. 2009. "The Repertoire of Official Sector Interventions in the Financial System: Last Resort Lending, Market-Making, and Capital." Speech at the 2009 International Conference: Financial System and Monetary policy Implementation, Bank of Japan, May 27–28, 2009: http://www.bankofengland.co.uk/publications/Documents/speeches/2009/speech390.pdf.

Turing, Alan. 1950. "Computing Machinery and Intelligence." *Mind* 59:433–60.

United States Government Accountability Office. 2011. *Federal Reserve System: Opportunities Exist to Strengthen Policies and Processes for Managing Emergency Assistance.* GAO-11-696.

Vanderblue, Homer. 1927a. "The Florida Land Boom, I." *Journal of Land and Public Utility Economics* 3 (2): 113–31.

Vanderblue, Homer. 1927b. "The Florida Land Boom, II." *Journal of Land and Public Utility Economics* 3 (3): 252–69.

Van Dyke, T. S. 1890. *Millionaires of a Day: An Inside History of the Great Southern California "Boom."* New York: Fords, Howard & Hulbert.

Van Vleck, George. 1943. *The Panic of 1857: An Analytical Study.* New York: Columbia University Press.

Vickers, Raymond B. 1994. *Panic in Paradise: Florida's Banking Crash of 1926.* Tuscaloosa: University of Alabama Press.

Volcker, Paul. 1984a. "Statement Presented at Hearings on Monetary Stability." U.S. Senate Joint Economic Committee, July 30.

Volcker, Paul. 1984b. "Statement before the Committee on Banking, Housing, and Urban Affairs." U.S. Senate, July 25.

Wagster, John D. 1996. "Impact of the 1988 Basle Accord on International Banks." *Journal of Finance* 51:1321–46.

Wagster, John D. 1999. "The Basel Accord of 1988 and the International Credit Crunch of 1989–1992." *Journal of Financial Services Research* 15 (2): 123–43.

Wall, Larry, and David Peterson. 1990. "The Effect of Continental Illinois' Failure on the Financial Performance of Other Banks." *Journal of Monetary Economics* 26:77–99.

Wallis, John Joseph. 2002. "An Internal Affair: Macroeconomic Instability and State Public Finance in the United States, 1836 to 1843." Working paper, University of Maryland.

Wallis, John Joseph. 2004. "Sovereign Default and Repudiation: The Emerging-Market Debt Crisis in the U.S. States, 1839–1843." Working paper, University of Maryland.

Wallis, John Joseph. 2005. "The Depression of 1839 to 1843: States, Debts, Banks." Working paper, University of Maryland.

Wallis, John Joseph, and Namsuk Kim. 2005. "The Market for American State Government Bonds in Britain and the United States, 1830 to 1843." *Economic History Review* 58:736–64.

Wallis, John Joseph, Richard Sylla, and Arthur Grinath. 2004. "Sovereign Debt Repudiation: The Emerging Market Debt Crisis in the United States, 1839–1843." Working Paper 10753, National Bureau of Economic Research.

Warner, John DeWitt. 1895. "The Currency Famine of 1893." *Sound Currency,* February 15.

Weber, Warren. 2010. "Bank Liability Insurance Schemes Before 1865." Federal Reserve Bank of Minneapolis Working Paper 679.

Wessel, David. 2010. *In FED We Trust: Ben Bernanke's War on the Great Panic.* New York: Crown Business.

Wheelock, David. 1992. "Regulation and Bank Failures: New Evidence from the Agricultural Collapse of the 1920s." *Journal of Economic History* 25 (4): 806–25.

Wheelock, David. 2008a. "Changing the Rules: State Mortgage Foreclosure Moratoria during the Great Depression." *Review—Federal Reserve Bank of St. Louis,* November/December, 569–83.

Wheelock, David. 2008b. "The Federal Response to Home Mortgage Distress: Lessons from the Great Depression." *Review—Federal Reserve Bank of St. Louis,* May/June, pt. 1, 133–48.

Wheelock, David. 2010. "Lessons Learned? Comparing the Federal Reserve's Responses to the Crises of 1929–1933 and 2007–2008," *Review—Federal Reserve Bank of St. Louis,* March/April, 89–108.

White, Eugene. 2009. "Lessons From the Great American Real Estate Boom and Bust of the 1920's." Working Paper 15573, National Bureau of Economic Research.

White, Lawrence J. 1991. *The S & L Debacle: Public Policy Lessons for Bank and Thrift Regulation.* New York: Oxford University Press.

White, Richard. 2011. *Railroaded: The Transcontinentals and the Making of Modern America.* New York: W. W. Norton.

Whitney, David. 1878. *The Suffolk Bank.* Cambridge, MA: Riverside.

Whitt, Joseph. 1996. "The Mexican Peso Crisis." *Economic Review—Federal Reserve Bank of Atlanta,* January/February, 1–20.

Wicker, Elmus. 2000. *Banking Panics of the Gilded Age.* Cambridge, UK: Cambridge University Press.

Wirth, Max. 1893. "The Crisis of 1890." *Journal of Political Economy* 1:214–35.

Wright, Carroll. 1886. *The First Annual Report of the Commissioner of Labor: Industrial Depressions.* Washington, DC: Government Printing Office.

Zane, John. 1900. *The Law of Banks and Banking.* Chicago: T. H. Flood.

Zarnowitz, Victor, and Lionel Lerner. 1961. "Cyclical Changes in Business Failures and Corporate Profits." *Business Cycle Indicators,* edited by Geoffrey Moore, 350–85. New York: National Bureau of Economic Research.

INDEX